Gifted Origins to Graced Fulfillment

Gifted Origins to Graced Fulfillment

The Soteriology of Julian of Norwich

Kerrie Hide

A Michael Glazier Book

THE LITURGICAL PRESS
Collegeville, Minnesota

www.litpress.org

A Michael Glazier Book published by The Liturgical Press

Cover design by Ann Blattner. Icon of Julian of Norwich by Robert Lenz. Used with permission.

1	2	3	4	5	6	7	8

Library of Congress Cataloging-in-Publication Data

Hide, Kerrie, 1954–
    Gifted origins to graced fulfillment : the soteriology of Julian of Norwich /
Kerrie Hide.
        p.   cm.
    Includes bibliographical references and index.
    ISBN 0-8146-5093-7 (alk. paper)
    1. Julian, of Norwich, b. 1343—Contributions in doctrine of salvation.
    2. Salvation—History of doctrines—Middle Ages, 600–1500.   I. Title.

BT752.H53   2001
234'.092—dc21

00-049742

To Col:

Love is God's Meaning

Contents

PART SIX
What Was the Meaning?

Acknowledgments

I wish to express my deep gratitude to Reverend Doctor Graeme Garrett, whose passion for theology, gift of words, and unstinting guidance have helped this study come to fruition. My gratitude extends to my companions, Elaine Farmer, Jane Foulcher, Marie Louise Uhr, Heather Thompson, Margaret Benson, and Sarah Macneil, who encouragingly journey with me, pray with me, celebrate with me in joy and console in sorrow. My spiritual direction group, Companions, also contribute to this sustenance. Thanks must also extend to colleagues in Theology at Australian Catholic University who create a vibrant theological environment in which to work and to students and colleagues at Signadou Campus of Australian Catholic University. Finally, I wish to thank my life-long companion Col, for sharing this journey into the *Revelations of Divine Love* with me.

The author is grateful to the following for permission for the use of quotations and illustrations:

Extract from the *Dictionary of Fundamental Theology*, edited by Rene Latourelle and Rino Fisichella, copyright © 1994 by The Crossroad Publishing Co. Extract from *The God of Jesus Christ*, Walter Kasper, copyright © 1984 by The Crossroad Publishing Co. Extract from *Content of Faith*, Karl Rahner, copyright © 1993 by The Crossroad Publishing Co. Extract from *The Trinity*, Karl Rahner, copyright © 1970 by The Crossroad Publishing Co. Used with permission of The Crossroad Publishing Co., New York City.

Extracts from *Julian of Norwich*, copyright © 1978 by Paulist Press, and from *Anchoritic Spirituality*, copyright © 1991 by Paulist Press. Used by permission of Paulist Press.

Excerpts from Brant Pelphrey and from Alexander Barratt, *Vox Mystica: Essays in Medieval Mysticism in Honour of Professor Valery M. Lagorio*, copyright © 1995 by D. S. Brewer, Cambridge. Used by permission of D. S. Brewer.

Excerpts from *The Confessions of St. Augustine*, translated by F. J. Sheed, copyright © 1949 by Sheed and Ward, London. Used by permission of

Sheed and Ward Publishing, an apostolate of the Priests of the Sacred Heart, Franklin, Wisconsin.

Excerpt from Hugh Kempster, "The Westminster Text," *Mystics Quarterly* (1997) 180, and from Roger Corless, "Comparing Cataphatic Mystics: Julian of Norwich and T'an-lum" 21 (1995) 20. Used by permission of the publisher.

Excerpt from Leanne van Dyk, "Vision and Imagination in Atonement Doctrine," *Theology Today* 50 (1993), 4. Used by permission of the publisher.

Excerpt from Jean Leclercq, *The Loving of Learning and the Desire for God*, © 1961 by Fordham University Press. Used by permission of Fordham University Press.

Excerpt from E. Ann Matter, *The Voice of My Beloved: The Song of Songs in Western Medieval Christianity*, © 1990 by University of Pennsylvania Press, Philadelphia. Used by permission of the University of Pennsylvania Press.

Excerpts from *The Prayers and Meditations of Saint Anselm*, translated by Benedicta Ward (Penguin Classics, 1973) copyright © by Benedicta Ward, 1993, and from *The Book of Margery Kempe*, translated by B. A. Windeatt (Penguin Classics, 1965) copyright © by B. A. Windeatt, 1965. Used by permission of Penguin Books Ltd, England.

Excerpts taken from *With Pity Not Blame* by Robert Llewelyn, published and copyright 1982 by Darton, Longman and Todd Limited, and used by permission of the publishers. Excerpts taken from *Theological Investigations* Vol. 3 by Karl Rahner S.J., published and copyright 1967 by Darton, Longman and Todd Limited, and used by permission of the publishers. Excerpts taken from *Foundations of Christian Faith* by Karl Rahner S.J., published and copyright 1978 by Darton, Longman and Todd Limited, and used by permission of the publishers.

Excerpts from *The Black Death in England*, edited by W. Mark Ormrod and Phillip G. Lindley, © 1996 by Paul Watkins, Stamford. Used by permission of Paul Watkins.

Excerpts from "Little Gidding," *The Oxford Book of Twentieth Century English Verse*, © 1973 by Oxford University Press, Oxford, and Brian Davies, *The Thought of Thomas Aquinas*, © 1992 by Clarendon Press, Oxford, are used by permission of Oxford University Press.

The author has made every effort to obtain all appropriate copyright permissions.

Preface

"And there he revealed a fair and delectable place, large enough for all mankind that will be saved and will rest in peace and in love" (10:24. 220).[1] Julian of Norwich believes in a God who saves. Belief in a God who saves, belief in a God who draws all human beings to God's self into the eternity of God's loving is a critical concept for a Christian. It is foundational for Christian hope. For as long as I can remember, this hope, embodied in Julian's statement, "all shall be well,"[2] has concerned me. Interested in the growth and development of the spiritual life, I wanted to articulate what salvation means in Christian terms. I aspired to explore the parameters of the human capacity for a life of communion with the transcendent mystery that pervades all reality.

My introduction to the writings of Julian of Norwich occurred when I was studying the history of Christian spirituality for a Master's degree. I realized that *The Revelations of Divine Love* was not simply a great spiritual classic that taught its readers how to live a life permeated with prayer. The text was more confronting. It presented the radically dynamic character of the human journey from God to God within the context of an all-pervading theology of trinitarian love. This was a theological classic that could stand the test of continued interpretation without its meaning being exhausted. I came to an awareness that Julian could inform my understanding of how God saves. She had something significant to say, something that was not ingrained in the Christian consciousness, about the relationship between God, Christ, Spirit, humanity, and creation, all within the context of salvation.

---

[1] All translations are from *Julian of Norwich Showings*. Translated by Edmund Colledge and James Walsh. Classics of Western Spirituality (New York: Paulist, 1978). Short text references will have roman numerals for chapter numbers; long text, arabic numerals.

[2] Because *shall* emphasizes both the present necessity and future dimension of making all things well, I will maintain this translation throughout the book. See Chapter 8, "*Oneing* Through the Holy Spirit."

Believing that the Christian community at large had not been given a clear articulation of this woman's ideas about salvation, I decided to pursue my study of Julian. Through that study I came to see that there was indeed a place for a systematic study of her understanding of salvation. Theologians such as Brant Pelphrey,[3] Joan M. Nuth,[4] Margaret Ann Palliser,[5] and Patricia Mary Vinje[6] laid the foundations. They demonstrated that Julian was a significant theologian in her development of a theology of divine love. They pointed to the importance of her soteriology. No one, however, had conducted a detailed analysis of the dimensions of the theology that informs Julian's doctrine of salvation. In a recent address Pelphrey remarked: "It is time to look carefully at this Julian. There is room for graduate students to explore every corner of mysticism here."[7] The corner of Julian's *Revelations of Divine Love* it is time to explore is soteriology.

Soteriology, however, is not simply a corner. The meaning of salvation is the central thesis of the *Showings*. All Julian's theology is grounded in soteriology. It is time for a formal reopening and reassessment of soteriological questions. It is time to look carefully within the tradition for soteriologies not given wide public access. It is time to redress the historical injustice that Julian's soteriology has not extensively informed the Christian tradition. Julian's vision of the saving grace of the Trinity addresses real existential questions that are at the heart of theology today.

Soteriology has its origins in the religious quest and the theology that accompanies this search. Soteriology addresses the perennial longings of human beings and asks how salvation can be a reality in a world

---

[3] Brant Pelphrey, *Love Was His Meaning: The Theology and Mysticism of Julian of Norwich.* Salzburg Studies in English Literature (Salzburg, Austria: Institut fur Anglistik und Amerikanistik, Universitat Salzburg, 1982); idem, *Christ Our Mother: Julian of Norwich* (Wilmington, Del.: Michael Glazier, 1989).

[4] Joan M. Nuth, *Wisdom's Daughter: The Theology of Julian of Norwich* (New York: Crossroad, 1991).

[5] Margaret Ann Palliser, O.P., *Christ, Our Mother of Mercy: Divine Mercy and Compassion in the Theology of the Shewings of Julian of Norwich* (Berlin and New York: Walter de Gruyter, 1992).

[6] Patricia Mary Vinje, *An Understanding of Love according to the Anchoress Julian of Norwich.* Salzburg studies in English literature. Elizabethan & Renaissance studies 92:8 (Salzburg, Austria: Institut fur Anglistik und Amerikanistik, Universitat Salzburg, 1983).

[7] Brant Pelphrey, "Afterword: Valerie's Gift," in Anne Clark Bartlett, ed., with Thomas Bestul, Janet Goebel, and William F. Pollard, *Vox Mystica: Essays on Medieval Mysticism in Honour of Professor Valery M. Lagorio* (Cambridge: D.S. Brewer, 1995) 234.

that knows so much destructive suffering. Soteriology arises from the human experience of the need for salvation. A technical theological term, derived from the Greek words *sōtēria* (deliverance, salvation) and *logos* (word or thought), soteriology is the study that aims to understand and interpret human hope for salvation or ultimate fulfillment. Soteriology is a dynamic practical aspect of theology that seeks to examine how we as spiritual/embodied beings become one with God. Soteriology is the study of God's action in Christ for our salvation.

The title of the book, *Gifted Origins to Graced Fulfillment*, sets the context in which we will examine Julian's soteriology. For Julian it is our gifted origins, who we are—created in the love of the Trinity with our being in God—that make salvation a reality. In origin, humanity is gifted with a relational responsiveness to the divine. This creates the potential for eschatological fruition in the fullness of God's time. Within history God continues to share divine life and love through Christ and the Spirit, renewing, re-creating, transforming, and increasing who we are in God. Grace abounds. The experience of divine love in this life in well-being and woe incorporates us within the love within the Trinity. This originating love draws us to be one in the fullness of trinitarian joy in the eschaton.

Because Julian's writings fall within the genre of mystical literature a systematic study of her soteriology presents its own difficulties. This is not the clearly structured text composed in question-and-answer dialogue that we are used to seeing in great theological authors such as Anselm and Aquinas. Julian's theology is integrated into vivid descriptions of her mystical experience of prayer, called *showings*. Mystical literature flows from a contemplative consciousness that is inherently creative, right-brain expression. It resists being constrained and systematized. Therefore, in order to be sensitive to the genre in which Julian composes and yet give some structure to her doctrine of salvation, I present a hermeneutic (Chapter 2) that gives guiding principles for interpreting Julian's soteriology. Julian's enunciation of the human journey of salvation, cast in a trinitarian framework, gives structure to the study. The formula is not imposed. It arises from within the text and draws all Julian's ideas about salvation into an interlaced unity.

Julian summarizes the history of human existence: ". . . all our life consists of three: In the first we have our being, and in the second we have our increasing, and in the third we have our fulfillment" (14:58.294). All of life "is in three." The trinitarian God of love is the centerpiece of the story of salvation. All of life is immersed within the love of the Father, Son, and Holy Spirit. We can only understand the meaning of existence within the dynamic threeness of the Godhead. The words "first," "second," and "third" simultaneously unite and distinguish the roles of each divine person of the Trinity in the work for salvation. The distinction between first, second, and third holds together the unity of the Trinity within the salvific process and the diversity within specific moments and activities of each divine person. The designation of time connects the beginnings and endings of salvation. Past, present, and future, historical time and eternity are united in the sharing of trinitarian love. The rhythmical unfolding echo, created by the rhyming of our being, our increasing, and our fulfilling, conveys the dynamic work of each person of the Trinity. The Trinity draws all creation into a relationship of love that is uncreated, created, and given. Within this harmonious unity, yet explicit diversity, the formula gives structure to the book.

Part One: The *Showings:* From Experience to Expression examines Julian's visionary experience and her expression of the experience that has led others to reflect on, record, and write about her text (Chapter 1) and presents a hermeneutic for interpreting the showings (Chapter 2). Part Two: A Soteriology of *Oneing* explores how all our life is in three by presenting Julian's soteriology as a trinitarian soteriology of *oneing* (Chapter 3). Part Three: In the First We Have Our Being delves into our gifted origins. Here we survey Julian's creation theology and her anthropology (Chapter 4). Part Four: In the Second We Have Our Increasing focuses on christology. This section presents Christ's role in redemption through the cross (Chapter 5), through his work as servant (Chapter 6), and through his function as mother (Chapter 7). In light of Christ's union with us we consider how Christ enables redemption, change, transformation, and re-creation. Part Five: In the Third We Have Our Fulfillment inquires into graced endings. The chapters examine the present experience of graced fulfillment in the power of the Holy Spirit (Chapter 8) and the hope for fulfillment in the eschaton (Chapter 9). Part Six: What Was the Meaning? draws together the understanding Julian comes to about salvation. It appraises the relevance of these teachings for today (Chapter 10).

Great soteriologies have arisen throughout the history of the Christian tradition. Authors such as Irenaeus († ca. 200), Origen († 254), Augustine (354–430), Anselm (ca. 1033–1109), and Thomas Aquinas (1225–1274) have made a valuable contribution to understanding this holiest of Christian mysteries, but these distinguished paradigms have, in the main, come from within a juridical framework. The classical expression of soteriology has tended to spiritualize salvation and place it on a supernatural plane where it loses contact with the existential lives of people. In the face of this heritage, questions arising from contemporary experience challenge the Christian tradition. Does life have meaning? Is love and the dynamic of sharing love at the core of all reality? Is all existence relational? Where does God stand in relation to human suffering and the incompletion of the cosmos? How do we remain open to growth, to change, and to transformation? How can we confront the non-being and non-doing of sin that creates so much despair and hopelessness? How do we keep hope alive? In search of some response to these questions about the salvific meaning of existence, I will demonstrate how Julian concludes that life does have meaning. Love and the dynamic of sharing love are at the center of all reality. Love is the harmonious wholeness that unites all things and draws them into a relationship with the divine. God is present: healing, transforming, renewing, re-creating, and drawing those who suffer to an awareness of everlasting joy. The research examines Julian's understanding of how "all shall be well."

I began this preface with Julian's expression of hope. Within God there is a place large enough for all humankind, who shall be saved, a place to rest in, in peace and in love. Is this a valid Christian response to who we are and how we will be saved? We will see how Julian can answer a firm "yes" to this question. Yet this is not a naïve "yes." The answer is found in the love within the Trinity: uncreated love, created and given. Salvation occurs within the communion of God, Son, and Spirit, engaging all creation in dynamic *oneing*. Gifted in origin, we are marked with the sign of the cross and formed through the experience of Christ's suffering, love, and joy. Salvation is partially experienced and prefigured by the reality of the glorious resurrection and the continuous presence of grace. Salvation is fulfillment in the joyous face-to-face vision of God in the eschaton.

Part One

The *Showings:*
From Experience to Expression

Here is a vision shown by the goodness of God to a devout woman, and her name is Julian (i:125).

1

Julian of Norwich

*What is impossible to you is not impossible to me. I shall
preserve my word in everything and I shall make everything
well* (13:32.233).

In 1373 a woman known as Julian of Norwich experienced a series
of *showings* or visions that she believed were a revelation from God. In
the midst of these visions she came to appreciate that, in spite of all the
woe that exists in creation, what looks impossible from a human point
of view is not impossible in the divine vision. She articulated one of the
most celebrated soteriological statements within the Christian tradition: "I will make all things well, I shall make all things well, I may
make all things well and I can make all things well; and you will see
that yourself, that all things will be well" (xv:151).

I. The Anchoress Julian of Norwich

Despite interest in Julian's theology and spirituality, we still know
very little about her life. In fact, not even her name is known for certain.[1] Our primary source of information comes from two versions of
her book, *The Revelations of Divine Love*, the short text (ca. 1373–74), and
the long text (ca. 1393). At the beginning of the long text she identifies
herself as "a simple, unlettered creature" (2:177).[2] She tells her readers

---

[1] Julian's epithet comes from the church where she was an anchoress. She was
also known as Dame Julian or Lady Julian.

[2] Colledge and Walsh (hereafter C&W) note that whatever unlettered may
mean it cannot be illiterate. Edmund Colledge and James Walsh, eds., *A Book of
Showings to the Anchoress Julian of Norwich*, 2 vols. (Toronto: Pontifical Institute of
Mediaeval Studies, 1978) 177 n. 1 (= *BSAJN*).

that she experienced a vision of Christ in "the year of our Lord one thousand, three hundred and seventy-three, on the thirteenth day of May (2:177).[3] This occurred when she was thirty and a half years old. A priest brings a crucifix before her as she thinks she is going to die. ("And when I was thirty and a half years old, God sent me a bodily sickness in which I lay for three days and three nights, and on the third night I received all the rites of Holy Church, and did not expect to live until day") (3:179). Suddenly Julian's pain subsides. She has a sense that she is one with Christ, one with divine love, and experiences a series of fifteen *showings* about the love of God: "the first began early in the morning, about the hour of four, and it lasted, revealing them in a determined order, most lovely and calm, each following the other, until it was three o'clock in the afternoon or later" (15:65.309-310). The following night she has the final vision that confirms the other fifteen: "and this sixteenth revelation was a conclusion and confirmation to all the fifteen" (16:66.310). Scholars disagree as to whether these details are historical or symbolic.[4] The details Julian gives suggest that she is reporting her actual experience. When she recovers, she records her insights about the experience.

Julian: Recluse at Norwich

We know little of Julian's life prior to her visionary experience.[5] All that we know is that she was interested in a prayerful life from an early age: "to receive three wounds in my life, that is, the wound of true contrition, the wound of loving compassion and the wound of longing with my will for God" (2:179). Some scholars suggest that she was a laywoman, others a Benedictine nun.[6] Whatever her status, however,

---

[3] The Sloane manuscript (S 1) says "the yeere of our Lord 1373, the eighth day of May" (II:41–42.39). Georgia Ronan Crampton, ed., *The Shewings of Julian of Norwich.* Teams Middle English Texts Series (Kalamazoo: Medieval Institute Publications, 1994). In accordance with this date, the Anglican calendar has Julian's feastday on May 8.

[4] Brant Pelphrey, *Love Was His Meaning: The Theology and Mysticism of Julian of Norwich* (Salzburg: Institut für Anglistik und Amerikanistik, 1982) 1 (= *LWHM*), notes that four in the morning would be about dawn for that time of year. Julian could have known the time with reasonable accuracy since there was a cathedral clock that regulated time throughout the city. C&W in contrast see the time as symbolic: *BSAJN* 65 n. 39; 631.

[5] Some suggest that Julian was educated by the Benedictine nuns at Carrow. Cf. Grace M. Jantzen, *Julian of Norwich: Mystic and Theologian* (London: S.P.C.K., 1987) 18.

[6] C&W believe Julian was a Benedictine nun (*BSAJN* 43). Grace Warrack, ed., *Revelations of Divine Love Recorded by Julian Anchoress at Norwich Anno Domini, 1373,*

she was well formed in Scripture and theology.[7] At the beginning of the short text the scribe names Julian: "Here is a vision shown by the goodness of God to a devout woman, and her name is Julian, who is a recluse at Norwich and still alive, A.D. 1413" (i:125). The finale to the Paris manuscript identifies the author as Julian, anchoress at Norwich: "Thanks be to God. Here ends the book of revelations of Julian the anchorite of Norwich, on whose soul may God have mercy" (16:86.343). *Recluse,* from the Old French *reclus,* enclosed, describes a person living in seclusion or isolation as a religious discipline.[8] *An(a)corite,* from the Latin *anchoreta* means someone who retreats or withdraws.[9] The medieval anchoress was enclosed by a bishop in a ceremony in which she entered the tomb of the anchorhold, usually attached to a church, and closed the door on the world. Her aim was to concentrate undistractedly on God by practising continual prayer through reciting the divine office, participating in Mass and the sacraments, spending time in silence, praying for humanity generally, and offering spiritual advice to people.[10]

The evidence of four wills[11] substantiates the comments made in the short text and the Paris manuscript, that Julian became an anchoress at St. Julian's Church in the parish of Conisford in the later part of her life, sometime before 1393. She was still alive in 1416.[12] Margery Kempe (b. 1373) corroborates these facts. Her autobiography records a visit to Julian in her anchorhold around 1415. In her autobiography Margery describes Julian as empathetic, wise, and discerning. Margery tells us she spoke to Dame Julian "and told her about the grace, that God had put into her soul . . . for the anchoress was expert in such things and could give good advice."[13] A much later reference in Bloomsfield's history of Norfolk also mentions Julian:

2d ed. (London: Methuen, 1907) xxi–xxii agrees with this point of view. Pelphrey considers that she was a lay woman (*LWHM* 18).

[7] For a discussion about being "unlettered" see *BSAJN* 43–59 and *LWHM* 18–28.

[8] Lesley Brown, ed., *The New Shorter Oxford English Dictionary on Historical Principles.* 2 vols. (Oxford: Clarendon Press, 1993) 2502 (= *NSOED*).

[9] *NSOED* 75.

[10] See Ritamary Bradley, *Julian's Way: A Practical Commentary on Julian of Norwich* (London: Harper Collins, 1992) 10–11 for an outline of the prayers recited by the anchoress.

[11] The wills of Roger Reed 1393 or 1394; Thomas Edmund, 1404; John Plumpton, 1415; Isabel Ufford, 1416 (*LWHM* 11–12).

[12] A bequest from a will of Walter Daniel suggests that a male anchorite occupied the anchorhold in 1423. Frances [Sister Anna Maria] Reynolds, *A Critical Edition of the Revelations of Julian of Norwich (1342–c. 1416) Prepared From All Known Manuscripts.* Ph.D. dissertation (Leeds: University of Leeds, 1956) x, n. 1.

[13] Margery Kempe, *The Book of Margery Kempe,* translated by B. A. Windeatt (Harmondsworth: Penguin, 1988) 77.

> In the east part of the church-yard stood an anchorage in which an ankress or recluse dwelt till the Disolution, when the house was demolished, though the foundations may still be seen (1768). In 1393 Lady Julian, the ankress here was a strict recluse, and had two servants to attend to her old age. This woman was in these days esteemed one of the greatest holinesses.[14]

There is general agreement that Julian was an anchoress, attached to St. Julian's Church, Norwich. She was known as a holy woman who could discern the ways of God and give good advice to people.

Julian gives little evidence of the day-to-day reality of her living as an anchoress in her text.[15] Although there is no direct evidence to suggest that she used the *Ancrene Wisse* it is certainly possible, since the rule was widely adopted by anchoresses in Julian's day.[16] In any case the text gives an indication of the style of life a person interested in holy living would have lived. Instructions given in the *Ancrene Wisse* give glimpses of what the particulars of Julian's life could have been like. It is important to note, however, that anchoresses felt at liberty to interpret this rule reasonably freely.[17] The rule explains the relationship of the anchoress to the Church, which Julian expresses as being "fastened and united [oned] to our mother Holy Church" (14:61.302). It gives directions to guide the internal disposition and outer observances

---

[14] Francis Bloomfield, *An Essay Towards a Typological History of the County Norfolk.* 4 vols. (London: Fersfield and Lynn, 1739–75) 4:81, quoted in Warrack, *Revelations of Divine Love* xvii.

[15] Julian may not have been an anchoress when she had her visions. It is likely that by the time she wrote the long text she lived the life of a recluse.

[16] Originally the rule composed in the dialect of the South West Midlands (ca. 1225–1230) was addressed to three female anchoresses in Hertfordshire. The writing was later revised and addressed to others. Cf. Elizabeth Robertson, *Early English Devotional Prose and the Female Audience* (Knoxville: University of Tennessee Press, 1990) 44. There were a large number of copies of this rule in circulation. Cf. *Anchoritic Spirituality. Ancrene Wisse and Associated Works*, translated by Anne Savage and Nicholas Watson (New York: Paulist, 1991) 41 (hereafter *AW*).

[17] The title *Ancrene Wisse* points to this freedom. Some editors translate *Wisse* as *Riwle*. *Wisse*, however, maintains the emphasis on guidance rather than strict rule. It advises the anchoress: "you should not in any way promise to keep any rules as though under a vow" (*AW* VIII: Outer Rule, 199). Robert W. Ackerman and Roger Dahood, editors and translators of *Ancrene Riwle. Introduction and Part 1.* Medieval & Renaissance Texts & Studies 31 (Binghamton, N.Y.: Center for Medieval and Early Renaissance Studies, State University of New York at Binghamton, 1984) comment (p. 5) that the rule was ancillary to the ultimate goal of the anchoress to model her life on Christ. Bradley, *Julian's Way* 15–59, agrees that Julian would have freely interpreted this rule.

of the anchoress. Julian's inner disposition was to focus on Christ, to have "a recollection of the Passion" (2:177). Her outer disposition expresses the same reality: "we are clad and enclosed in the goodness of God" (1:6.186).

Fastened and Oned to Our Mother Holy Church

The *Ancrene Wisse* describes the relationship of the anchoress to the Church, which she experiences both physically and spiritually. Physically the anchoress lived beside but attached to the church. Although there is no record of the physical appearance of Julian's anchorhold as it stood in the fourteenth century, Warrack, writing in 1910, gives a description of the anchorhold before its bombing on June 27, 1942: "The little Church of St. Julian (in use at this day) still keeps from Norman times its dark round tower of flint rubble, and still there are traces about its foundation of the anchorage built against its south-eastern wall."[18] These foundations suggest that there was a cell or house of perhaps two or three rooms that Julian never left after her enclosure. Llewelyn describes the renovated cell:

> The site of Julian's cell today is still marked by two fragments of stone jutting out from the walls of the church, dating back to Julian's time or before. These have been incorporated into the present cell, which is now furnished as a chapel and is rather more than twice the size of the estimated hundred square feet of the original.[19]

Small in size, the recluse's chamber generally had three windows, one looking into the adjoining church so she could participate in liturgy, one so that she could communicate with her maids, and one opening to the outside. The parlor window where Julian communicated with the world looked onto the street. Today it is a garden.[20] The *Ancrene Wisse* advises: "Love your windows as little as you possibly can. Let them all be little, the parlour smallest and narrowest" (*AW* II: Outer Senses, 66). To be gazed through wisely, the window was the connecting link with the outside world.

---

[18] Warrack, *Revelations of Divine Love* xviii. The church was thought to have been founded before the Conquest and given to the nuns of Carrow by King Stephen.

[19] Robert Llewelyn, *With Pity Not Blame. The Spirituality of Julian of Norwich and the Cloud of Unknowing for Today* (3d. ed. London: Darton, Longman and Todd, 1994) 7.

[20] Llewelyn, *With Pity Not Blame* 7.

The stones jutting out from the walls of St. Julian's suggest more than a physical fusing with the church building. They signify a significant spiritual connection to the body of Mother Church. The rule also shows just how significant a role the anchoress played in the Church:

> The bird of the night under the eaves symbolizes recluses, who dwell under the eaves of the church because they understand that they should be of so holy a life that the whole of Holy Church, that is, Christian people, can lean upon them and trust them, while they hold her up with their holiness of life and their blessed prayers. This is why an anchoress is called an anchoress, and is anchored under a church like an anchor under the side of a ship, to hold that ship so that waves and storms do not overturn it. In the same way all Holy Church, which is called a ship must anchor on the anchoress. (*AW* III: Inner Feelings, 204).

The image of the recluse being like the anchor of a ship, particularly relevant in a seaport such as Norwich, suggests that, like an anchor under a ship, the prayerful, stable anchoress holds the Church steady in stormy times. Julian expresses this unity as being "fastened and united [oned] to our mother Holy Church" (14:61.302), yielding herself into the arms of the mother Holy Church: "And now I submit myself to my mother, Holy Church, as a simple child should" (14:47.259). As an anchoress, under the eaves of St. Julian's Church, Julian was valued and supported by the Church.

A Mind of the Passion

Within the *Showings* Julian tells us that she prays for a "recollection of the Passion" (2:177). Her emphasis on the Passion reflects the guidelines of the *Ancrene Wisse:*

> Keep him (Christ) in your nest, that is your heart. Think how much pain he suffered in his flesh outwardly, how sweet hearted he was, how soft within. . . . Whoever cannot have or hold this gemstone in the nest of her heart should at least have its likeness that is the crucifix in the nest of her anchorhouse; let her look on it often and kiss the places of the wounds in sweet memory of the true wounds which he patiently suffered on the true cross (*AW* III: Inner Feelings, 99).

Christ is central in explicating Julian's understanding that "all shall be well."

Clad and Enclosed in the Goodness of God

Julian gives little attention to outer observances in the *Showings*. She only refers to exterior materiality in images that reflect the goodness of God: "For as the body is clad in the cloth, and the flesh in the skin, and the bones in the flesh, and the heart in the trunk, so are we, soul and body, clad and enclosed in the goodness of God" (1:6.186). This reference to the body "clad in cloth" implies a possible interest in fabric. At the service of seeing all things as clad and enclosed in the goodness of God, the *Ancrene Wisse* gives guidelines for the cloth that clothes the anchoress:

> [I]t does not matter if your clothes are white or black, so long as they are plain, warm and well-made, the skins well tanned; and have as many as you need for your bed and to wear. . . . In winter let your shoes be soft, large and warm. In summer you have leave to walk and to sit barefoot, or to wear light shoes. Whoever wishes may wear stockings without feet to lie down in; do not sleep in shoes and sleep nowhere but in bed. . . . If you can go without wimples and are fully willing to, wear warm caps, and on them white or black veils (*AW* VIII: Outer Rule, 202).

The guideline for clothing suggests that Julian was modestly and warmly attired. The rule also provides details for harsh mortification of the body, but we will see there is no evidence in Julian's *Showings* that she engaged in such practices.

The *Ancrene Wisse* informs us that although the anchoress was to follow the days of fasting outlined by the Church she was not to be extreme in this asceticism. Food was to be nutritious and plain:

> You must not eat meat or fat, except in the case of great illness, or unless someone is very weak. Eat vegetable stew willingly, and accustom yourself to little drink. Nevertheless dear sisters, your food and drink have often seemed less to me than I would want you to have. Do not fast on bread and water any day unless you have leave (*AW* VIII: Outer Rule, 202).

The anchoress could have two servants to help with daily chores: "An anchoress who does not have food at hand must be careful to have two women, one who always stays at home and another who goes out when necessary" (*AW* VIII: Outer Rule, 204). The will of Thomas Edmund left to Julian in 1404 mentions a servant Sarah, while another left by John Plumpton in 1415 mentions a maid Alice.[21]

---

[21] *LWHM* 11–12.

Pets were limited to a cat: "[U]nless need drives you and your director advises it, you must not have any animal except a cat. An anchoress who has animals seems more like a house wife than Martha was; she cannot easily be Mary, Martha's sister with peace in her heart" (*AW* VIII: Outer Rule, 201).

She was not to conduct business: "An anchoress fond of bargaining, that is one who buys to sell for gain, sells her soul to the merchant of hell. Things that she makes, with her directors advice, she may sell for her needs. Holy people often used to live by their hands" (*AW* VIII. Outer Rule, 201). She was to make Church vestments and poor people's clothes: "do coarse kinds of handiwork. Do not make purses to win friends, but only for those for whom your director gives you leave, nor caps, silk bandages nor lace without leave; but cut out and sew and mend church vestments and poor people's clothes" (*AW* VIII: Outer Rule, 203).

The *Ancrene Wisse* helps us create a picture of Julian's daily life. In general we can conclude that Julian lived a simple life focused on a daily routine of prayer and concern for the poor. There is no suggestion in the rule or in Julian's text that observance of external rules was ever an end in itself. Her daily living focused on an appreciation that all of life was clad and enclosed in the goodness of God.

I Often Beheld the Woe That Is Here

In the short text suffering seems ever-present to Julian. Immersed in suffering, she remarks: "for often I beheld the woe that there is here" (xx:160). While we will see how Julian tries to resolve the tension between well-being and woe, I will briefly sketch here the historical background that could enable Julian to be so consciously aware of woe. The world outside the anchorhold, fourteenth-century pre-Reformation England, was a world that knew the waves and storms of suffering. Julian was born during the reign of Edward III (1327–1377), shortly before the Hundred Years' War between England and France. Because so much energy went into war, the administration of English agriculture declined, resulting in poor organization, failed crops, and famine. The war exacerbated an already tense situation between feudal lord and laborer. Discontented with a collapsing economy and lack of justice, peasants rebelled against secular and ecclesial lords. In Norwich this rebellion was led by Geoffrey Litster, who seized Norwich Castle. Subsequently he was captured and sentenced to death by the Bishop of Norwich, Henry Despenser.[22]

---

[22] May McKissack, *Oxford History of England*. Vol. 5, *The Fourteenth Century 1307–1399* (Oxford: Clarendon Press, 1959) 418.

At the same time as England was ravaged with social disruption, it also suffered endemic disease. There were at least three outbreaks of the Black Death in Julian's lifetime: in 1349 when she would have been seven, in 1351 when she would have been nineteen, and in 1369 when she would have been thirty-seven.[23] Norwich was particularly hard hit by its ravages, the population of 13,000 being halved. The aftermath was so devastating that Norwich barely regained its population by the end of the sixteenth century.[24] Although Julian does not mention these events in her text, she refers to the image of "the foul black death" (2:10.194) when she describes the suffering body of Christ, and also again when she describes a child's decaying body in images reminiscent of the black death (15:64.306). Bishops ordered services and processions to pray for relief from the plague and to avert God's anger at the sins of the people. Because priests visiting the sick became so susceptible to the plague, with forty-five percent of them dying,[25] the bishop of Bath and Wells in 1349 ordered: "if anyone on their death bed did not have access to a priest, they should make their confession to a layman, or even to a woman, and such confession would be most beneficial for the remission of their sins."[26] There is no doubt that the plague instigated a climate of suffering, crisis, and change. It is obvious that Julian often "beheld the woe that is here."

Theological controversies raged. We see glimpses of Julian's knowledge of these controversies in her repeated comments about being loyal to mother Church and her image: "Holy Church will be shaken in sorrow and anguish and tribulation in this world as men shake a cloth in the wind" (13:28.226). The image of cloth in the wind draws on the contrast between the fragile nature of woven cloth and the bitterness of the freezing, brawny wind that would blow from the North Sea over Norwich. It vividly describes the turmoil in the Church. A further reference: "for one single person may often be broken" (14:61.301) hints at individuals being broken over controversies of politics and heresy. Her reference in the short text to "paintings of the Crucifixion . . . which are made by God's grace, according to Holy Church's teaching, (i:125) could refer to the Lollard attack on the use of art objects for devotional or meditative purposes.[27] Yet Tanner's research suggests that

[23] See Jantzen, *Julian of Norwich* 7–8.

[24] Mark Ormrod, "The Politics of Pestilence: Government in England After the Black Death," in Mark Ormrod and Phillip Lindley, eds., *The Black Death in England* (Stanford: Paul Watkins, 1996) 141.

[25] Christopher Harper-Bill, "The English Church and English Religion After the Black Death," in Ormrod and Lindley, eds., *The Black Death in England* 86.

[26] Ibid. 79.

[27] Cf. *BSAJN* 202 n. 14.

Norwich was relatively free of accusations of heresy during Julian's lifetime.[28] While there is no evidence to conclude that the city had a continuous Lollard tradition as London had, it is possible that Julian would have been aware of the theological controversies instigated by John Wycliff and his followers. Margery Kempe vividly records her detention, stating that "if the Mayor could have his way, he would have [her] burnt."[29] It is possible that Margery visited Julian to inform her of her trial at Leister in 1417.

A major crisis in spiritual authority occurred in 1378 with the Great Schism, when a group of French cardinals challenged the legitimacy of Pope Urban IV and elected Clement VII pope. It is possible that Julian knew of the controversy because the bishop of Norwich, Henry Despenser, supported Urban and led a crusade promising indulgences for the families of those who participated. The campaign failed and Bishop Despenser returned home in disgrace.[30] Though Julian makes no mention of Church hierarchy, she has one reference to the sin of pride that indirectly relates to the Church: "I shall completely break down in you your empty affections and your vicious pride, and then I shall gather you and make you meek and mild, pure and holy through union *[oneing]* with me" (13:28.226-227). Excommunications and depositions continued for forty years (1378–1417). Rivalry among the leadership weakened authority in the Church. Yet, true to the title of anchoress who holds the Church steady in turbulent times, Julian remained faithful to the Church.

A Medley of Well-being and Woe

Contrasting with this litany of sickness, war, violence, poverty, and discontent, however, there were signs of well-being. Norwich, well positioned at the mouth of a river and close to a major highway, was able to develop into a center of cultural and intellectual exchange. It became a prosperous city with a vibrant textile trade, beautiful buildings, especially a cathedral, many churches, religious houses, and beguinages.[31] Within the walls of Norwich there were at least twenty religious houses

---

[28] The earliest cases come from records of trials of suspected Lollards between 1428 and 1431. See Norman P. Tanner, *Heresy Trials in the Diocese of Norwich 1428–31: Edited for the Royal Historical Society From Westminster Diocesan Archives MS.B.2* (London: Offices of the Royal Historical Society, 1977) 7–31.

[29] *The Book of Margery Kempe* 152.

[30] McKissack, *The Fourteenth Century* 432.

[31] See Norman P. Tanner, *The Church in Late Medieval Norwich: 1370–1532* (Toronto: Pontifical Institute of Medieval Studies, 1984) 57–58.

served by Austin Canons, Franciscans, Dominicans, Benedictines, and Carmelites.[32] They built significant libraries.[33] Churches were rebuilt in the perpendicular style. Craftspeople embellished and decorated, carving stone, painting colorful frescoes, designing altar pieces and fitting stained glass windows. The school of East Anglian art became famous for the delicacy of its illuminations. Great literary works emerged such as Chaucer's *Canterbury Tales,* Langland's *Piers Ploughman, The Pearl,* and *Sir Gawain and the Green Knight.* Mystical texts were composed, such as the anonymous author's *Cloud of Unknowing,* Walter Hilton's *Scale of Perfection* and Richard Rolle's *Fire of Love.* In the midst of pain and turmoil, the place was alive with creativity. From this brief historical sketch arises the question: How is it that Julian comes to conclude that "all shall be well" while living in this medley of well-being and woe?

II. THE MANUSCRIPTS OF *THE REVELATIONS OF DIVINE LOVE*

There is no extant copy of the manuscript of *The Revelations of Divine Love.* Copies made in later centuries come to us in two versions: the short and long texts. The short text (25 chapters), known as the Amherst Text, is in the British Museum.[34] Scholars generally agree that Julian recorded the short text immediately after her visionary experience in 1373.[35] It has a descriptive, immediate quality and presents a vivid portrayal of Julian's visionary experience and the beginning of her search for meaning.

The longer version (86 chapters) occurs in two copies: Paris Bibliothèque Nationale MS Fonds anglais 40, known as "Paris" (P), and the London British Library MS Sloane manuscript No. 2499, known as "Sloane 1" (S1). Paris and Sloane 1 represent two different manuscript traditions. There is a second Sloane text, London British Library MS

---

[32] Ibid. map 1, xii–xiv.

[33] See Patricia Mary Vinje, *An Understanding of Love According to the Anchoress Julian of Norwich* (Salzburg: Institut für Anglistik und Amerikanistik, 1983) 45–46.

[34] British Museum, Additional Manuscripts No. 37790, fols. 97–115. The short text belongs to an anthology of devotional pieces possibly compiled for use by a religious community. See Frances Beer, ed., *Julian of Norwich's Revelations of Love: The Shorter Version.* Middle English Texts 8 (Heidelberg: Carl Winter, 1978) 7–37.

[35] Dundas Harford first advanced the theory that the short text was a separate document, with the long text being the outcome of twenty years' reflection on the meaning of her visions. See Dundas Harford, editor and translator, *Comfortable Words for Christ's Lovers: Being the Visions and Voices Vouchsafed to Lady Julian, Recluse at Norwich in 1373* (London: R. A. Allenson, 1911) 8.

Sloane 3705 (Sloane 2), which is an eighteenth-century modernization of Sloane 1. Evidence in the long text suggests that Julian takes some time to reflect on the meaning of the *showings* before she composes the long text. She notes "fifteen years after and more, I was answered in spiritual understanding" (16:86.342). She also makes the aside: "twenty years after the time of the revelation except for three months" (14:51.270). Thus the long text was recorded around 1393.[36] Julian claims more authority for herself as an author in the long text. She omits the reference that denigrates herself as a teacher recorded in the short text: "God forbid that you should say or assume that I am a teacher, for that is not and never was my intention; for I am a woman, ignorant, weak and frail" (vi:135). The long text is a mature theological treatise on the meaning of love composed by a theologian. I concentrate on the long text because it gives most insight into Julian's understanding of salvation.

The Long Text

There are significant differences between the Paris and the Sloane 1 copies of the long text that raise questions among scholars. The Paris text, belonging to the late sixteenth to mid-seventeenth century,[37] is scribed on paper in a style of calligraphy popular around 1500. It was designed as a companion volume in a library for medieval devotional manuals.[38] The language is sometimes modernized and it contains a few passages not in Sloane 1. Through her study of all Julian's manuscripts, Frances Reynolds concludes that the original of P was close to Julian's first record of her showings.[39] Edmund Colledge and James Walsh make a contrary judgment of its value. They condemn it as: "the work of a not especially gifted antiquarian, more concerned . . . with appearance and form than meaning."[40] Yet they conclude: "There was never any serious question but that P must be chosen as the basic text."[41] Walsh gives reasons for this choice, citing Reynolds: "that the

---

[36] Cf. Nicholas Watson, "The Composition of Julian of Norwich's Revelations of Divine Love," *Speculum* 68 (1993) 637–83, for an argument that suggests a later dating of the texts.

[37] Glasscoe dates this as late sixteenth to early seventeenth century. C&W suggest ca. 1650. Cf. Marion Glasscoe, "Visions and Revisions: A Further Look at the Manuscripts of Julian of Norwich," *Studies in Bibliography* 42 (1989) 105; *BSAJN* 7.

[38] *BSAJN* 25.

[39] Reynolds, *Revelations of Julian of Norwich* xxiii.

[40] *BSAJN* 17.

[41] *BSAJN* 26.

Paris MSS. represents more nearly the MS. tradition."[42] They chose it for their critical edition because it appeared a more accurate copy of Julian's original text than the Sloane 1 manuscript.

Marion Glasscoe in contrast argues for the priority of Sloane 1 because it preserves linguistic forms closer to Julian's day.[43] It is written on poor quality paper in a sprawling hand. Colledge and Walsh characterize Sloane 1 as "marred throughout by the persistent omission of words and phrases which the scribe (or his copy) had deemed superfluous to the sense, but which destroys Julian's rhetorical figures, which are integral to her thought."[44] Furthermore, although Sloane 1 has more linguistic forms similar to the language of Julian's day, the scribe takes a more dominant role. There are chapter headings summarizing the main theme in each chapter. There is a lengthy postscript concerned that: "[T]his book come not but to the hands of them that will be his faithful lovers, and to those that will submit themselves to the faith of holy Church, and obey the wholesome understanding and teaching of those [men] that are of virtuous life, serious age, and profound learning" (86:163). These comments suggest that the text has been more carefully scrutinized in terms of heresy. One wonders whether the "men that be of virtuous life, serious age, and profound learning" do not include the scribe.[45] The omission of Julian's name and the authority given to the judgment of the scribe present enough evidence for us to wonder whether the scribe has edited the text to some degree according to his or her theological perspective. We see examples of possible editing in the passages about the body as a purse and Christ as mother.

The disagreement is not an easy one to resolve. Both texts are post-Reformation copies that could have been amended accordingly. I am not arguing a clearly conclusive case for the superiority of Paris over Sloane 1. Each is significant in that it represents a different manuscript

---

[42] *The Revelations of Divine Love of Julian of Norwich*, translated by James Walsh (London: Burns and Oates, 1961) v. Walsh also suggests that the Westminster florilegium supports this conclusion. Whether this collection is based on Paris is debatable.

[43] Glasscoe, "Visions and Revisions," 105. Although Reynolds adheres to the linguistic forms close to Julian's day she is cautious because the text is "frequently illegible and has numberless doubtful readings." Reynolds, *Revelations of Julian of Norwich* xx.

[44] *BSAJN* 26.

[45] C&W, *BSAJN* 8, suggest that the copyist was Mother Clementia Cary, a Benedictine nun. The scribe's comment at the end of the text implies a copyist with more authority.

tradition.[46] Nevertheless, I use Colledge and Walsh's translation of the Paris text[47] because it presents a tradition of Julian scholarship that has credibility within Catholic theology. The care taken to copy it in ornate calligraphy could suggest accuracy rather than inaccuracy. Moreover, it is possible that Paris is an earlier copy than Sloane 1. Because it left England in the seventeenth century[48] it is less likely to have been edited according to concerns of reformers who were suspicious of mystical literature. The first printed edition of the revelations was based on it. Paris names Julian as the author. Significantly, in terms of soteriology, the theology in Paris is more arresting in that it has a number of unique features regarded as significant for theology today.

Other Manuscripts

Other manuscripts that have come to the attention of scholars recently are extracts of Julian's texts in *The Upholland Anthology,* which has brief selections from the Paris tradition of the long text,[49] and the Westminster text, a heavily abridged adaptation of the long version.[50] Palaeographic studies assign the Westminster text to the late fifteenth or early sixteenth century. In his examination of the Westminster text Hugh Kempster claims that Colledge and Walsh assert that the text belongs to the Sloane tradition.[51] Glasscoe maintains that Westminster belongs to the Paris tradition. Neither sees a place for Westminster in their manuscript heritage. Kempster concludes: "I propose that neither is correct in positioning W on their branch of their own well-studied text. A comparative study of W, P, and S1 points to the existence of a

[46] Cf. Marion Glasscoe, ed., *Julian of Norwich. A Revelation of Love* (Exeter: University of Exeter Press, 1986) ix.

[47] A translation of the Paris text is used to make the theology accessible to contemporary readers. However, at times it is important to keep the Middle English words as represented in the Paris critical edition in order to appreciate some of the nuances of Julian's soteriology. I place these in brackets beside the translation when necessary.

[48] C&W point out (*BSAJN* 7) that the collection that this copy belongs to was begun in the first half of the seventeenth century by Jean Bigot and increased by his son Émeric until 1689.

[49] Hywel Wyn Owen and Luke Bell, eds., "The Upholland Anthology: An Augustine Baker Manuscript," *Downside Review* 107 (1989) 274–92.

[50] Hugh Kempster, ed., "Julian of Norwich: The Westminster Text of a Revelation of Love," *Mystics Quarterly* 23 (1997) 177–245.

[51] Although, as we noted above, they have related Westminster to the Paris text. See Walsh, ed., *Revelations of Divine Love* v–vi.

third distinct branch of the LV tree."[52] If Kempster is correct and there is a third manuscript tradition that the Westminster text represents, this can be helpful in deciding whether an idea in the Paris tradition that is not in Sloane 1 belongs to Paris alone or is reflected more widely in the tradition. Therefore I will refer to Westminster when such discrepancy arises.

III. THE AIMS OF THIS STUDY

This book presents a study of Julian's trinitarian soteriology as expressed in the Paris manuscript. The research demonstrates that Julian is a distinguished theologian who has something to say about the greatest of Christian questions, the meaning of salvation. Her book is not simply the mystical ponderings of an unknown anchoress. This is solid, orthodox, trinitarian theology that gives a reliable perspective on the meaning of salvation. In what follows I will

- place Julian in her historical context,
- present a hermeneutic that gives guiding principles for how we can interpret the theology elucidated in Julian's mystical text,
- organize Julian's ideas so that a contemporary audience may comprehend her soteriology,
- examine what Julian means by her trinitarian enunciation of the human journey from God to God described as "in the first we have our being, in the second we have our increasing and in the third we have our fulfilling,"
- show how in essence Julian's soteriology is a soteriology of *oneing,*
- analyze each aspect of Julian's trinitarian soteriology of *oneing* by investigating the role each person of the Trinity, Father, Son, and Holy Spirit, plays from gifted origins to graced fulfillment,
- demonstrate how Julian's soteriology is creation-centered,
- explore Julian's idea of the relationship between nature and grace, and
- assess aspects of Julian's soteriology and illustrate how her ideas can inform a contemporary understanding of salvation.

---

[52] The Westminster Text, 180. (W = Westminster; P = Paris; S1 = Sloane 1; LV = Long Version.)

2

A Hermeneutic for Interpreting the *Showings*

Here he says: Behold and see, for by the same power, wisdom and
goodness that I have done all this, by the same power, wisdom
and goodness I shall make all things well which are not well and
you will see it (1.176).

The art of understanding the *Revelations of Divine Love* must be informed by the time in which the text was composed and the genre of
literature to which these writings belong. Julian's writing is in the tradition of medieval visionary mystical literature. The aim of this chapter
is to demonstrate how we may interpret Julian's text by examining the
information Julian presents about interpretation in her writing. This
includes how her ideas came to fruition and how this influences the
interpretative process. Throughout the chapter I will demonstrate how
all Julian's thought occurs within a trinitarian framework. Interpreted
through the prayer of *beholding,* her writing invites a hermeneutic of
beholding. In *beholding* an image of the crucified Christ, Julian distinguishes three ways of seeing: through bodily sight, words forming her
understanding, and spiritual sight, all of which influence how we
might interpret the text. With the presence of Christ the main catalyst
for her writings, Julian also integrates Scripture and other sources into
her text. Consequently, because of the way Julian expresses her theology, the interpreter becomes engaged in a hermeneutical circle of ongoing interpretation. Although this text may be classified as private
revelation, Julian's theology is of value as public revelation.

I. MYSTICAL LITERATURE

Mystics are people who are aware of a sense of ultimate mystery
that is inherent in, yet transcends creation. Mystical literature gives

expression to both the experience[1] and the meaning of the experience, the perception that all of creation is part of a transcendent, unifying, meaningful whole. Christian mystical literature is grounded in a belief that union between human beings and God is possible in this life. It describes Christian belief and practice of what constitutes the immediate or direct presence of God.[2] Julian's book is a classic example of belief in, consciousness of, and reflection on the meaning of the presence of the divine.

A climax in the discernment that grounds Julian in ultimate mystery occurs when she gazes at the crucifix. Contemplation of this devotional object leads to union between her life experience and the story of Christ's Passion. This union, which she believes has divine origin, occurs through vivid visual and auditory phenomena. The value she attached to the experience led her to write about her encounter with Christ, and in doing so she created a genre of visionary literature. Visionary experience was expected in the medieval world.[3] The conditions of monastic life and instruction in prayer[4] encouraged the formation of mental images as an aid to prayer. Meditative techniques created a sensitivity to visualization and a receptivity to visionary perception as a way of expressing insights into the sacred. Naturally, the ideas that suffused the consciousness through visions were reflected in images from the visionary's tradition.

Julian's expression of her theology in the genre of visionary literature is not as irregular as it may seem. The theology that emerges from the subjectivity of her personal experience resonates with Lonergan's idea of transcendental method: it is not the intrusion into theology of alien matter from an alien source. Its function is to advert to the fact that theologies are produced by theologians, that theologians have

---

[1] I use experience as outlined by Gerald O'Collins, *Fundamental Theology* (London: Darton, Longman and Todd, 1981) 33–36. Experience has an aspect of immediacy; it implies direct contact that must be entered into and lived. Experience and reflection on the experience, though distinct, are not separable. Experience points to our being alive. It affects our whole existence.

[2] Cf. Bernard McGinn, *The Presence of God: A History of Western Christian Mysticism. Vol. 1: The Foundations of Mysticism* (New York: Crossroad, 1991) xvii.

[3] Elizabeth Petroff, ed., *Medieval Women's Visionary Literature* (Oxford: Oxford University Press, 1986) 5–20, shows how prolific visionary experience was in women's piety.

[4] For example, *lectio divina* or Franciscan meditation. Cf. *Meditations on the Life of Christ: An Illustrated Manuscript of the Fourteenth Century*, translated by Isa Ragusa, edited by Isa Ragusa and Rosalie B. Green (Princeton: Princeton University Press, 1961); Kerrie Hide, "The Showings of Julian of Norwich as a *Lectio Divina*," *Tjurunga* 49 (1996) 39–50.

minds and use them, that their doing so should not be ignored or passed over, but explicitly acknowledged in itself and in its implications.[5]

Julian's revelations express her understanding of the mystery of God. They incorporate doctrinal expressions blended with familiar images from nature, paintings, stained glass windows, crucifixes, and illuminations from Psalters or books of hours. Her theology is the fruit of her view of reality informed by the culture she lived in, her way of thinking, her woman's view of reality. Thus in order to interpret this literature we must be aware of how theology was communicated to Julian and the way she gave concrete expression to understanding. This awareness enables the reader to engage in Julian's way of interpretation and facilitates interpretation in this generation.

Julian begins her *Showings* with a dramatic description of her illness. She thinks she is going to die. A priest attends her bedside and places a crucifix before her: "The parson set the cross before my face and said: Daughter, I have brought you the image of your savior. Look at it and take comfort from it, in reverence of him who died for you and me" (ii:128).[6] A fifteenth-century bone crucifix, with a serene face, a muscular body, and a concentration on the five wounds of Christ in his hands, feet, and side illustrates the type. From this experience of contemplating the meaning of divine love expressed so poignantly on the cross Julian unfolds her theology of love. The priest invites Julian to observe "the image of your savior." The description continues: "I agreed to fix my eyes on the face of the crucifix if I could" (ii:128). She vividly recounts the experience: "my sight began to fail, and it was all dark around me in the room, dark as night, except that there was ordinary light trained upon the image of the cross, I never knew how" (ii:128). In darkness Julian begins to see with a special kind of light that illuminates her understanding of reality. In the deepest darkness of suffering she comes to understand how all things have meaning through the love of Christ.

---

[5] Bernard Lonergan, *Method in Theology* (New York: Seabury, 1972) 24–25.

[6] It is uncertain whether this crucifix was made of wood, bone, or bronze. An extant bone crucifix (ca. 1460), sixteen centimeters long, shows the realism typical of a Gothic figure of Christ. The style is quite like the crucifixion illumination found in the Abingdon Missal, dated 1461. See Peter Lasko and Nigel J. Morgan, eds., *Medieval Art of East Anglia 1300–1520* (London: Thames and Hudson in association with Jarrold and Sons, 1974) 55. Brant Pelphrey, *Love Was His Meaning: The Theology and Mysticism of Julian of Norwich* (= *LWHM*) (Salzburg: Institut für Anglistik und Amerikanistik, 1982) xviii, provides a sketch of a gilded and enameled crucifix (ca. 1400–1450).

While Julian gazes single-mindedly at the face of the savior the image acquires characteristics reminiscent of a medieval crucifixion image from an illuminated manuscript.[7] "[S]uddenly I saw the red blood running down from under the crown, hot and flowing freely and copiously, a living stream, just as it was at the time when the crown of thorns was pressed on his blessed head" (1:4.181). The emphasis on red blood flowing creates an empathetic mood that helps the reader comprehend the depth of divine love. Julian presents a collection of Passion scenes, with pictorial qualities that depict the transition from Christ's suffering and dying to his glorified rising.

Thus the soteriology that emerges throughout the *Showings* is grounded in an experience of suffering (Julian's suffering mirrored in Christ's suffering). Walter Kasper points to the significance of such an inception: "a theology that takes the human experience of suffering as its starting point, starts, therefore, not with a borderline phenomenon but with the center and depth of human experience."[8] Julian is concerned with that center and depth, with how God relates to humanity in suffering. Immersed as she is in her own suffering and the suffering of Christ, her major concern becomes the question of salvation.

II. A Trinitarian Framework

Julian's text is far more complex than a simple description of the crucified Christ: it presents the salvific meaning of the paschal mystery. In the long text she makes it clear that the principal insight she has from looking at the crucifix is an interconnection between the paschal mystery and the Trinity: "This is a revelation of love which Jesus Christ, our endless bliss, made in sixteen showings, of which the first is about his precious crowning of thorns; and in this was contained and specified the blessed Trinity" (1:175). This link between Christ's Passion, death, and resurrection and the Trinity gives Julian's theology a unique flavor. Her *Showings* do not simply record a vision of Christ suffering; they communicate trinitarian theology. The vision marks the way her theology will proceed. There is no distinct separation of theology into discrete areas with one section of the revelations devoted to interpreting christology, one devoted to trinitarian theology, and one to

---

[7] See for example the Gorleston Psalter, Richard Marks and Nigel Morgan, *The Golden Age of English Manuscript Painting 1200–1500* (New York: George Braziller, 1981) 79. I am indebted to Denise N. Baker for pointing to the likely connection of this Psalter to Julian. Denise Nowakowski Baker, *Julian of Norwich's Showings: From Vision to Book* (Princeton, N.J.: Princeton University Press, 1994) 43.

[8] Walter Kasper, *The God of Jesus Christ* (New York: Crossroad, 1984) 160.

redemption. All elements of her theology intersect. All her theology is trinitarian. All her theology is soteriological. All that she will express as the revelations continue occurs within the context of a trinitarian doctrine of God. She explains in more detail:

> And in the same revelation, suddenly the Trinity filled my heart full of the greatest joy, and I understood that it will be so in heaven without end to all who will come there. For the Trinity is God, God is the Trinity. The Trinity is our maker, the Trinity is our protector, the Trinity is our everlasting lover, the Trinity is our endless joy and our bliss, by our Lord Jesus Christ and in our Lord Jesus Christ. And this was revealed in the first vision and in them all, for where Jesus appears the blessed Trinity is understood, as I see it (1:4.181).

Julian's added reflection presents principles that govern interpretation of her theology. She encounters Christ, experiences trinitarian joy, and understands that Christ reveals the Trinity. Life experience and theology converge. The rhythmical formula that identifies the trinitarian nature of her doctrine of God, "the Trinity is God and God is the Trinity," informs every *showing* that follows. Furthermore, and reflecting the mystical nature of her starting point, the terminology she uses in reference to the Trinity is sometimes explicit, sometimes implicit. There are no hard and fixed doctrinal formulations about the inner life of the Trinity; rather she adopts her own way of expressing beliefs about the presence of the Trinity to humanity through images that are inclusive, free, and rhythmical.

III. Beholding

Julian comes to appreciate the immediate presence of God through *beholding*. The first reference to the significance of *beholding* occurs in the introduction that summarizes the *Showings:* "Here he says: Behold and see, for by the same power, wisdom and goodness that I have done all this, by the same power, wisdom and goodness I shall make all things well which are not well, and you will see it" (1:176). Julian gives sight or contemplative vision an important role, but her *beholding* is more than ordinary seeing. The *Middle English Dictionary* defines *beholding* as looking, gazing, or seeing a visual appearance, applying the mind in thought, meditation, or contemplation, and being in a state of relationship or connection.[9] Although this definition reflects Julian's

---

[9] Hans Kurath, Sherman Kuhn, and Robert Lewis, eds., *Middle English Dictionary* (Ann Arbor: University of Michigan Press, 1954–) (= *MED*) 835–38. Cf. Paolo Molinari, *Julian of Norwich; The Teaching of a 14th Century English Mystic* (London

use of the word, she expands its meaning to its limits. For Julian *behold-ing* involves the ability to see with the highest inner sensitivities of the soul. *Beholding* is a way of interpreting revelation. *Beholding* reveals the underlying truth of all reality. *Beholding* incorporates truth, wisdom, and love: "Truth sees God, and wisdom contemplates God, and of these two comes the third, and that is a marvellous delight in God, which is love" (14:44.256). *Beholding* communicates a "lesson of love." This creates a response in the soul: "For of all things, contemplating (beholding) and loving the Creator makes the soul to seem less in its own sight, and fills it full with reverent fear and true meekness, and with much love for its fellow Christians" (1:6.187). *Beholding* enables Julian to participate in what Christ's Passion signifies, to become one with it, and to be transformed by it. Related to loving, *beholding* is see-ing with the "eye of the heart" (Eph 1:18) or seeing with a felt under-standing of love. *Beholding* creates a sense of "reverent fear," which Julian later qualifies as "gentle; For the more it is obtained, the less is it felt, because of the sweetness of love" (16:74.324).

Julian explains the process of *beholding*:

> God showed me this in the first vision, and he gave me space and time to contemplate [*behold*] it. And then the bodily vision ceased, and the spiritual vision persisted in my understanding. And I waited with reverent fear, rejoicing in what I saw and wishing, as much as I dared, to see more, if that were God's will, or to see the same vision for a longer time (1:8.190).

Though the corporeal vision was the catalyst for her emerging insights, space and time cause this to fade. An intermediary time is essential to her expressing herself in words:

> (B)efore God revealed any words, he allowed me to contemplate [*be-hold*] him for a fitting length of time, and all that I had seen, and all the significance that was contained in it, as well as my soul's simplicity could accept it. And then he, without voice and without opening of lips, formed in my soul this saying: With this the fiend is overcome (5:13.201).

Fundamental to *beholding* is time to contemplate beyond bodily sight, beyond seeing Christ suffering, into "spiritual sight." *Beholding* enables Julian to interpret meaning, to create theology, and to articulate her soteriology.

---

and New York: Longmans, Green, 1958) 104–39, and Robert Llewelyn, *With Pity Not Blame. The Spirituality of Julian of Norwich and the Cloud of Unknowing for Today* (3d. ed. London: Darton, Longman and Todd, 1994) 73–74.

Although Julian's repeated use of *beholding* tends to privilege see-ing as the most important sense that leads to understanding, she also makes reference to the other senses: "I had touching, sight and feeling of three properties of God, in which consist the strength and the effect of all the revelation" (16:83.339). Initiated by God, touching, sight, and feeling create mutual contact or common ground, which deepens understanding. Nevertheless, understanding the mystery of divine loving is always partial. There is always something of the mystery yet to be revealed. Touching, sight, and feeling point to the presence of the divine in the act of interpretation that is intimate and familiar.

When Julian describes the deepest knowledge of God that human beings will have in the face-to-face beatific vision she includes all the senses:

> And then we shall all come into our Lord, knowing ourselves clearly and wholly possessing God, and we shall all be endlessly hidden in God, truly seeing and wholly feeling, and hearing him spiritually and delectably smelling him and sweetly tasting him. And there we shall see God face to face, familiarly and wholly. The creature which is made will see and endlessly contemplate God who is the maker (14:43.255).

Knowledge of God flows from both an intellectual vision of clearly knowing and a non-cognitive, intuitive understanding of experiencing love. In attempting to describe what this involves, Julian makes direct reference to the spiritual senses.[10] Seeing and *beholding* God involves "truly seeing, wholly feeling, spiritually hearing, delectably smelling" and "sweetly tasting." Thus for Julian the more complete the *beholding* the more all the senses are involved. Julian's reference to the senses, however, includes more than bodily knowing. The senses are "organs of mystical knowledge."[11] They convey a combined bodily, spiritual, and intellectual way of understanding. The senses communicate how she is awakened and sensitized to the originating presence of God within her being.

Julian further associates *beholding* with being *oned* into the God-head:

[10] This is a doctrine that goes back to Origen, who identified mystical senses of the soul that become Christ. See Origen, "The Mystical Senses," in Harvey Egan, ed., *An Anthology of Christian Mysticism* (Collegeville: The Liturgical Press, 1991) 29. For Origen the senses are always spiritual. Julian, in contrast, leaves the imagery more open to both a physical and a spiritual interpretation.

[11] This is Rahner's phrase. See Karl Rahner, "The 'Spiritual Senses' According to Origen," *Theological Investigations* 16, translated by Karl-Heinz and Boniface Kruger (New York: Seabury, 1979) 97.

> [W]hen our courteous Lord of his special grace shows himself to our soul, we have what we desire, and then for that time we do not see what more we should pray for, but all our intention and all our powers are wholly directed to contemplating [*beholding*] him. And as I see it, this is an exalted and imperceptible prayer; for the whole reason why we pray is to be united [*oned*] into the vision and contemplation [*beholding*] of him to whom we pray, wonderfully rejoicing with reverent fear, and with so much sweetness and delight in him that we cannot pray at all except as he moves us at the time (14:43.254).

Beholding diminishes the gap between the human and the divine. Although imperceptible, *beholding* creates an ability to see partially as God sees, and to understand as God understands. *Beholding* makes the human and the divine one. The fruits of *beholding* are joy, reverent fear, sweetness, and delight.

Significantly, then, Julian's interpretation of her experience does not come from thought that engages in analysis of the meaning of the Passion, as we would find in scholastic writing. Her insights express wisdom felt, experienced, and intuited in the deepest levels of her being. In *beholding* Julian engages her whole being in seeing, tasting, feeling, hearing, savoring, and touching the mystery of divine love revealed in Christ. *Beholding* enables her to have a deep sense of reverent fear that expresses itself in love that is beyond feeling. *Beholding* also enables her to know in wisdom and truth that all human beings are part of a meaningful whole that will make all things well. Thus *beholding* creates what might be called a mystical rather than systematic soteriology.

IV. ALL THIS WAS SHOWN IN THREE PARTS

Division into three parts is a recurring theme in Julian's writing.[12] The space and time to *behold* lead to three levels of understanding. In the short text she identifies these as teachings: "All this blessed teaching of our Lord was shown to me in three parts" (vii:135). Both texts describe the three parts. The vision occurs "by bodily vision and by words formed in my understanding and by spiritual vision. But I may not and cannot show the spiritual visions as plainly and fully as I should wish" (1:9.192). These parts are not isolated ways of interpreta-

---

[12] We will examine three manners of understanding charity, three *beholdings* of suffering, and three *beholdings* of motherhood later in the text. Pelphrey, *LWHM* 103, suggests that Julian's references to three demonstrate her awareness of the Trinity as the central and most important element of her visions. Cf. J.P.H. Clark, "Nature, Grace and the Trinity in Julian of Norwich," *Downside Review* 100 (1982) 203.

tion, but rather interact and interrelate with each other and together make a whole. Never left to stand alone or presented as literal truth, the bodily sight reveals something deeply hidden. Therefore, although Julian spends a considerable portion of the text describing bodily sights of the Passion, this is always at the service of the deeper meaning communicated by the images. The understanding she receives from reflecting on these sights becomes paramount. Julian's version of visionary literature is not simply a depiction of what she sees. It presents what she comes to understand through seeing. The visions are not significant because they represent a state of consciousness surpassing ordinary human experience. Their validity rests on the value they have as a means of communicating an intensive realization of the mysteries of God in words that convey unfathomable levels of meaning.

The movement in understanding "by bodily sight, by words forming in my understanding," and "by spiritual sight" is not linear. It is a blending together like colors on a canvas creating an integrated whole. At the beginning of the long text Julian explains how the parts interrelate:

> This is a revelation of love which Jesus Christ, our endless bliss, made in sixteen showings, of which the first is about his precious crowning of thorns; and in this was contained and specified the blessed Trinity, with the Incarnation and the union between God and man's soul, with many fair revelations and teachings of endless wisdom and love, in which all the revelations which follow are founded and connected (1:175).

The whole sixteen *showings* are one revelation of love, all founded and connected within the bodily sight of Christ crowned with thorns. There is an essential unity in the revelation that draws all that is communicated into an integrated whole. Central facets of theology, an understanding of the Trinity, the Incarnation, the union between God and humanity's soul, and teachings of endless wisdom become one within the visual image. Skinner's translation of the Sloane 1 manuscript, "in which all the showings that follow are grounded and oned" (1:1) captures this well.[13] The *showings* are ultimately an example of *oneing* where all parts become one. The verbs in the Paris text, "contained" and "specified," suggest that the theology is included, defined, and delineated within the whole. The scribe's warning at the end of this manuscript[14] accentuates the same unity: "And beware that you do

---

[13] John Skinner, *Julian of Norwich: A Revelation of Love.* Newly translated from Middle English (Evesham: Arthur James, 1996).

[14] This comment is also recorded at the end of the Sloane 1 manuscript.

not accept one thing which is according to your pleasure and liking, and reject another, for that is the disposition of heretics. But accept it all together, and understand it truly."[15] To understand what Julian is saying about salvation we must take everything together and apply her method of *beholding*. Taking everything together includes not only *beholding*. Within these bodily sights are spiritual sights and words formed in her understanding that express theology.

In order to explain how Julian's method of interpretation works I will apply the threefold process she outlines to one of her Passion scenes as an example of how levels of meaning interconnect. As we focus on each aspect of the scene, however, we must be mindful that each facet is part of an undivided whole. When we concentrate on the crown of thorns or the sea-bed it is like focusing on a small detail within a whole painting. Similarly, when we center on words that form in her understanding we are concentrating, for the moment, on one element that is essential to the composition of the whole canvas.

Bodily Sight

Julian begins by telling us that she sees the face of the crucifix with *bodily sight*:

> I looked with bodily vision into the face of the crucifix which hung before me, in which I saw a part of Christ's Passion: contempt, foul spitting, buffeting, and many long-drawn pains, more than I can tell; and his color often changed. At one time I saw how half his face, beginning at the ear, became covered with dried blood, until it was caked to the middle of his face, and then the other side was caked in the same fashion, and meanwhile the blood vanished on the other side, just as it had come (2:10.193).

Continual *beholding* of the figure hanging before her leads to partial sight of the Passion. She presents a litany of pains that she sees Christ experience, which leads to a strange, dispassionate portrayal of Christ's face caked in a mask of dried blood. There is a mystical, timeless quality about the portrait, an enigmatic ambience that incorporates the tangible with the transcendent. Though the image is corporeal, there is no sense that this is a historical account of Christ's suffering. Julian points to the depth of meaning it evokes as she sees "more than she can tell."

---

[15] Edmund Colledge and James Walsh, eds., *A Book of Showings to the Anchoress Julian of Norwich*, 2 vols. (= *BSAJN*) (Toronto: Pontifical Institute of Mediaeval Studies, 1978) 734 n. 23.

Julian emphasizes the corporeal nature of her seeing: "This I saw bodily, frighteningly and dimly, and I wanted more of the light of day, to have seen it more clearly" (2:10.193). Her words enable us to picture a crucifix and see Christ's body on the cross dimly, and yet lit by changing light as if tinged with the colors of stained glass windows. But Julian is answered in her reason, and the seeing that evolves from *beholding* the cross is not the consequence of ordinary light. Seeing comes through the light of divine revelation. Marion Glasscoe captures the manner in which Julian interprets the Passion scenes: "They [Julian's bodily sights of the Passion] hang as if vividly lit in a silent darkness for contemplation, and function sacramentally in that they crystallise forms which allow a depth of insight into the inner realities of human existence as perceived in Christian terms."[16] Roger Corless expresses a similar sentiment. The visions are for Julian "sacraments of the un-image-able, outward and visible signs of inward and spiritual truths."[17] Julian sees the crucified body of Christ, and the seeing begins to function sacramentally: it works mysteriously on her consciousness and begins to suggest more than she can clearly describe or define.

Words Formed in My Understanding

The scene changes abruptly: "Once my understanding was let down into the bottom of the sea" (2:10.193). We are now in the area of Julian's *understanding*. Elsewhere in the text she refers to looking with the eye of her understanding: "I looked at it with the eye of my understanding and thought" (1:5183); "this revelation was given to my understanding to teach our souls wisely" (1:6.184); and "this vision was shown to teach me to understand" (7:15.205). Understanding expresses her thought, the wise learning of her soul, how she grasps the meaning of a vision. In this instance her understanding draws her on to visualize a possibly familiar experience of observing the sea-bed. Her understanding moves down to the sea floor, a traditional image for the unconscious. She evokes a colorful scene with surprising detail: "and there I saw green hills and valleys, with the appearance of moss strewn with seaweed and gravel" (2:10.193) before describing her understanding in a convoluted manner that is not easy to interpret:

[16] Marion Glasscoe, *English Medieval Mystics: Games of Faith* (London and New York: Longman, 1993) 223.
[17] Roger Corless, "Comparing Cataphatic Mystics: Julian of Norwich and T'an-luan," *Mystics Quarterly* 21 (1995) 20.

> Then I understood in this way: that if a man or woman were there
> under the wide waters, if he could see God, as God is continually with
> man, he would be safe in soul and body, and come to no harm. And
> furthermore, he would have more consolation and strength than all this
> world can tell (2:10.193).

The passage suggests that no matter where men and women find themselves, if they are aware of the continual presence of God they will feel
safe in body and soul and experience no harm.

As words form in Julian's understanding she tries to articulate further her theology of divine presence. Consequently she expresses her
teaching more explicitly: "For it is God's will that we believe that we
see him continually, though it seems to us that the sight be only partial;
and through this belief he makes us always to gain more grace"
(2:10.194). She gives this teaching authority by qualifying that God
wishes us to believe it. A teaching becomes clear: "for God wishes to be
seen, and he wishes to be sought, and he wishes to be expected, and he
wishes to be trusted" (2:10.194). Julian experiences more sight and
there is another rhythmical movement in the text. She relates this back
to her original vision of Christ's face: "And then several times our Lord
gave me more insight, by which I understood truly that it was a revelation. It symbolized and resembled [*was a figure and a likeness of*] our foul,
black death, which our fair, bright, blessed Lord bore for our sins"
(2:10.194). More sight reveals that Christ resembles the *black death.*[18] The
image is sacramental because Christ does not simply show signs of
human suffering: he *is* human suffering. He is the definitive form of the
Black Death. This *beholding* of Christ as the figure of human suffering
draws her to think of another veil:

> It made me think of the holy Vernicle at Rome,[19] which he imprinted
> with his own blessed face, when he was in his cruel Passion, voluntar-
> ily going to his death, and of his often-changing color, the brownness
> and the blackness, his face sorrowful and wasted. Many marvelled how
> it could be the case that he imprinted this image with his blessed face,
> which is the fairest of heaven, the flower of earth and the fruit of the
> virgin's womb (2:10.194).

[18] It is noteworthy that the Sloane 1 text refers to the Black Death as the *foule dede
hame* (X:374.51). This places less emphasis on the historical experience of suffering
due to the Black Death and more on sin. Christ is, however, still the image and likeness of harmful deeds.

[19] Based on tradition rather than Scripture, the vernicle was a handkerchief
believed to have been lent to Christ by Veronica on the Via Dolorosa. This cloth subsequently bore the impression of Christ's face. This relic was venerated in the
Middle Ages, and was often mentioned in sermons and popular devotional books.

The face veiled in blood, the face that is the figure of the Black Death, and the face imprinted on the vernicle subconsciously interrelate and become pregnant with a depth of meaning that is evoked rather than stated. The crucifix becomes "a sacrament of divine darkness"[20] that transmits meaning. Thus Julian's interplay of images that express darkness and light, ugliness and beauty, pain and joy reveals that light exists in darkness, healing in suffering, love in wretchedness, and well-being in woe. This integration of well-being and woe enfolded in each other in a paradoxical unity is characteristic of her style.

Julian then brings in a teaching from the Church: "We know in our faith and our belief, by the teaching and preaching of Holy Church, that the blessed Trinity made mankind in their image and their likeness" (2:10.194). The echoes of *figure and likeness* and *image and likeness* fuse the two ideas, enabling them to interact in the imagination of the reader. Julian continues to add theological insights that she places side by side without fully explaining the connection:

> In the same way we know that when man fell so deeply and so wretchedly through sin, there was no other help for restoring him, except through him who created man. And he who created man for love, by the same love wanted to restore man to the same blessedness and to even more (2:10.194).

Julian then links the ideas more directly through her words *in the same way we know.* She places together two more theological positions about salvation. The first, that there was no other help for restoring humanity but through the one who created humanity, reflects the idea that a God-man was needed to respond to the sin of humanity. The second reference, to the one who created humanity *for love,* focuses on Christ becoming human for love. This juxtaposition creates a rhythm between different theological perspectives that enables her readers to appreciate the value of both positions. By placing a series of images side by side and connecting them with the repetition of imagery Julian creates a thread of unity between the creation story, the incarnation of Christ, the problem of sin, the suffering that humans experience on account of the Black Death, the suffering Christ experienced at the crucifixion, and the new creation brought to fruition in Christ. This interspersal of dogmatic Church teaching within the imagery occurs throughout the text.

[20] This is a term used by Dermot A. Lane, *Christ at the Centre: Selected Issues in Christology* (New York: Paulist, 1991) 77.

Therefore in order to understand what Julian is saying about salvation we need to hold the eclectic gathering of doctrines in dialectical tension. Though at times Julian seems to contradict herself, her method invites us to take everything together and find meaning in the intersections that are not, however, easily pinned down. At the end of this revelation she reminds us of the difficulty of attempting to access the inaccessible: "For he works in secret, and he will be perceived, and his appearing will be very sudden. And he wants to be trusted, for he is very accessible, familiar [homely] and courteous, blessed may he be" (2:10.196). The revelation of God is *secret,* but she confidently advises: "he will be perceived."

Spiritual Sight

Though the second revelation provides a good example of bodily sight and words forming in Julian's understanding, it does not give an example of what Julian identifies as *spiritual sight.* She reserves her category of *spiritual sight* for times when she attempts to describe the meaning of divine love. Her first reference to a *spiritual sight* coincides with a bodily sight: "At the same time as I saw this sight of the head bleeding, our good Lord showed a spiritual sight of his familiar [homely] love" (1:5.183). Later in the text *spiritual sights* become more ethereal: "[O]ur good Lord opened my spiritual eye, and showed me my soul in the midst of my heart" (16:68.312). In both cases, however, she uses concrete imagery, namely cloth and a city, to describe the *spiritual sight.* Yet when she "is answered in spiritual understanding" that "love was his meaning" (16:86.342) there is no reference to concrete imagery: instead, the idea of love becomes personified. The spiritual teachings point beyond the words that attempt to express them.

Spiritual in Bodily Likeness— More Spiritual Without Bodily Likeness

Within the *Showings* Julian recounts a significant parable about a lord and a servant that contains *spiritual sights.* Like a preacher's exemplum,[21] the parable presents theological insights in the form of an alle-

---

[21] An exemplum is a story used by preachers to illustrate the points to be made in a sermon. See Gerald Robert Owst, *Preaching in Medieval England: An Introduction to Sermon Manuscripts of the Period 1350–1450* (Cambridge: Cambridge University Press, 1926). Gerald Robert Owst, *Literature and Pulpit in Medieval England: A Neglected Chapter in the History of English Letters and of the English People* (New York: Barnes and Noble, 1961).

gorical narrative that unlocks the meaning of the revelations. She points to the centrality of the example in developing her understanding of salvation: "I have teaching within me, as it were the beginning of an ABC, whereby I may have some understanding of our Lord's meaning, for the mysteries of the revelation are hidden in it, even though all the showings are full of mysteries" (14:51.276). The example contains the mysteries of the revelation. During the presentation of the parable Julian explains the process she uses to understand its meaning:

> And then our courteous Lord answered very mysteriously, by revealing a wonderful example of a lord who has a servant, and gave me sight for the understanding of them both. The vision was shown doubly with respect to the lord, and the vision was shown doubly with respect to the servant. One part was shown spiritually, in a bodily likeness. The other part was shown more spiritually, without bodily likeness (14:51.267).

Mysterious and mystical, the parable gives sight to her understanding. She experiences the sight in two ways: spiritually "in bodily likeness" and "more spiritually without bodily likeness." In other words, these seem to be spiritual, dream-like sights that resemble bodies but become more spiritual and ineffable without bodily likeness. Faithfulness to interpreting these two kinds of visions inspires three levels of understanding:

> The first is the beginning of the teaching which I understood from it at the time. The second is the inward instruction which I have understood from it since. The third is all the whole revelation from the beginning to the end, which our Lord God of his goodness freely and often brings before the eyes of my understanding. And these three are so unified [*oned*], as I understand it, that I cannot and may not separate them (14:51.269).

The parable unlocks three levels of meaning: the instruction that Julian understands immediately as she receives the vision, the inward learning that she gradually comes to after the event, and the condensation of the meaning of the whole revelation in the example. Julian notes that these are not separate levels of meaning: they are *oned*. The integration of these three levels occurs as she presents the example of a description in bodily likeness, recapitulates her immediate response to the images, and adds her subsequent interpretation. Julian receives instruction: "to take heed to all the attributes, divine and human, which were revealed in the example, though this may seem to you mysterious and ambiguous" (14:51.270). Though the parable has an unreal quality, each detail conveys insight into the meaning of salvation expressed in the revelations as a whole.

In order to interpret her spiritual *sight*, spiritual "in bodily like-ness" and "more spiritual without bodily likeness," we must engage the hermeneutic of *beholding*. We must behold Julian's images and fol-low the explanations of meaning that arise. Yet Julian reminds us: "I may not and cannot show the spiritual visions as plainly and fully as I should wish" (1:9.192). Julian tells what she can of her *spiritual sights* and surrounds them in interconnecting silences that leave room for mystery. *Spiritual sights* inspire revelation in the imagination of her readers.

Understanding Meaning

Julian's preoccupation with the visionary experience could lead to an easy labeling of her as an affective theologian. There is no doubt that Julian believes that God is love and that love unites humanity with God. But the intellect also plays an important role. Julian gives another threefold body of principles that governs how she comes to understand salvation:

> Man endures in this life by three things, by which three God is honored and we are furthered, protected and saved. The first is the use of man's natural reason. The second is the common teaching of Holy Church. The third is the inward grace-giving operation of the Holy Spirit; and these three are all from one God. God is the foundation of our natural reason; and God is the teaching of Holy Church, and God is the Holy Spirit (16:80.335).

Julian's ground of knowledge includes three things: reason, Church teaching, and grace. At times Julian interprets her experience through existing teachings of the Church, as when she comments: "We know in our faith and our belief, by the teaching and preaching of Holy Church" (2:10.194). At other times interpretive elements occur in her personal experience: "And in this I was taught by the grace of God" (32:13.233). New insights emerge within the *Showings* themselves. Julian points to the importance of integrating reason, "the teaching of Holy Church and the inward gracious operation of the Holy Spirit." Both the collec-tive horizon of the Church and her own personal horizon shape and color her understanding.

Judiciously, however, Julian qualifies the place of reason. Although "[o]ur reason is founded in God" (14:56.290), she warns: "we cannot profit by our reason alone, unless we have equally memory and love, nor can we be saved merely because we have in God our natural foundation, unless we have, coming from the same foundation, mercy and grace" (14:56.290). Memory and love must complement reason. Therefore although reason is important to Julian she does not limit knowledge to a rationalism that believes reason alone can grasp the mysteries of faith, nor does she suggest that uncritical faith is sufficient to grasp God's revelation. Knowledge is not based on reason alone, but on the memory of the history of God's fidelity in working for our salvation, the memory of our true nature and the ongoing work of mercy and grace called to consciousness in love.

Knowledge occurs not in abstract thinking about God, but by means of attention to our nature in God through the power of the Holy Spirit. In Julian's interpretative framework knowledge transpires through direct, immediate, intuitive experience that occurs in mediation between knower and known. Brant Pelphrey identifies this as knowing "in an intimate, familial sense implied by 'homely loving'."[22] When Julian becomes certain of this knowing she gives it authority by associating her insights with the will of God: "It is God's will, as I understand it, that we contemplate his blessed Passion in three ways" (8:20.214). This certainty comes through experiencing deep communion in God.

Beholding with bodily sight, words forming in her understanding, spiritual sight, spiritual sight in bodily likeness, and spiritual sight without bodily likeness enable Julian to communicate her theology in a dialectical interaction of images and ideas from a variety of sources. She combines the instruction she understands immediately as she receives the vision, the inward learning that she gradually comes to after the event, and the meaning of the whole revelation in the visions, while always leaving room for mystery. She integrates ideas from Scripture and other sources. She draws on reason, Church teaching, and grace.

V. SCRIPTURE AND OTHER SOURCES

Scripture plays a major role in Julian's thought and the composition of the *Showings*. As a woman interested in a life of prayer, possibly trained in the monastic method of *lectio divina*,[23] Julian would have memorized large sections of Scripture, enabling instant recall. Edmund Colledge and James Walsh suggest that Julian was "deeply familiar with all four gospels, the Pauline and Johannine epistles and Hebrews,

---

[22] *LWHM* 121 n. 17.

[23] *Lectio divina* consists of four phases in a single movement: *lectio* (active reading), *meditatio* (meditating), *oratio* (speaking), and *contemplatio* (contemplation), involving the mind, the heart, the will, and the body.

the Psalms, the sapiential books and Deutero-Isaias."[24] These were most probably in a translation from the Vulgate.[25] Naturally, her visionary experience and interpretation of the experience include references and images from Scripture.

Jean Leclerq's description of the characteristics of the monastic use of Scripture popular in the Middle Ages resembles Julian's methodology:

> It is this deep impregnation with the words of Scripture that explains the extremely important phenomenon of reminiscence whereby the verbal echoes so excite the memory that a mere allusion will spontaneously evoke whole quotations and, in turn, a scriptural phrase will suggest quite naturally allusions elsewhere in the sacred books. Each word is like a hook, so to speak; it catches hold of one or several others which become linked together and make up the fabric of the exposé.[26]

We see an example of this integration in Julian's reference to Christ, the deep wisdom of the Trinity. In the image of *wisdom* there are possible allusions to Wisdom literature, particularly the book of Proverbs and the book of Wisdom,[27] *logos* theology from John 1:1-18, and wisdom theology in 1 Cor 1:17-25. In her images Julian integrates multiple scriptural allusions into her text freely, without references. These create verbal echoes, excite the memory, and evoke quotations, phrases, and images. Although we know this integration is occurring, it is impossible to say concisely how many allusions Julian's echoes evoke.

Julian also infuses her text with patristic ideas, integrating these sources in much the same way. Commenting on this way of writing, E. Ann Matter explains:

> . . . originality is here the process of borrowing, re-working, using old material in new ways to show the imagination and talents of a given author. . . . They did not distinguish between borrowing and the creation of new ideas. True creativity was often seen in the way disparate sources were conceived to fit together.[28]

---

[24] *BSAJN* 43.

[25] The Vulgate was commonly used in Julian's time. See Grace M. Jantzen, *Julian of Norwich: Mystic and Theologian* (London: S.P.C.K., 1987) 16–17.

[26] Jean Leclercq, *The Love of Learning and the Desire for God: A Study of Monastic Culture,* translated by Catherine Misrahi (2nd ed. New York: Fordham University Press, 1961) 91.

[27] E.g., Prov 1:20-33; 8:1-8; Wis 1:6-7.

[28] Ann E. Matter, *The Voice of My Beloved: The Song of Songs in Western Medieval Christianity* (Philadelphia: University of Pennsylvania Press, 1990) 6.

Without mentioning her sources, Julian freely borrows and reworks theological insights from patristic classics. It cannot be determined whether Julian actually read the works of the most important Fathers or whether she integrated their ideas into her thought processes through listening to homilies or to the works being read. Nevertheless, her writings show the influence of years of accumulated theological insights. We see a clear example when "beholding" evokes whole quotations from patristic literature in her question: "What is sin? For I saw truly that God does everything, however small it may be, and that nothing is done by chance, but it is of the endless providence of God's wisdom. Therefore I was compelled to admit that everything which is done is well done" (viii:137). Compare Augustine: "Whence then is evil, since God who is good made all things good? It was the greater and supreme Good who made these lesser goods, but Creator and Creation are alike good."[29] Julian's question about sin echoes Augustine's text in format and content. In this example the word *sin* either consciously or unconsciously awakens her memory and becomes a "hook" that links her own thought with Augustine's. This leads to a delicate process of fusion of language. Each time Julian considers the question of sin, Augustine's ponderings become part of the network of interlocking images. Tracing possible sources to Julian's theology is a task that could never be concluded.

VI. The Hermeneutical Circle

As much as we can understand of Julian's own intention will always be the primary concern in interpreting her theology. It is possible, however, that the reader of the text extracts further meaning from it not necessarily obvious to Julian herself. As we examine Julian's theology, informed by the unfolding of history, implications about salvation will emerge that may not have been apparent to Julian. Too often we can assume that Julian knows exactly what she is communicating. Unless she states categorically that it is God's will that we know a certain teaching I would argue that Julian invites the reader into the continual reflection and analysis she models. Furthermore, as Friedrich Schleiermacher suggests, we can never totally objectify an author or her ideas:

> Since speaking and writing is an "act" that almost leaves the "I" on one
> side, so the circle of understanding never closes itself because the

---

[29] Augustine, *The Confessions of St. Augustine*, translated by Frank J. Sheed (London: Sheed and Ward, 1949) 7.5.106.

inventiveness of the interpreter finds in the text truths not understood
by the author; through the very act of comprehension these truths
become fresh historical happening and thus a way of interpretation in
different circumstances.[30]

The purpose of engaging in the art of theological interpretation is to attempt to be true to Julian's meaning and to transfer meaning from one
cultural language to another. This includes becoming part of the hermeneutical circle, engaging in theology as Julian engages in theology.
Still, the hermeneutic we employ must heed Leanne Van Dyk's warning about atonement theology:

> The dark mystery, the holy secret of the atonement must always serve
> as a caution and reminder to the theologian. The atoning death of Jesus
> Christ will not be reduced to a formula of scholars or a possession of
> the church. The tragic elements of the story, the inescapable judgement
> on human self-deception, and the mysterious salvific impact of the
> atonement must never be muted or dimmed in the legitimate interest of
> theological clarity and precision.[31]

Although we are interested in clarity and precision, Julian's theology
always leaves room for the mysterious salvific impact of divine presence to continue to reveal itself. The key to a hermeneutic for interpreting
the visions is that the theology expressed in the text is first contained in
the visions. The pictures created by her words interact with the words
that form in her understanding. They act sacramentally as they crystal-
lize insights about divine love perceived in Julian's understanding.
Therefore in order to interpret Julian's soteriology I will attempt to
draw together images presented throughout the text on thematic lines
so that we may see more clearly the subtle links in images and the
words that form in her understanding. For clarity's sake I will attempt
to define words as Julian defines them, or where this is not possible
point to their general meaning in Middle English. I will highlight the
theology contained within the visions and express this in terms of or-
ganizing ideas to stress her understanding of soteriology.

---

[30] Prosper Grech, "Hermeneutics," in René Latourelle and Rino Fisichella, eds.,
Dictionary of Fundamental Theology (New York: Crossroad, 1994) 419. This is in contrast
to the argument that the true meaning of a passage is only the meaning intended by
the author.

[31] Leanne Van Dyk, "Vision and Imagination in Atonement Doctrine," *Theology
Today* 50 (1993) 4.

VII. This is a Revelation of Love

Julian's text is concerned with revelation. It is "a revelation of love." This leads to the question of the significance of these revelations for the Christian community and Christian theology: are these personal revelations that have no relevance for the wider community? I would argue that Julian's revelations belong to a corpus of public literature that seeks to give insight into the mystery of the divine. While Julian's revelations may be classified as private,[32] they are not addressed only to her. The comment she makes toward the beginning of her text about the general nature of the revelation reinforces the value of the text as a more public document: "I was greatly moved in love towards my fellow Christians, that they might all see and know the same as I saw, for I wished it to be a comfort to them, for all this vision was shown for all" (1:8.190). From Julian's perspective these are not private revelations solely addressed to her. The vision was shown for all. She repeats this opinion and gives it weight by suggesting that it is God's will that her readers *behold* God in it:

> . . . disregard the wretch to whom it was shown, and that mightily, wisely and meekly you contemplate upon *[behold]* God, who out of his courteous love and his endless goodness was willing to show it generally, to the comfort of us all. For it is God's will that you accept it with great joy and delight, as Jesus has shown it to you (1:8.191).

With humility, Julian counsels her readers not to focus on her experience of the vision but on the revelation of God that occurs through the experience and reflection on the experience. She advises her readers to *behold* God in the vision, which is a revelation given to the community for the comfort of all.

Although it is difficult to categorize Julian's writing, I wish to suggest that it belongs to the category of public revelation. Julian believes that her visions are an action of God that she experiences and interprets in language and images familiar to her. More specifically the revelation Julian seeks to describe is what Gerald O'Collins calls "dependent" revelation, as distinguished from "foundational" revelation.[33] Foundational revelation describes the original apostolic experience of and witness to Jesus. Dependent revelation names revelation that is grounded in this primordial experience and continues to occur in history in the

---

[32] "Private revelation" is a term used by Rahner. See Karl Rahner, *Visions and Prophecies,* translated by Charles Henkey and Richard Strachan (London: Burns and Oates, 1963) 13–14.

[33] O'Collins, *Fundamental Theology* 102.

lives of believers. According to this distinction Julian's revelations are *dependent* because they express her understanding of the continual revelation of God in her lifetime.

The revelation that occurs in the presentation of bodily sights, words forming in her understanding, and spiritual sights resonates with Avery Dulles' definition of revelation as symbolic disclosure. In Dulles' model revelation is never considered to be a purely internal experience or unmediated encounter with God. It is always mediated through an experience in the world. Specifically it is communicated through symbol, through externally perceived signs that work mysteriously on human consciousness.[34] "Revelatory symbols," he concludes, "are those which express and mediate God's self communication."[35] Julian's revelations are not simply a subjective experience of God mediated through the prayer of *beholding* the crucifix. The crucifix becomes a symbol, an externally perceived sign that works mysteriously on her consciousness and enables her to interpret levels of meaning that objectively reflect orthodox Christian thought on the nature of reality. The experience belongs to the community's body of knowledge. Julian deserves to take her place among the community of theologians who seek to interpret divine revelation in their times. Just as she had something to say to her own times, she has something to contribute to a deeper understanding of salvation today. Some consider her vision of value; others will not. Ultimately the criterion Christian theology can judge her by is "by their fruits you will know them" (Matt 7:16a; 20).

VIII. A SUMMARY OF JULIAN'S STYLE AND METHOD

Julian gives primacy to her personal experience of God. This starting point, grounded in life experience, is highly significant for the theology that emerges. Negatively, her emphasis on her own visionary experience of God could lead to concern about authenticity, bias, and introspection. Positively, however, Julian's *Showings* resonate with some of the best expressions of Catholic theology. She displays an ability to record her personal experience of God and to give fresh insights into the nature and meaning of revelation. She invites her readers to enter her experience, to journey with her as insights emerge, to encounter the story of salvation in a fresh, dynamic way.

The theology that emerges from *beholding* integrates insights that arise from contemplative gazing. This seeing comes from knowing that

---

[34] Avery Dulles, "Symbolic Structure of Revelation," *TS* 41 (1980) 55–56.
[35] Ibid. 56.

integrates wisdom felt, experienced, and intuited in the deepest levels of her being. Insights surface as Julian engages her whole being in seeing, tasting, feeling, and hearing the mystery of divine love revealed in Christ. This allows for the expression of ideas missed or disregarded in a more scholastic approach to theology. The contemplative nature of the theology balances other works within Western theology that stress a strictly philosophically fashioned doctrinal approach.

The threefold way of interpretation that Julian describes—bodily sight, words formed in understanding, and spiritual sight—enables her to weave together diverse strands of *kataphatic* and *apophatic* knowing[36] and leaves room for the creation of a new fabric. The bodily sights emphasize the similarity between God and the created world while the spiritual sights retain the incomprehensibility of God. Such language is inherently imprecise. It relies on context to express meaning. It is susceptible to ambiguity and vulnerable to misinterpretation. Yet language that creates images and concepts that point beyond itself is sensitive to the problem of limiting the mystery of God to the language that defines the mystery. It maintains complexity inherent in theological articulation.

The crucifix becomes a symbol for Julian, an externally perceived sign that works mysteriously on her consciousness and enables her to interpret levels of meaning that objectively reflect orthodox Christian thought on the nature of reality. The composition of a text enables Julian to formulate a theology. Thus the text becomes sacramental because it encourages participation in the meaning that unfolds. In the telling of her experience and interpretation of the experience Julian's personal experience becomes communal. It becomes part of the Christian community's reflection on the divine.

IX. IMPLICATIONS OF THE HERMENEUTIC FOR THIS STUDY

The unique way in which Julian presents her theology has consequences for the way I will proceed with interpretation. The first relates to the presentation of ideas as a whole. The ideas that emerge must not be isolated from each other. All must be taken together. While these interconnected ideas may not seem very clear at first, neither are they confused: they relate to each other as ripples form on the surface of a pond. This means that systematizing individual aspects of Julian's

---

[36] The *kataphatic* tradition emphasizes a similarity between creatures and the Creator. The *apophatic* tradition emphasizes the incomprehensibility of God. See Harvey Egan, "Christian Apophatic and Kataphatic Mysticism," *TS* 39 (1978) 405.

work creates a disharmony within its wholeness. At the same time, however, the reader needs some system and direction in order to comprehend aspects of her theology. Therefore, in order to aid interpretation, I attempt to remain true to the mystical wholeness of the work and yet to identify and thematize her theology. This inevitably creates tension between the inexpressibility of mystical consciousness and its resistance to being contained within a system and the desire to present Julian's soteriology with some clarity.

The second consequence arises from the fact that Julian does not divide her theology into discrete segments or concentrate on a single theme; rather she interconnects all the mysteries of Christian faith, placing them within a framework of trinitarian love. Negatively this necessitates repetition when presenting an analysis of a single theological theme because often a single image communicates more than one theological idea. Positively the fruit of this infusion of different theological fragments into a trinitarian schema is that there is an underlying homogeneity that connects each dimension of theology. Thus a study of Julian's soteriology necessitates some repetition in order to remain consistent with her method.

The third consequence is the result of Julian's eclectic integration of Scripture and other sources. This makes the theology extremely dense. It invites the synthesis of a wide range of images, doctrines, and theological perspectives. This creates problems in that it is difficult to pin Julian down, to trace sources with any certainty, or to place her within any specific theological school. Positively this intricacy leaves room for the paradoxical nature of theology and the complexity of revelation.

The fourth consequence involves hermeneutics. We can explain the language expressed by use of the historical and literary means available to understand any author. However, the interpreter also plays a role in the hermeneutical circle. Although Julian's own intention and theological interpretations are always paramount, the contemporary interpreter plays a role in the interpretive process. In other words, as author of the book I bring my own cultural, religious, and personal perspectives on reality into play. Keeping all these things in mind, we are now ready to address the soteriology expressed in the *Showings*.

Part Two

A Soteriology of *Oneing*

By virtue of that precious oneing (14:58.293).

$$\overline{\hspace{6cm}}\underbrace{\qquad\mathbf{3}\qquad}$$

Oneing Through the Trinity

For all our life consists of three (14:58.294).

Julian's doctrine of salvation is a theology of love that has its foundation in the love within the Trinity. Although Julian never explicitly develops a doctrine of the Trinity or systematically outlines her trinitarian theology, the mystery of trinitarian love is behind all the key elements in her soteriology. Every word in *The Revelation of Divine Love* creates a network of interwoven images that reveals the certainty of salvation because there is an eternal ontological and existential relationship founded in love between the Trinity and all people that creates an ontology of being-in-relationship. The purpose of this chapter is to present an overview of this central doctrine, which forms the foundation of Julian's soteriology: the love within the Trinity. The exegesis will situate Julian's theology of love, described as "uncreated charity," "created charity," and "given charity," in a totally trinitarian context. After examining Julian's threefold understanding of charity we will discern how this interpretation of salvation history is a soteriology of *oneing*, with a movement that is similar to the Plotinian notion of *exitus* (exit), and *reditus* (return). Thus the exegesis will create a framework through which we can examine in more detail what it means to be saved by the God of love, in Christ, through the grace of the Holy Spirit.

I. LOVE WAS HIS MEANING

Toward the end of the long text in the sixteenth revelation, which Julian says confirms the other fifteen *showings,* she summarizes the understanding she came to about the meaning of salvation: "in the end everything will be charity" (16:84.340), and "love was his meaning"

45

(16:86.342). It took Julian fifteen years of prayerful reflection to come to know that the heart of God's meaning is love:

> . . . and it was said: What, do you wish to know your Lord's meaning in this thing? Know it well, love was his meaning. Who reveals it to you? Love. What did he reveal to you? Love. Why does he reveal it to you? For love. Remain in this, and you will know more of the same. But you will never know different, without end. So I was taught that love is our Lord's meaning (16:86.342).

This famous exposition on love comes to Julian in the form of *spiritual understanding* in language that points beyond words. Through analytical questioning Julian appraises the theological consequences of the assertion that "God is love" (1 John 4:8). She repeats the word "love," emphasizing that love is the essence of the Godhead. What is God's meaning? Love. Who revealed it? Love. Why did God create? Out of love. How does God communicate? In love. To know our Lord's meaning is to know God's love, to know the creative, redemptive, ecstatic, unitive love of the Trinity. Divine love does not stay self-enclosed but shares itself in love. She summarizes the journey from love to love: "In our creation we had beginning, but the love in which he created us was in him from without beginning. In this love we have our beginning, and all this shall we see in God without end" (16:86.142-143). Love goes forth from God. God creates the world in love. God dwells within humanity in love. God provides a protective presence that redeems creation from within, making an eternal gift through the gift of God's self. Thus life is a journey in love from God to God.

II. Uncreated Charity, Created Charity, Given Charity

Immediately before presenting love as the meaning that underlies all reality, Julian gives a reflection on charity. Her insights about charity emerge as she experiences a "touching, sight and feeling" (16.83.339). Julian delineates "three kinds of understanding in this light of charity" (16:84.341):

> The first is uncreated *[unmade]* charity, the second is created *[made]* charity, the third is given charity. Uncreated charity is God, created charity is our soul in God, given charity is virtue, and that is a gift of grace in deeds, in which we love God for himself, and ourselves in God, and all that God loves for God (16:84.341).

Contrasting experiences of divine light and the darkness of woe reveal the nature of charity. Charity is a light in the darkness. The threefold repetitive formula creates a dialectical relationship between the unmade, eternal nature of divine love and finite created love as given. For Julian, the word charity incorporates a range of nuances. Charity enables human beings to live "meritoriously, with labor" (16:84.340). Charity is one of the theological virtues: "So charity keeps us in faith and in hope. And faith and hope lead us in charity" (16:84.340). In this trinitarian context, however, the use of the qualifiers uncreated, created, and given associate charity with the being and action of the Godhead. Charity has ontological status. Uncreated charity, created charity, and given charity are three ways in which divine love originates and shares itself. The passage grounds every *showing* in love.

The first way of understanding divine love, *uncreated charity*, accentuates that there is no beginning to God's loving. God has no other source except God's self from which God loves. God does not possess love; God is love. *Uncreated charity* establishes a trinitarian ontology grounded in love, which places the whole of reality in relationship to the love within the Trinity. Julian sees no beginning to the loving of *uncreated charity:*

> God never began to love mankind; for just as mankind will be in endless bliss, fulfilling God's joy with regard to his works, just so has that same mankind been known and loved in God's prescience from without beginning in his righteous intent (16:84.283).

There is one history of love, founded in the eternity of God that begins before the creation of human nature. At the end of the *Showings* Julian asserts her certainty of the eternal nature of God's loving: "that before God made us he loved us, which love was never abated and never will be. And in this love he has done all his works, and in this love he has made all things profitable to us, and in this love our life is everlasting" (16:86.342). The nature of *uncreated charity* is not to stay self-enclosed but to unite human beings in the love within the Godhead. This union in love creates an ontological bond that can never be destroyed. The eternity of God's loving is the background in which God creates.

The second way of understanding divine love, *created charity*, shows how completely divine love is shared with humankind:

> . . . before he made us he loved us, and when we were made we loved him; and this is made only of the natural substantial goodness of the Holy Spirit, mighty by reason of the might of the Father, wise in mind of the wisdom of the Son. And so is man's soul made by God, and in the same moment joined [*knit*] to God (14:53.283-284).

From eternity each divine person shares love with *created charity*. We receive love from the "kindly substantial goodness" of the Holy Spirit, the "might" of the Father, and the "wisdom" of the Son. The unusual placement of the Holy Spirit first in the formula emphasizes the dynamic role of the Spirit in imparting love. The sharing of trinitarian love means that humanity is made of God, and at the same time knit to God.[1]

The third way of understanding divine love, *given charity*, includes "virtue, and that is a gift of grace in deeds, in which we love God for himself, and ourselves in God, and all that God loves for God" (16:84.341). *Given charity* suggests that *uncreated charity* gives love to humanity gratuitously. Julian further characterizes the gift thus given as *virtue*. In popular usage *virtue* characterizes worth and moral perfection. It also describes the power inherent in a divine being.[2] But this does not adequately define Julian's theological use of the term. In reference to divine love, *given charity* is love within the Trinity, which works in human lives as grace and activates the theological virtues of faith, hope, and love. These virtues enable us to love God, ourselves in God, and all that God loves.

III. HOMELY AND COURTEOUS QUALITIES OF DIVINE LOVE

Another dimension of the *touching* that enables Julian to understand that "love is his meaning" is her identification of the qualities of divine love as *homely* and *courteous*. She sees and feels:

> three properties of God, in which consist the strength and the effect of all the revelation. . . . The properties are these: life, love and light. In life is wonderful familiarity *[homeliness]*, in love is gentle courtesy, and in light is endless nature *[kindness]*. These three properties were seen in one goodness (16:83.339).

The three properties, *life*, *love*, and *light*, underlie and inform the entire revelation. Julian identifies the strength and effect of these properties as "marvelous homeliness,"[3] "gentle courtesy," and "endless kind-

---

[1] *Knitting* is an important image for Julian, which the translation *joined* does not convey dynamically enough. We will examine her use of the word in the next section.

[2] Lesley Brown, ed., *The New Shorter Oxford English Dictionary on Historical Principles*. 2 vols. (Oxford: Clarendon Press, 1993) (= *NSOED*) 3586.

[3] *Homely* is equivalent in meaning to the Latin word *familiaris*, introduced into theological language by Gregory the Great, which denotes being familiar and later comes to be a synonym for mystical union. See Wolfgang Riehle, *The Middle English Mystics*, translated by Bernard Standring (London and Boston: Routledge & Kegan Paul, 1981) 97. Because American audiences associate *homely* with being plain or ordinary, C & W have translated *homely* as "familiar" (*BSAJN* [Toronto: Pontifical Institute of Mediaeval Studies, 1978] *ad loc*). I prefer *homely* as understood in Middle

ness."[4] Every *showing* reveals the quality of divine love to be *homely* and *courteous*.

Julian often couples *homely* and *courteous* love as two essential dimensions of divine love: "For our Lord himself is supreme familiarity [*homeliness*], and he is as courteous as he is familiar [*homely*], for he is true courtesy" (16:77.331). Together the expressions of love create a "marvelous melody of endless love." They harmonize with each other to reveal the intimate as well as the majestic and polite qualities of divine love. *Homely* and *courteous* love signifies the trustworthiness of God: "And he wants to be trusted, for he is very accessible, familiar [*homely*] and courteous, blessed may he be" (2:10.196).

Homely and *courteous* love is shared with us through each person of the Trinity:

> For the greatest abundance of joy which we shall have, as I see it, is this wonderful courtesy and familiarity [*homeliness*] of our Father, who is our Creator, in our Lord Jesus Christ, who is our brother and our saviour. But no man can know this wonderful familiarity [*homeliness*] in this life, unless by a special revelation from our Lord, or from a great abundance of grace, given within by the Holy Spirit. But faith and belief together with love deserve the reward, and so it is received by grace (1:7.189).

The love of the Father is *homely* and *courteous* in Christ. Human beings participate and gain further understanding of *courtesy* and *homeliness* through grace given by the Holy Spirit. *Courtesy* and *homeliness* bestow the joy human beings partially experience in this life and look forward to in our final return to God in the beatific vision. To know and experience the fullness of *homely* and *courteous* trinitarian love is the goal of the spiritual journey: "our soul will never have rest till it comes into him, acknowledging that he is full of joy, familiar [*homely*] and courteous and blissful and true life" (12:26.223). We will fully see *homely* and *courteous* love in eternity.

In Life is Marvelous Homeliness

Julian gives a concrete image of what she means by "homely loving," which she identifies as a "spiritual sight": "I saw that he is to us

---

English because it emphasizes the human person as the home or dwelling place of divine love.

[4] *Kindness* has a specific theological meaning for Julian that "nature" does not fully convey. See Chapter 4.

everything which is good and comforting for our help. He is our clothing, who wraps and enfolds us for love, embraces us and shelters us,
surrounds us for his love, which is so tender that he may never desert
us" (1:5.183). The image of clothing enclosing the body creates a sense
of being surrounded in Christ, held in Christ, and comforted by Christ.
The quality of *homely* love is tender. It never leaves us. Later in the text
Julian describes Christ making a home in humanity: "The place which
Jesus takes in our soul he will nevermore vacate, for in us is his home of
homes and his everlasting dwelling" (16:68.313). "Homely loving" describes Christ's intimate presence to humanity, his being at home and
endlessly dwelling within humanity.

The "homely love" that these images describe resonates with the
interpretation of *homely* that comes from the concrete Germanic words
homli, homlihed, homlines.[5] *Homely* in this sense means belonging to a
home or household, becoming as one of a household, intimate, at home
with. It characterizes home as a place where one receives kind treatment.[6] It is also linguistically related to the word "humble," or could
even be a variant spelling of the same word,[7] as in: "a simple soul
should come naked, openly and familiarly *[homely]*" (1:5.184). Thus
homely integrates a sense of being friendly, humble, personable, and
hospitable. It includes the word home and expresses the coziness and
lack of formality of a home. It denotes the permanence of family life.
Theologically, then, "homely loving" emphasizes the constancy of intimate, tender divine love, at home in humanity, giving life to humanity.

In Love is Gentle Courtesy

Julian complements *homely* love with the quality of *courtesy.* She
associates courtesy most often with God's response to sin: "And this is
a supreme friendship of our courteous Lord, that he protects us so tenderly whilst we are in our sins" (13:40.246). Subsequently, in the language of courtly love, Julian relates the idea of courtesy to the mystical
love between God and the soul:

> . . . our courteous Lord shows himself to the soul, happily and with
> the gladdest countenance, welcoming it as a friend, as if it had been in
> pain and in prison, saying: My dear darling, I am glad that you have

[5] Riehle, *Middle English Mystics* 97.

[6] James Walsh, "God's Homely Loving: St. John and Julian of Norwich on the
Divine Indwelling," *The Month* 19 (1958) 165.

[7] Brant Pelphrey, *Christ Our Mother: Julian of Norwich.* Way of the Christian Mystics 7 (Wilmington, Del.: Michael Glazier, 1989) 108.

come to me in all your woe. I have always been with you, and now you
see me loving, and we are made one in bliss (13:40.246).

With no hint of blame because of sin, the "courteous Lord" offers humanity a friendship that surpasses all others. The friendship is revelatory, as the "courteous Lord" addresses human beings as lovers, calms
their woe, and draws them to be one in bliss. In a later passage Julian
associates courteous love with grace: ". . . grace works with mercy,
raising, rewarding, endlessly exceeding what our love and labor deserve, distributing and displaying the vast plenty and generosity of
God's royal dominion in his wonderful courtesy" (14:48.262-263). *Courteous* love is grace offered in friendship that draws humanity into union
with the Trinity. Gracious *courteous* love returns human beings to their
origin in God, to "be one in bliss."

Many scholars have noted the significance of *courtesy* in Julian's
writing.[8] Often associated with courtly love, particularly the wooing of
a lady by a knight, *courtesy* points to nobleness and benevolence. It
describes politeness or consideration toward others. *Courtesy* also distinguishes a relationship of inheritance, as it represents the tenure that
a husband held after his wife's death whereby he inherited certain
kinds of property.[9] When associated with God, however, *courtesy* not
only denotes the way in which divine love is shared, but describes the
essence of God's nature. It points to the nobility of divine love. It conveys the radical character of God's intimacy, which places all persons
in a courtly love relationship. *Courteous* love, grounded in the very
being of God, is trinitarian love manifest in the Father, Son, and Holy
Spirit. This relationship between humankind and the Trinity as creator,
savior, and bestower of grace characterized by courteous love creates
an indissolvable inheritance of love.

In short, the threefold nature of uncreated charity, created charity,
and given charity suggests that in Julian's theology there is no distinction between who God *is* as love and how God *acts* in love. There is a
unity between the being and work of the Trinity. God's being is love,
and the nature of love is to be self-giving. Thus in Julian's trinitarian
theology it is impossible to conceive of God's inner life without seeing
how God relates in *homely* and *courteous* love. What Julian implicitly
says is the principle Rahner made famous centuries later: "no adequate
distinction can be made between the doctrine of the Trinity and the

---

[8] E.g., Joan M. Nuth, *Wisdom's Daughter: The Theology of Julian of Norwich* (New
York: Crossroad, 1991) 74. Mary Olson, "God's Inappropriate Grace: Images of
Courtesy in Julian of Norwich's Showings," *Mystics Quarterly* 20 (1994) 47–59.

[9] *NSOED* 533.

doctrine of the economy of salvation."[10] Grounded in her own experience of trinitarian presence, her teaching about the Trinity is not simply a doctrine of received formulations about the inner life of God that do not inform the realities of life. Julian's doctrine of the Trinity explains who human beings are and how salvation is an essential element in what it means to be in relationship with God. She shows that there is always an identity between the immanent Trinity, God's nature as uncreated charity, and the economic Trinity, the historical manifestation of the sharing of this love in the world through created charity and given charity. We will now see how this sharing of *homely* and *courteous* love is in essence a soteriology of *oneing*.

IV. BY VIRTUE OF THAT PRECIOUS ONEING

The movement of uncreated charity, created charity, and given charity that draws humanity into relationship with the Trinity is a soteriology of *oneing*. This includes ontological *oneing*, which God establishes for all time in sharing divine love at creation, and existential *oneing*, which increases human relationship with God and leads to the progression of humanity into the being of God. Each of these dimensions of *oneing* takes place through the work of the Trinity. In images that are difficult to envisage, Julian outlines her progressive understanding of *oneing*:

> And in our creating he joined and united [*knit and oned*] us to himself, and through this union [*oneing*] we are kept as pure and as noble as we were created. By the power of that same precious union [*oneing*] we love our Creator and delight in him, praise him and thank him and endlessly rejoice in him. And this is the work which is constantly performed in every soul which will be saved (14:58.293).

Human beings are *knit* and *oned* to the Trinity at creation and are kept in a relationship of *oneing*. Julian then summarizes each divine person's involvement in *oneing*: "in our making, God almighty is our loving [*kindly*] Father, and God all wisdom is our loving [*kindly*] Mother, with the love and the goodness of the Holy Spirit, which is all one God, one Lord" (14:58.293). In our being *knit* and *oned* to God our loving Father and Mother, intertwined in the love and goodness of the Holy Spirit, there is an originating, ontological *oneing* that can never be eradicated. The constant increasing or deepening of this *oneing* occurs in "every soul which will be saved, creating an existential oneing" until

---

[10] Karl Rahner, *The Trinity* (New York: Herder and Herder, 1970) 24.

the human being becomes the beloved spouse of the divine: "And in the joining [knitting] and the union [oneing] he is our very true spouse . . . for he says: I love you and you love me, and our love will never divide in two (14:58.293). Through the relationship of *knitting* and *oneing* humanity is in a permanent ontological and existential relationship with divine love.

Oneing

Julian's concept of *oneing* is virtually untranslatable. To be *oned* in Middle English means to be one, united, joined, blended, or fused,[11] yet none of these words conveys the sense of this primordial interpenetration of the divine and the human that preserves difference in identity. The concept is so extraordinary that Julian uses *oneing* to describe the union between Christ's humanity and his divinity: "because the union [oneing] in him of the divinity gave strength to his humanity to suffer" (8:20.213). There is something mystical and indefinable about the union that *oneing* conveys. In the Sloane 1 text *oneing* describes the divine indwelling in humanity: "For in us is his homeliest home and His endless wonyng."[12] *Wonyng*, translated as dwelling, distinguishes the *homely* presence of Christ in the human soul. It also includes the activity of "homely loving" that makes humanity Christ-like. *Oneing* gathers human beings and makes them holy: "I shall gather you and make you meek and mild, pure and holy through union [oneing] with me" (13:28.226-227). *Oneing* continues the process of profound identification until the union we share with Christ is complete. Thus the translation *union* does not adequately convey the indissolubility of our original *oneing* in uncreated charity or the dynamism of the love that is shared in the continuation of this *oneing*.

Brant Pelphrey points out that *oneing* is a forerunner of the modern word "atonement." Literally this term means *at-one-ment* with God.[13] Julian's concept of *oneing* is literally *at-one-ment*. Pelphrey rightly suggests, however, that the word atonement generally assumes separation, subsequent reconciliation, and the mending of the division.[14] Although Julian is concerned with sin and reconciliation, this is not her concept of *oneing*. At creation humanity is *knit* and *oned* to the Trinity and kept

---

[11] *NSOED* 1998.

[12] lxvii:2800,134. *Wonyng* appears as *dwellyng* in the Paris manuscript.

[13] Pelphrey, *Christ Our Mother* 42.

[14] Brant Pelphrey, *Love Was His Meaning: The Theology and Mysticism of Julian of Norwich* (Salzburg, Austria: Institut für Anglistik und Amerikanistik, Universität Salzburg, 1982) (= *LWHM*) 132–34.

in this inviolable *oneing*. Humanity is always one with divine love. God never disengages from this original *oneing* in any way that would separate the divine and the human. Yet *oneing* also increases and fulfills this destiny of being one with God. The movement is paradoxical. We are one and are becoming more completely one. We begin as children of God who is Father and Mother to us and become the adult spouse of God. Thus salvation is intrinsic to what it means to be human because God creates humanity *one* with the Godhead within a relationship of *oneing*.

Knitting

The image of *knitting* that Julian often couples with *oneing* helps clarify her use of *oneing*: "[the] beloved soul was preciously knitted to him in its making, by a knot so subtle and so mighty that it is united [*oned*] in God. In this uniting [*oneing*] it is made endlessly holy" (14:53.284). We observe how Julian engages the very concrete image of knitting to picture humanity's original *oneing* in Christ. Underlying this image are multiple representations of union. In the first instance, on a literal level the word *knit* draws on the craft of sewing or knitting suggesting interlocking, tying, bonding, threading, linking, or interlacing.[15] The knitter draws the yarn closely and firmly together so that it may knot with the other thread. From this multiple interlocking a cloth is created. The image also reflects Pauline theology of the mystical body of Christ (1 Cor 6:15a; 12:12-27; Rom 12:4-6). Knit to Christ, humankind is one body in Christ and individuals are parts of one another. *Knit* can further denote the mending of broken bones as the bones grow together to become one. *Knitting* draws on other images of union. It describes the intertwining of thread that forms a secure fastening. In a personal sense, to tie a knot means to join people together intimately, to establish a covenant of peace or a marriage bond, and to make or have a binding obligation.[16] *Knitting* suggests forming and maintaining union.

The image of *knitting* shows how the divine and the human interact with each other to form a fabric. The image maintains the interconnection between the divine and the human, yet it preserves difference in identity. There are always at least two threads in knitting and forming a knot. Thus *oneing* does not mean total absorption of humanity into the Godhead, or creating a fusion such that human beings are God or become God. Rather, *oneing* brings to completion who human beings

[15] Hans Kurath, Sherman Kuhn, and Robert Lewis, eds., *Middle English Dictionary* (Ann Arbor: University of Michigan Press, 1954–) 566–69.

[16] *NSOED* 1502.

truly are in God, "knit in this knot, and oned in this oneing, and made holy in this holiness" (14:53.284). *Knitting* and *oneing* is about being made holy. They point to a permanent intertwining of humanity with God that is so subtle it would be impossible to separate the two individual threads. Though the two remain distinct, there is a connectedness between the divine and the human that is constitutive of our being.

Enclosed in the Trinity

A further image that helps us interpret Julian's concept of *oneing* is her depiction of mutual enclosure between the Trinity and humanity. The vision seems spiritual in its presentation, being neither pictorial nor completely abstract. The description communicates the oneness between God and humanity and the *oneing* that brings this oneness to fulfilment:

> For the almighty truth of the Trinity is our Father, for he made us and keeps us in him. And the deep wisdom of the Trinity is our Mother, in whom we are enclosed. And the high goodness of the Trinity is our Lord, and in him we are enclosed and he in us. We are enclosed in the Father, and we are enclosed in the Son, and we are enclosed in the Holy Spirit. And the Father is enclosed in us, the Son is enclosed in us, and the Holy Spirit is enclosed in us, almighty, all wisdom and all goodness, one God, one Lord (14:54.285).

Julian begins by distinguishing the attributes of each divine person. She assigns *truth* to the first person of the Trinity, the Father, *wisdom* to the second person, the Mother, and *goodness* to the third person, our Lord. Then her image of enclosure almost collapses the assignment of attributes in stressing trinitarian unity. Insights emerge as if one is gazing at an iconographic portrait of the Trinity such as the "Trinity" in the Bedford Hours, which depicts Christ and the Father embracing each other, forming a center of enclosure, with the Holy Spirit, in the form of a dove, nesting between the two.[17] As if beholding such a portrait, Julian's understanding moves beyond imagery into knowing that comes from the depths of her being. She perceives that human beings not only participate in this trinitarian life but belong to it and are enclosed in it. Conversely each person of the Trinity shares divine love in such a profound way that each becomes enclosed in every man and woman.

---

[17] "Hours of the Trinity (for Sunday): the Holy Trinity, with Scenes of Creation," in Janet Bakehouse, *The Bedford Book of Hours* (London: The British Library) Plate 23. See Margaret M. Manion and Bernard J. Muir, eds., *Medieval Texts and Images. Studies of Manuscripts from the Middle Ages* (Sydney: Harwood Academic Publishers, 1991) 41.

Julian's use of the image of enclosure rings with hauntingly expressive power over the entire *Showings*. It contains all other images of human beings in relationship to the Trinity. Her repetition of "(en)closed" emphasizes oneness in God and oneness between God and us. *Closed* reminds us of our ultimate origin and completion in the Trinity, while *enclosed* gives a more dynamic sense of movement within the life of the Trinity. *Enclosed* embodies both deep stillness and dynamic movement, thus creating a sense of being surrounded by, contained within, and sharing life with one another. This suggests that human beings partake in divine life. Human beings literally exist in the Trinity. Mutual enclosure elucidates the indissolubility of the unity between human beings and the Trinity.

Julian's image of mutual enclosure is an example of *oneing*. It is a prototype of her version of the doctrine of *perichoresis,* which maintains the reciprocal presence or indwelling of the three divine persons in one another. The persons of the Trinity are within one another; they contain one another. At the same time they open their personhood to the other. But Julian's image of mutual enclosure goes much further than suggesting *perichoresis* within the Trinity.[18] It creates a sense of *perichoresis* in the God-human relationship. The image of mutual enclosure locates *perichoresis* not only in the inner life of the Trinity but in the mystery of one communion of love between all persons, divine and well as human.

This emphasis on mutual enclosure between the Trinity and humanity is, I suggest, a most significant theological assertion. Through this image of mutual enclosure Julian creates an ontology of being-in-relationship. She confirms that it is intrinsic to God's nature not to stay self-enclosed but to reach out to human beings in relationship. She reinforces that there are not two sets of trinitarian relationships, one within the divine being and the other with human beings. The one mystery of communion includes humanity and God engaged in a relationship of *oneing*. God and humanity are one, or enclosed in each other, and are *oneing* or enclosing each other. This suggests that the relationship of *oneing* with human beings is essential for God's life of communion. It implies an inherent relationship between theology and anthropology.

[18] Scholars generally agree that this idea of trinitarian relations is similar to the Greek tradition of *perichoresis* or the Latin *circumincessio* or *circuminsessio*. These technical terms highlight the dynamic and vital character of each divine person of the Trinity as well as the coherence and immanence of each person in the other two. Cf. *LWHM* 105. J.P.H. Clark, "Nature, Grace and the Trinity in Julian of Norwich," *Downside Review* 100 (1982) 206; 217 n. 29; Brant Pelphrey, "The Trinity in Julian of Norwich," 527–35, at 528; Nuth, *Wisdom's Daughter* 88.

Julian's soteriology is a soteriology of *oneing*. *Oneing* is a hermeneutical principle that designates salvation as a dynamic process of being one and becoming one in God. Humanity is one with divine love and continually drawn into a vibrant process of further *oneing* until humanity finally returns to the Trinity, and at the end all is charity. The relationship of *oneing* creates an ontology of being-in-relationship. In the *oneing* that occurs through the reciprocal sharing of divine love the Father, Son, and Holy Spirit fulfill the potential in human beings established at creation to become divinized or participate fully in the life of God.[19]

V. EXITUS REDITUS

The pattern of the sharing of love as uncreated charity, created charity and given charity that creates *oneing* in love between human beings and the Trinity reveals how in "love we have our beginning, and all this shall we see in God without end." The sharing of divine love expresses the pattern of salvation history identified in the tradition as *exitus reditus*. Essentially, *exitus* implies emanation, going out from.[20] *Reditus* means returning.[21] All reality is understood in relation to God in the view that all things come from God and all things return to God. Because I am conscious that Julian never uses this technical language I am not suggesting that Julian knew directly the source of the Plotinian principle of *exitus reditus*.[22] It is, however, a concept that had wide currency in Christian theology, and Julian seems to have inherited it and integrated it into her theology.

Briefly, in Plotinian cosmology[23] *exitus reditus* is a cyclic vision. The idea implies that it is intrinsic to the nature of "the One" to share itself with human beings. In this sharing, however, there is never any diminishment in the One. Plotinus suggests that the One can no more not

[19] This reflects 2 Peter 1:3-4a.

[20] Charlton T. Lewis, *A Latin Dictionary. Founded on Andrew's Edition of Freund's Latin Dictionary Revised, Enlarged and in Great Part Rewitten* (Oxford: Clarendon Press, 1984) 689 (= *LD*).

[21] *LD* 1542.

[22] Plotinus was born in Egypt ca. 205, went to Rome in 244, and died there in 270. His life was written by Porphyry, who gathered his writings together and edited them in six *Enneads*. See *Plotinus: The Six Enneads*, translated by Stephen MacKenna and B. S. Page. Robert Maynard Hutchins, ed., Great Books of the Western World (Chicago: Encyclopedia Britannica, Inc., 1952). Plotinus's work was popular in medieval theology: Thomas Aquinas structured his *Summa theologia* around the pattern of *exitus reditus*.

[23] Andrew Louth, *The Origins of the Christian Mystical Tradition* (Oxford: Clarendon Press, 1981) 38.

produce some sort of offspring than the sun can fail to produce light or the fountain water.[24] Everything derives from the One and everything returns to the One.[25] Due to the relationship of our nature to the One, the movement is circular, including emanation and return. Human beings can return to the One because they possess qualities of the One. Although return to the One involves conversion, this return is so intrinsic to human nature that Plotinus cannot conceive of the soul as having totally fallen. The journey of return to the One occurs through turning inward and entering more and more deeply into contemplation of the mind. This is a staged ascent that involves union with the *nous* or intellect, as well as a higher uniting with what is beyond all thought and being, the unknowable One.[26] Although this ascent is primarily intellectual, love also plays a dominant role.

Julian reflects a similar understanding of salvation history. As with the One who cannot help but share itself, it is intrinsic to the nature of uncreated charity not to stay self-enclosed but to share divine love with human beings as created charity. When the Trinity shares itself with human beings there is no diminishment in the love within the Trinity. This sharing in divine love means that it is intrinsic to the nature of created charity to long to return to its source. We will see in the following chapters that knowledge of self in the journey inward is an essential component of this return. Although sin hinders the return and could even block it, essentially human beings return to the Trinity because they are ontologically one with the Trinity and experience further existential *oneing* in the Trinity. While for Plotinus the soul attains this return to the One without any assistance from the One, the involvement of the Trinity in human lives is absolutely integral to Julian's soteriology. For Julian, *oneing* is an ontology of being-in-relationship that the Trinity initiates and constantly participates in. *Oneing* occurs because of the gratuitous involvement in creation of the Father, Son, and Holy Spirit. This is a deeply personal, homely, and courteous relationship of love. All things originate from the Trinity, are one with the Trinity, and are drawn into a relationship of further *oneing* with the Father, in the Son, through the Holy Spirit that ensures return to the Trinity. Through possessing trinitarian love and receiving trinitarian love humankind return to their origin.

[24] Cheslyn Jones, Geoffrey Wainwright, and Edward Yarnold, *The Study of Spirituality* (Oxford: Oxford University Press, 1986) 98.

[25] *Enneads* 2.1.40-41.

[26] Bernard McGinn, *The Foundations of Mysticism*. The Presence of God: A History of Western Christian Mysticism 1 (New York: Crossroad, 1991) 44–55.

In one sense the *exitus reditus* is a single dynamic sharing of divine love, yet in another sense there are three distinct moments in sharing love associated with each person of the Trinity. "I contemplated the work of all the blessed Trinity," Julian affirms (14:58.293). She then delineates the three distinct roles and ways of working of each person. Essentially, through the "Father we have our protection *[keeping]* and our bliss, as regards our natural substance, which is ours by our creation from without beginning" (14:58.293). At creation we are *oned* to the Father in substance. In the Son "we have our perfection, as regards our sensuality, our restoration and our salvation, for he is our Mother, brother and savior" (14:58.293). The Son continues our *oneing* with the Trinity by restoring and saving human beings from the effects of sin in the world. Finally, in the Holy Spirit we have "our reward and our gift for our living and our labor, endlessly surpassing all that we desire in his marvelous courtesy, out of his great plentiful grace" (14:58.294). The Holy Spirit gives us the gift of grace for our living until we finally return to our source. The movement is from God to God through the work of all the Trinity.

Subsequently Julian creates a memorable trinitarian formula that summarizes the role of each person of the Trinity in the *oneing* in love that is human salvation. This informs the soteriology that unfolds throughout the *Showings:* "For all our life consists of three: In the first we have our being, and in the second we have our increasing, and in the third we have our fulfillment. The first is nature, the second is mercy, the third is grace" (14:58.293-294). The one ecstatic movement of uncreated charity, created charity, and given charity that flows freely from emanation to return has three specific dimensions that involve each person of the Trinity, Father, Son, and Holy Spirit. First, God creates human beings one with God. Second, this *oneing* is increased during our lifetime, and third, this *oneing* is fulfilled at the end when all becomes charity. The importance of Julian's concept of *oneing* for her soteriology cannot be overemphasized.

Julian's doctrine of salvation is a theology of love that has its foundation in the love within the Trinity. Trinitarian love shares itself as uncreated charity, created charity, and given charity. Divine love is *homely* and *courteous*. Because we are reciprocally enclosed in divine love in a relationship of *oneing*, there is a *perichoresis* between God and us. Salvation is intrinsic to who we are as human beings: we are *one* with God and in a relationship of *oneing*. Furthermore, the movement of love from uncreated charity to created charity to given charity reveals that everything comes from the uncreated love of God and returns to God through Christ in the Holy Spirit. This cyclic movement of divine love, or *exitus reditus*, takes place from all eternity. It is manifested at every moment of creation until human beings finally return to the Trinity. Mindful that ultimately "all life consists of three," we are now ready to address the first movement in the *exitus reditus*, "in the first we have our being."

Part Three

In the First We Have Our Being

. . . in the first we have our being (14:58.294).

4

Oneing in Being

. . . everything has being through the love of God (1:5.183).

Central to Julian's soteriology is the belief that human beings are in a permanent relationship with divine love. We originate in God and will return to God. Divine love initiates an originating presence that increases during human lives, fulfilling and substantiating God's salvific promise that "all shall be well." This chapter focuses on our gifted origins. The determinant of our gifted origins is our being in God, for "in the first we have our being." Significantly, being in God is not limited to an anthropocentric viewpoint; being in God includes all things. Alongside this universal perspective on all things as having being through the love of God, Julian uses the image of knitting to describe the reciprocal nature of the distinctive relationship between God and human beings. Human beings are *knit* to God in the making and God is *knit* to humanity in taking flesh. In presenting the reciprocal nature of being *knit* to God, Julian shows that the understanding of human existence is grounded in the *imago Trinitatis* and in the *imago Christi*. In each of these dimensions of Julian's soteriology there is a *oneing* that places all being in relationship with divine love.

I. IN THE FIRST

We recall Julian's trinitarian formula that expresses how we are in a permanent relationship of *oneing* with divine love: "all our life consists of three: In the first we have our being, and in the second we have our increasing, and in the third we have our fulfillment. The first is nature, the second is mercy, the third is grace" (14:58.294). Our first focus, then, is on salvific origins: "in the first we have our being."

63

Julian does not define the phrase, but gives hints of its meaning by the way she uses it. The word "first" is equivocal. It refers primarily to the first person of the Trinity, the Father, and designates the role of the Creator in sharing divine love through creating humankind. "In the first" also refers to the collective creation of humanity when humankind "was made like the Trinity in our first making" (2:10.194). Thus "in the first" denotes the first moment in history when charity uncreated extends to charity created and the eternity of God's loving embraces humanity. This idea of a "first making" bears some resemblance to Augustine's doctrine of original creation, which he describes in two phases:

> one in the original creation when God made all creatures before resting from his works on the seventh day, and the other in the administration of creatures by which he works even now. In the first instance God made everything together without any moments of time intervening, but now he works within the course of time.[1]

Julian's reference to "in the first" echoes Augustine's distinction between original creation and God's providence. As in Augustine, "in the first" refers to the collective creation of humankind as portrayed in the book of Genesis. Julian adapts Augustine's idea of continuous creation when she refers to God's work that continues to sustain creation as "making again: our Creator wished us to be like Jesus Christ our savior in heaven forever, through the power of our making again" (2:10.195). We will see that for Julian creation does not mean that God created at an appointed time in the past. Creation is continuous. God sustains creation in being through the presence and action of Christ and the Holy Spirit transforming or re-creating us again and again until we are fully Christlike. Never disconnected from "making again," "in the first" refers to God's original act of creation. "In the first" lays the foundations for the bringing-together of creation and "making again," of origins and destiny. "In the first" refers to the originating gift of God's creative activity that institutes a continuity between past, present, and future. At the same time it leaves room for change and transformation.

Being has a theological meaning for Julian. In secular Middle English *being* refers to existence, material or immaterial life. It is the substance, nature, constitution, or essence of persons.[2] Julian's meaning

---

[1] Augustine, *The Literal Meaning of Genesis: A Commentary in Twelve Books.* Vol. 1. Translated by John Raymond Taylor (New York: Newman, 1982) 5.11 (p. 162). I am not suggesting that Julian was consciously familiar with this source but, as we noted in Chapter 2, there are many echoes of Augustine in her work.

[2] Lesley Brown, ed., *The New Shorter Oxford English Dictionary on Historical Principles.* 2 vols. (Oxford: Clarendon Press, 1993) (= *NSOED*) 208.

reflects this perception when she concludes: "and thus everything has being through the love of God" (1:5.183). But there is a further theological connotation to the term *being* that associates our being with the divine being. God's being is "everlasting being . . . eternal form without beginning" (14:58.293). Thus God is being. When God creates, God shares being so that all things have being through the love of God. All things exist because they come from God, who is being. All things participate in the divine being.

II. ALL THINGS HAVE BEING THROUGH THE LOVE OF GOD

"A little thing, like a hazelnut" reveals how all creation has being in God. This is a foundational image recorded toward the beginning of both the short and long texts. Described as "a spiritual sight of Christ's homely love" (1:5.183), the vision has an intangible quality that hints at the oneness between God and creation:

> And in this he showed me something small, no bigger than a hazelnut lying in the palm of my hand, as it seemed to me, and it was as round as a ball. I looked at it with the eye of my understanding and thought: What can this be? I was amazed that it could last, for I thought that because of its littleness it would suddenly have fallen into nothing (1:5.183).

Julian examines this spiritual sight "with the eye of [her] understanding," her interior eye, and sees a little thing like a hazelnut, "round as a ball." She understands that this is a vision of "all that is made." The image communicates a paradoxical meaning. Creation is so small in relation to God. It looks worthless, fragile, as if it could insignificantly fall into nothingness, and yet creation is of inestimable value, is precious, and belongs to God. Creation is eternally enfolded in the love of God. Julian unlocks the paradoxical nature of the image in words that become central to her soteriology: "It lasts and always will, because God loves it; and thus everything has being through the love of God" (1:5.183). She appreciates the oneness of all reality because all created reality extends from the divine being through love.

As Julian continues to contemplate the vision of the hazelnut with the eye of her understanding she sees three properties within it: "The first is that God made it, the second is that God loves it, the third is that God preserves [*keeps*] it.[3] But what did I see in it? It is that God is the

---

[3] I will use the Middle English *keep/keeper* here, as the activity of God as keeper occurs in other passages about creation. It creates a link between God's protection of creation and of humanity.

Creator and the protector *[keeper]* and the lover" (1:5.183). It is note-worthy that these properties are within creation and are not separate from creation. The presence of the properties of *making, loving,* and *keeping* reveals how all creation bears the mark of the Trinity. These activities indicate that creation is one and in a relationship of *oneing* with the Trinity. "That God made it" reveals God's role as creator in the foundational event of creation. "That God loves it" shows that this is a continual creation. It places divine love within creation. "That God keeps it" reinforces the constant presence of divine love and the faith-fulness of God in drawing the divine plan for salvation to completion. The properties express the role of the Trinity in all that is made, from being to fulfillment, from *exitus* to *reditus.* The properties convey that the shared love of the Trinity expressed as *maker, keeper,* and *lover* en-sures salvation.

Through the vision of the hazelnut Julian makes some important theological conjectures about how creation has being in God. God does not create and leave creation to its own resources; rather, God's creat-ing involves continuous involvement in creation as *maker, keeper,* and *lover.* This work is a natural process of *oneing* that never isolates God's work of creating from God's work of keeping and loving in history. *Making-keeping-loving* establishes a oneness between Creator and crea-tion formed at the original moment of creation and continued. This im-plies an evolutionary view of creation. Creation is not static or passive but, like a hazelnut, it has a potentially active kernel of growth within it. Creation responds to God's making, keeping, and loving.

Julian extends the notion of making, keeping, and loving when she says: "I saw God in a poynte" (3:11.3, 336).[4] This is an even more inef-fable sight than the vision of the hazelnut, for she sees it in her under-standing. Consequently she gives a more concrete qualifier to explain

---

[4] "I saw God in an instant of time." Edmund Colledge and James Walsh, eds., *A Book of Showings to the Anchoress Julian of Norwich.* 2 vols. (Toronto: Pontifical Insti-tute of Mediaeval Studies, 1978) 336 n. 3. Note the discrepancy in the translation because Colledge and Walsh consider that Julian means she saw God at a point of time, or in a fleeting moment. In contrast Frances Reynolds, "Some Literary Influ-ences in the Revelations of Julian of Norwich," *Leeds Studies in English and Kindred Languages* 7 (1952) 24, and Brant Pelphrey, *Love Was His Meaning: The Theology and Mysticism of Julian of Norwich* (Salzburg: Institüt für Anglistik und Amerikanistik, 1982) (= *LWHM*) 112–13, suggest that Julian is referring spatially to a point or the center of a circle. In this sense God is likened to the unity at the center of a circle that is in relationship to all the points on the circle. Ritamary Bradley, *Julian's Way: A Practical Commentary on Julian of Norwich* (London: Harper Collins, 1992) 94, consid-ers that the point signifies the reality of God at the heart of all things.

what she means: "for he is at the center *[mid point]* of everything, and he does everything" (13:11.197). God in a *point* reveals the dynamic presence of God as the *mid point* of all things, and all God does. God is at the heart of all reality. Julian clarifies further: "by which vision I saw that he is present in all things. I contemplated *[beheld]* it carefully, seeing and recognizing through it that he does everything *[all]* which is done" (3:11.197). This comment emphasizes that this theology is not conjecture on her part. She knows the truth of the statements: "he is present in all things and does all that is done." *All* becomes predominant. Graeme Garrett suggests that "all" presumably means what it says. "Not nearly all, or all important features, or all human beings, but all in the universal sense, simply every aspect, function, being, system —the whole creation—is situated in relation to God."[5] God is in relationship with all. *Things* is similarly inclusive because in Middle English it refers to an entity of any kind, including the immaterial and abstract, material substance, living beings.[6] *Things* for Julian includes all reality. That God is *in all things* is almost a paraphrase of "for you created all things" (Rev 4:11) with one significant change, however. God not only creates all things; God is actively present in all things. "All things" precludes a divorce between the human and the natural, between humanity and all created reality. Julian concludes: "For in mankind which will *[shall]* be saved is comprehended all, that is to say all that is made and the maker of all. For God is in man and in God is all" (1:9.192). We can understand all within human nature, "which shall be saved." This is possible because human beings are in God and in God is all. To love God means to love all things. Thus Julian's theology of divine presence extends beyond a personal mysticism that neglects social and cosmic responsibilites. Her theology of presence encompasses all creation, all that is. Furthermore, there is an intrinsic connection between God being in all things and God doing all that is done. God cannot be present to all things without actively participating in all that is done. Such an intense theology of gifted origins and divine presence, however, highlights the problem of sin.

In stark contrast to all things having being through the love of God and God continuing to be in all things, sin is the opposite of *all*. Sin has no being. Very early in the short text Julian confronts the dichotomy between being and nonbeing. She inquires into the existence of sin:

> O, wretched sin, what are you? You are nothing. For I saw that God is in everything; I did not see you. And when I saw that God has made

---

[5] Graeme Garrett, "Finding God in All Things," *The Way* 33 (1993) 3.
[6] *NSOED* 3281.

everything, I did not see you. And when I saw that God is in everything, I did not see you. And when I saw that God does everything that
is done, the less and the greater, I did not see you. And when I saw our
Lord Jesus Christ seated in our soul so honorably, and love and delight
and rule and guard all that he has made, I did not see you. And so I am
certain that you are nothing (xxiii:166).

Momentously, when Julian confronts the tension between the presence of God in all things and the problem of sin, instead of engaging in
beholding that leads to the spiritual sight of a little thing like a hazelnut
and God in a point, Julian engages in a hermeneutic of not seeing and
not understanding. In opposition to being, "sin is nothing *[nouzt]*"
(viii:226). In the tradition of Augustine,[7] Julian differentiates between
the being of God and the nonbeing of sin. Sin has no being. Sin is a
nothing with no ontological status, no substance, and no existence in
God. Therefore Julian does not see sin because sin is an absence of
being. The fivefold repetition of "I did not see you" emphasizes the
nothingness of sin. It leaves no doubt that Julian cannot *behold* sin. She
concludes: "and all those who love you and delight you and follow you
and deliberately end in you, I am sure that they will *[shall]*[8] be brought
to nothing with you and eternally confounded. Amen, for love of him"
(xxiii:166). The use of the word *shall* points to the certainty that sin will
lead sinners to what does not exist. Sin results in an abyss of nothingness and endless disorder.

Although Julian sees the nonbeing of sin as a contradiction to the
divine presence in all things, years of reflection reinforce her theology
of divine presence. She adds an important passage to the long text that
emphasizes the immanence of God:

> See, I am God. See, I am in all things. See, I do all things. See, I never
> remove my hands from my works, nor ever shall without end. See, I
> guide all things to the end that I ordain them for, before time began,
> with the same power and wisdom and love with which I made them
> (3:11.199).

---

[7] For example, see Augustine, *Confessions* 3.7.12; 7.12.18; Cf. Thomas Aquinas,
Summa theologica 1, q. 48.1-6; q. 49.1-3 (*Summa Theologica*, translated by the Fathers
of the English Dominican Province. 3 vols. [New York: Benziger, 1947] 248–56). This
philosophical tradition also exists in the East. See *Pseudo-Dionysius: the Complete
Works*, translated by Colm Luibheid. Classics of Western Spirituality (New York:
Paulist, 1987) 4.19 (p. 85). Cf. *Plotinus: The Six Enneads*. Translated by Stephen
MacKenna and B. S. Page (Chicago: Encyclopedia Britannica, 1952), *First Ennead* 8.1-
12 (pp. 27–34).

[8] *Shall* conveys a greater sense of necessity in Middle English than *will*.

The fivefold repetition of *see* invites a hermeneutic of seeing that encourages deeper interpretation. The words "in all things," "do all things," and "never remove my hands from my works" expand the meaning of *loving* and *keeping*. They describe the constant presence of God and the faithfulness of God in working to bring creation to its goal in God. "I guide all things to the end that I ordain them for" accentuates God's *keeping* or providential care. The concluding rhetorical question: "how should anything be amiss?" (3:11.199) inspires hope that God will complete what God initiated in the act of creation. I must emphasize that Julian's theology of divine presence is not pantheistic. She does not identify all created reality with God. Julian can say that God is in all things, does all things, and never becomes detached from creation, but there is always a distinction between Creator and creation. Julian is consistent in taking a middle ground between pantheism and a theism that separates God from the world and sees God as the irrelevant first cause of creation distant from the world. Furthermore, in pointing to God's providential care Julian is not setting up a doctrine of predestination that diminishes freedom of response from human beings. Her accent is on *oneing* that follows the pattern of *exitus reditus*. The pattern of life that God originates at creation is grounded in all things having being through the love of God. Thus being in God ensures a continuity between beginnings and endings. All things will return to God.

The images of "the little thing like a hazelnut" and "God in a point" imply a cosmic vision of all reality. The images present the universe dependent on God, the maker, keeper, and lover. In this unified cosmic picture all creation bears the mark of the Trinity. All creation exists in a relationship of *oneing* from origin in the Trinity to return to the Trinity. Although I am not suggesting that Julian had any idea of evolution as we know it, there is a sense in which there is a final convergence of all things in God. In her creation theology Julian undermines the dualism between God and creation. She binds the transcendence and immanence of God in such a way that the immanence of God is predominant. She sees creation as both gift and promise. God, the source and ground of all things, is creation's hope and destiny. Within the perspective of all creation having being in God we are now ready to focus on human nature.

III. Human Beings Have Being Through the Love of God

The first insight that the vision of the hazelnut reveals is God's role as creator: "the first is that God made it," or as Julian says in relation to human beings, "in the first we have our being." She qualifies: "the first is kind [nature]." Julian sees human nature in a relationship of *oneing* with the Godhead:

> . . . our nature *[kind]* is wholly in God, in which he makes diversities flowing out of him to perform his will, which nature *[kind]* preserves and mercy and grace restore and fulfill. And of these none will be destroyed, for our nature *[kind],* which is the higher part, is joined *[knit]* to God in its creation, and God is joined *[knit]* to our nature *[kind],* which is the lower part in taking flesh (14:57.291).

Without distinguishing what type of seeing this is, Julian describes humanity as "wholly in God." Humanity is *in* God, included in God, enclosed in God. *Wholly* emphasizes the oneness of this inclusion, the ontological unity between God and human nature. There is also dynamic movement in this enclosure, "our *kind,* which is the higher part, is *knit* to God in its creation." Reciprocally, "God is *knit* to our *kind* in taking flesh." God becomes one with the lower part of our nature in the Incarnation. The movement is dialectical. We are in God and God is in us. We are knit to God and God is knit to us. We recall the significance of Julian's image of *knitting,* which points to a permanent intertwining of humanity with God that is so subtle it would be impossible to separate the two individual threads. The imagery creates a sense of *perichoresis* in the God-human relationship. There is one reciprocal communion of love between the divine and human. A look at Julian's definition of *kind* and the two ways we are *knit* to God—at creation and in God's becoming flesh—will show how Julian comes to such a strong sense of *our kind* being *wholly in God,* human nature being *knit* to God, and God being *knit* to human nature.

IV. And Thus is Kind Made

Julian uses the word *kind* theologically: "God is essence *[kind]* in his very nature *[being];* that is to say, that goodness which is natural *[kind]* is God. He is the ground, his is the substance, he is very essence or nature *[the same thing that is kindness],* and he is the true Father and the true Mother of natures *[kinds]*" (14:62.302).

The first reference to *kind* in this passage portrays God as "*kind* in his *being.*" Thus *kind* delineates the being or nature of God. In the context of the created order Julian further defines *kind* as "that goodness that is kind, it is God." *Kind* reflects the goodness of God and *kind* is the ground and substance of all being.[9] In the second passage, "he is the same thing that is kindness," the meaning of *kindness* becomes more

---

[9] Julian is using the word "substance" here in a theological sense to describe the essence of God. In substance the three persons of the Trinity are one. This was a common Middle English usage. See *NSOED* 3123. Julian gives substance another meaning in the context of her anthropology, which we will examine shortly.

ambiguous. *Kindness* still seems to refer to the nature of God, but it also characterizes the quality of God's nature as compassionate, generous, and benevolent. Significantly for our understanding of human nature, the *kind* or nature of God that reflects the goodness of God is the "true Father and true Mother of *kinds*."

Brant Pelphrey points to possible sources for Julian's theological use of the word *kind*, integrating a sense of nature, goodness, and benevolence. He demonstrates that the term has roots in the German word *Kind*, meaning child or offspring, and suggests that in a familial sense *kind* relates to a family, class, or group:

> In Julian's usage "kinds" can also indicate the various "families" of nature, i.e., of animal life. There is a further meaning in Julian however, which is significant for her theology. We shall see that to be properly "kind" (i.e., to be human or natural) really means to be kind in the modern adjectival sense as well, that is to be courteous or loving.[10]

Kind is a polysemous word that Julian utilizes to communicate shades of meaning. It indicates that human nature is *one* with the nature of God. Human nature has familial ties with the Creator, ties that are bound by love. Humankind is true to this identity, truly natural, when it reflects the goodness of the divine nature, that is, when human nature is *kind*. Although human nature designates familial relationship with God, Julian maintains a distinction between God and humanity by referring to the Godhead as *kind unmade*: "and so is created nature *[kind made]* rightfully united *[oned]* to the maker, who is substantial uncreated nature *[kind unmade]*" (14:53.284). What Julian is stressing in these passages is that human lives ultimately come from God and have familial ties with God that make human nature like God. This entry into divine relationship that begins at creation, as I have noted earlier, should not be mistaken for pantheism, in which humans disappear or are God, or where God is identified with human nature. Julian always maintains a distinction between *kind made* and *kind unmade*. Through our creation our *kind* has a familial relationship in *kind* with the Creator.

---

[10] *LWHM* 88. Cf. Marion Glasscoe, ed., *Julian of Norwich. A Revelation of Love* (Exeter: University of Exeter Press, 1976) xvii–xviii; M. Diane F. Krantz, *The Life and Text of Julian of Norwich: The Poetics of Enclosure* (New York: Peter Lang, 1997) 97–109. It is noteworthy that in *Piers Plowman* William Langland also uses the word *kind* with similar semantic richness, where *kind* refers not only to nature, but to kindness (Hugh White, *Nature and Salvation in Piers Plowman* [Cambridge: D. S. Brewer, 1988] 1–2).

Creation

Julian invites her readers into the realm of her understanding about the creation of *kind* or human nature by presenting a myth-like depiction of God begetting human beings. The exposition incorporates a number of creation stories, more abstract doctrines that she has heard or been taught, and some of her own imagery:

> I understood that man's soul is made of nothing, that is to say that it is made of nothing that is made, in this way: When God was to make man's body, he took the slime of the earth, which is matter mixed and gathered from all bodily things, and of that he made man's body. But to the making of man's soul he would accept nothing at all, but made it. And so is created nature [*kind made*] rightfully united to the maker, who is substantial uncreated nature [*kind unmade*], that is God. And so it is that there may and will be nothing at all between God and man's soul. And in this endless love man's soul is kept whole (14:53.284).

In this eclectic rendering of the creation story Julian speculates about the creation of *kind*. She distinguishes the creation of the soul and the creation of the body. Julian does not make any reference to creation as a literal history of seven days. Rather she integrates two themes from the biblical creation myths, the Yahwist tradition (Gen 2:7) that God fashioned human beings from the earth, and the Priestly tradition that affirms the goodness of creation (Gen 1:1-25). To these myths she adds the later interpretation of *creatio ex nihilo*.[11] The phrase "just as the blessed Trinity created all things from nothing" (13:32.233) complements, or at least stands in tension with, her references to the immanence of God. This protects the distinction between Creator and creatures. *Creatio ex nihilo* affirms the transcendent, uncreated nature of God.

The Soul

Julian begins with the creation of the soul. She does not give a precise definition of what she means by soul, although in a later passage she identifies it thus: "the soul is a life, which life of his goodness and his grace will last in heaven without end, loving him, thanking him, praising him" (14:53.284). This understanding of the soul as the life-giving principle reflects the definition of the soul or *anima* popularized

---

[11] This was a common idea found in Origen, Tertullian, Irenaeus, and the Shepherd of Hermas. Julian probably synthesized the idea from Augustinian theology. She may simply be using a formula she is familiar with without being aware of the implications for other aspects of her creation theology.

by Thomas Aquinas as "that which makes living things live."[12] Also in keeping with Aquinas, Julian identifies this life-giving principle as immortal. She uses a series of metaphors to describe the soul: "as wide as if it were an endless citadel . . . as if it were a blessed kingdom . . . I understood that it is a fine city" (16:68.312-313). In emphasizing that God creates this life-giving principle from nothing Julian alludes to the spiritual, transcendent nature of the human soul.

Significantly, then, in creation we see that human beings are ontologically one with God because from the first moment of creation nothing can come between God and the soul: "Our soul is united [oned] to him who is unchangeable goodness. And between God and our soul there is neither wrath nor forgiveness in his sight. For our soul is so wholly united [oned] to God, through his own goodness, that between God and our soul nothing can interpose" (14:46.259). The repetition of oned/wholly oned emphasizes the copiousness of the oneing between God and the soul. Julian pushes her point about the oneing between the soul and God so far that separation from God is impossible. Her assertion "that between God and our soul nothing can interpose" indirectly links into her image of the nonbeing of sin. Nothing, not even "wrath nor forgiveness," can come between the soul and God. Toward the end of the Showings Julian confirms how valuable the human soul is in the eyes of God:

> . . . if the blessed Trinity could have created man's soul any better, any fairer, any nobler than it was created, the Trinity would not have been fully pleased with the creation of man's soul. But because it made man's soul as beautiful, as good, as precious a creature as it could make, therefore the blessed Trinity is fully pleased without end in the creation of man's soul (16:68.314).

The human soul could not be more meritorious than it was created. The Trinity is pleased with the making of the soul. Thus we can see that there is no doubt in Julian's mind of the intrinsic goodness of the human soul created one with God in a relationship of oneing that cannot be severed, even by sin. The human soul is oned to God.

The Body

In contrast to the soul made from nothing, God creates the body from the slime of the earth. Julian integrates this comment into the text as if it is a doctrine she knows. Traditionally this way of describing the

[12] Brian Davies, *The Thought of Thomas Aquinas* (Oxford: Clarendon Press, 1993) 212.

body created from "slime" points to the material nature of the human body considered sinful or base and in need of controlling.[13] I register a note of caution in interpreting this reference negatively, however, as the word *slyppe*[14] in the Sloane 1 manuscript implies that the reference alludes to the silt of the earth rather than slime. Thus *slime/slyppe* echoes Gen 2:7 where God begets human beings from the dust of the soil. This emphasis on the body "as a matter mixed and gathered from all bodily things" relates the body to the hazelnut image. We are reminded that "all things have being through the love of God." Julian's appreciation of the *oneing* that occurs between God and the body becomes clearer when we consider one of her first references to the body. She presents a unique image that defies beliefs about the impurity of the body:

> A man walks upright, and the food in his body [*soule*][15] is shut in as if in a well-made purse. When the time of his necessity comes, the purse is opened and then shut again, in most seemly fashion. And it is God who does this, as it is shown when he says that he comes down to us in our humblest needs (1:6.186).

In this image that Julian observes (she says it "came to my mind" [1:6.186]), the body is like a purse that opens and closes as it eliminates waste from the body. She points out that it is God who does this. The divine presence in the human body is so intimate that God is involved in the digestion of food and the elimination of waste. This implies that the elimination of waste is not something to be despised. It reveals how close God is to human physicality. God creates our bodies, loves our bodies, and continues to serve us in the humblest of our bodily needs because our soul is made in the likeness of God. Julian leaves no doubt about God's attitude to human physicality: "For he does not despise what he has made, nor does he disdain to serve us in the simplest natural functions of our body, for love of the soul which he created in his own likeness" (1:6.186). In contrast to many of her predecessors and contemporaries, Julian presents the body as good. The human body is of value to God because God made it in love.

---

[13] *NSOED* 2899.

[14] Sloane 1; liii:2191, 113.

[15] Colledge and Walsh point out that *soule*, from the Old English *sofol*, means cooked digested food. Though this usage was rare in Julian's day it appears in the *Ancrene Wisse*. See *BSAJN* 306 n. 35. There have been a number of translators who give this a spiritual meaning: cf. *LWHM* 157. The use of the same word *soule* translated as food and *soule* translated as soul is noteworthy. This could be a deliberate word play on Julian's behalf to emphasize that the whole of human nature is made in the image and likeness of the Trinity.

It is significant that the Sloane 1 manuscript does not have the image of the body as a purse.[16] Although this could cast doubt on whether this is Julian's image, the Westminster florilegium, a highly abridged collection of Julian's *Showings*, does contain this image.[17] The text clearly describes the presence of God in the opening and closing of the body for the elimination of waste. If Kempster is correct and this is a third manuscript tradition, the statement that "the food in his body is shut in as if in a well-made purse" suggests that this image was known by more than one heritage of Julian's texts. Thus the reference could be Julian's and not the interpolation of a scribe. Moreover, the image is too unusual to be made up by anyone and simply added to the text. It is possible that the controversial nature of the image induced the scribe of the Sloane 1 text to remove it. The image is important for Julian's soteriology because it suggests that the body plays a role in salvation. It counteracts any implied images of the body as base, sinful, and carnal. Salvation is not spiritualized.

Julian remains silent on whether anything can come between the body and God. She makes no comment about chastity and gives no cautions about sexuality. Neither does she advocate fasting, bodily mortification, or other ascetical practices. She preserves this silence on the subject of denial or mortification of the body when she states towards the end of the book: "As to the penance which one takes upon oneself, that was not revealed to me" (16:77.330). Julian has nothing to say about inflicting penance on the body. Moreover, she emphasizes the collective nature of the creation of humanity when she concentrates on the creation of the body. She refers to "man's body" in the generic sense of humankind and does not distinguish the creation of women. This subtly eliminates common medieval gender distinctions that associate women with the body or evil and men with the intellect, transcendence, or divinity. It is all humanity, the bodies and souls of women and men, that is normatively human. Julian uses bodily imagery extensively to describe the human relationship with God.

In the act of creation there is a distinction between the creation of the soul and the creation of the body. There is no doubt that nothing can come between the soul and God. In contrast, some ambiguity clouds the creation of the body in that Julian does not distinguish how the

[16] Cf. Sloane 1: vi:203–210, 45. The text simply refers to "the simplest office that to our body longyth in kinde."

[17] See Hugh Kempster, ed., "Julian of Norwich: The Westminster Text of a Revelation of Love," *Mystics Quarterly* 23 (1997) 107–14, p. 215. Even if this is not a third tradition, and is an eclectic gathering of both Paris and Sloane sources, it is significant that the compiler chose to include the reference.

body in *oned* in God. Still, the convoluted depiction of the creation of soul and body leaves room for the creation of both as the subject of her theological statement: "and so is *kind* created rightfully *oned* to the maker, who is substantial *kind* uncreated, that is God" (14:53.284). There is enough evidence that Julian values the body to conclude that our *kind* is the whole of human nature as God intends it to be. Soul and body, our *kind,* is *oned* to God.

Julian's treatment of the doctrine of the creation of soul and body *oned* to God in creation presents a paradox. From one perspective there is a Platonic and Neoplatonic dichotomy between soul and body. The soul, created first, is made from nothing whereas the body is made from slime of the earth. Yet Julian does not persist with these traditional metaphysical definitions of human nature defined as body and soul. She moves in the direction of appreciating the wholeness of the human person as a unity of soul and body. Her thought resonates with Church teaching based on the statement of Thomas Aquinas that the soul is "that which makes living things live." Strictly speaking, this philosophical approach[18] precludes ever dealing with soul or body independently, in life or in death. In short, for Julian God creates a *oneing* of humanity in God that includes the whole of human nature, both body and soul. Gifted origins include our body and soul.

Within this general context of the creation of human nature as a soul and a body, *"kind created oned* to *kind uncreated,"* Julian focuses on the "higher part" of human nature that is *"knit* to God at creation." It is important to note at this stage, however, that Julian does not simply equate the "higher part" with the soul. In what follows we will see how we have being in God in the "higher part."

V. KNIT TO GOD

We have noted that from Julian's perspective the whole human person, soul and body, is *oned* to the Creator in creation. This *oneing* institutes a bond that can never be broken. Moreover, in this understanding of how we have being in God there is a higher part that makes this *oneing* inviolable: for our nature *[kind]*, which is the higher part, is joined *[knit]* to God in its creation" (14:57.291). We will see explicit facets of this *knitting* in the higher part by examining Julian's understanding of the *imago Dei,* "substance," the "Godly will," and the "kindly will." In each of these aspects of our nature God creates a *oneing* that lays the foundation for our return to God.

---

[18] See Thomas Aquinas, *De Anima* 2.1.234, in Davies, *The Thought of Thomas Aquinas* 209.

Our Soul Is a Made Trinity

The doctrine of the *imago Dei* is foundational in Julian's anthropology. It is in fact *imago Trinitatis*.[19] She gives weight to this teaching by stating that this is not simply her idea. It is the teaching of Holy Church. She reiterates: "We know in our faith and our belief, by the teaching and preaching of Holy Church, that the blessed Trinity made mankind in their image and their likeness" (2:10.194). When Julian interprets this doctrine further she places the *imago Dei* in the soul[20] and describes human nature as "a created trinity, like the uncreated blessed Trinity, known and loved from without beginning, and in the creation united [*oned*] to the Creator, as is said before. This sight was sweet and wonderful to contemplate, peaceful and restful, secure and delectable" (14:55.287). Multiple images of joy describe the wonder of the image of God in humanity. She repeats her theological position: human nature is *oned* to the maker, *like* the maker. Julian's reference to "likeness" emphasizes the capacity for actualization of the image of God. *Like* suggests that we bear a faithful resemblance to the Trinity. We share qualities that are God-like so that we may perfect our image of God.[21]

The likeness to God is so authentic that human nature possesses trinitarian qualities that will assist it in returning to the Trinity. Julian sees and understands that "the high might of the Trinity is our Father, and the deep wisdom of the Trinity is our Mother, and the great love of the Trinity is our Lord; and all these we have in nature [*kind*] and in our substantial creation" (14:58.294). This passage expresses truth as Julian understands it: the Trinity is Father, Mother, and Lord to humanity. Because of this familiarity we are uniquely gifted with trinitarian qualities of high might, deep wisdom, and great love. Julian's repetition of this idea reinforces the teaching: "For God is endless supreme truth, endless supreme wisdom, endless supreme love uncreated; and a man's soul is a creature in God which has the same properties created" (14:44.256). Made like the Trinity, we possess trinitarian qualities.

---

[19] See Joan Nuth, *Wisdom's Daughter: The Theology of Julian of Norwich* (New York: Crossroad, 1991) 104–16, where she argues that Julian's anthropology follows Augustine.

[20] We need to be careful about Julian's use of the word "soul" here. I will show in the next section that our sensuality, the more bodily part of human nature, is also considered a soul. Note that in the first passage she uses the generic term "mankind." Therefore humankind or human nature is a more accurate translation. See Wolfgang Riehle, *The Middle English Mystics*. Translated by Bernard Strandring (London: Routledge and Kegan Paul, 1981) 148; 211 n. 60.

[21] *Lyke* in Middle English suggests having the same characteristics or qualities. *NSOED* 1588.

Anthropologically this suggests that God-like qualities are intrinsic to human nature. Furthermore, the sharing of properties implies that God does not create human nature in order to rule over human nature. God creates in order to share divine life with human nature. For Julian the *imago Dei* is a defining imprint in the human soul that determines the inviolable *oneing* between us and the Trinity. The image of the Trinity in the human soul initiates an originating participation in God that can never be destroyed.

Oneing *in Substance*

Julian uses an additional image to point to the *oneing* that occurs between *created kind* and *uncreated kind*. She refers to the "substance" of humankind. "Substance" has a specific meaning for her that she finds difficult to define clearly. She tells of her inability to describe it fully:

> . . . there was a perception and a secret inward vision of the higher part, and that was shown at the same time when I could not, in response to the intermediary's suggestion look up to heaven. And that was because of that same mighty contemplative vision *[beholding]* of the inward life, which inward life is that high substance, that precious soul which is endlessly rejoicing in the divinity (14:55.288).

In "a secret inward vision" Julian discerns that substance has to do with the "inward life." Possibly reflecting the inner life outlined in the *Ancrene Wisse,* the inner life is the deepest yearning of the human heart to be focused on Christ.[22] Her reference to the qualifier "high" suggests that "substance" describes the most exalted part of human nature. Substance is the "precious" soul that endlessly enjoys God. It is the life-giving principle that enables us to know divine joy.

Julian is certain that our substance extends from the being, creating, loving, and keeping of God. There is no beginning to our substance's having being in God: "In our almighty Father we have our protection and our bliss, as regards our natural substance, which is ours by our creation from without beginning" (14:58.293). We always dwell in God in substance: "I saw no difference between God and our substance, but, as it were, all God; and still my understanding accepted that our substance is in God, that is to say that God is God, and our substance is a creature in God" (14:54.285). Because our soul dwells in God in sub-

---

[22] See *Anchoritic Spirituality Ancrene Wisse and Associated Works.* Translated by Anne Savage and Nicholas Watson (New York: Paulist, 1991), *AW* III. Inner Feelings, 93–113.

stance we derive existence from the Trinity, share life with and belong
to the Trinity. Julian stresses the union between God and our substance
so strongly that she makes an almost pantheistic statement: "I saw no
difference between God and our substance." Then she moderates her
position by clarifying her statement: "God is God and our substance is
a creature in God." Although at creation our substance is created a
creature in God and in union with God for all time, it is not fully identified with God. She makes another clear statement about human *oneing* with God: "in it a substance was kept which could never and
should never be parted from him, and that through his own good will
in his endless prescient purpose" (14:53.283). Through God's providential plan for salvation there is an indissoluble unity between human
beings and the Trinity because our substance is "kept" in the Trinity.
Congruent with the insights that emerge from the hazelnut image,
Julian appreciates that God's "endless prescient purpose" ensures that
our substance can never be parted from God. "Kept" in the Trinity, our
substance is enclosed in God and dwells in God in eternal *oneing*.

Nebulously, Julian alludes to what she understands by substance:

> It is a great understanding to see and know inwardly that God, who is
> our Creator, dwells in our soul, and it is a far greater understanding to
> see and know inwardly that our soul, which is created, dwells in God in
> substance, of which substance, through God, we are what we are *[we be
> that we be]* (14:54.285).

Humanity dwells in God in substance. In our substance *we be that
we be*, or as the Sloane 1 text says, "we are all that we are" (54.108).[23] *Be
that we be* echoes the hazelnut image, where all things have being in the
love of God. In our substance we are who we are. Although Julian has
described substance as "high" and has identified it with the inward
life, she does not maintain an emphasis on substance as the exclusively
spiritual part of human nature. In this statement where she makes a
further qualification, "of which substance, through God, we are what
we are," substance describes how we exist. Thus it would be incorrect
to limit the definition of substance to the demarcation of the highest
faculty of the soul, or only to the soul, our spiritual nature, or the deep
self, although these are a dimension of what she means by substance.

[23] See *LWHM* 89–90; Susan Mahan, *The Christian Anthropology of Julian of Norwich.*
Ph.D. dissertation, Marquette University (Ann Arbor: UMI Disertation Services,
1988) 194; Grace M. Jantzen, *Power, Gender and Christian Mysticism* (Cambridge:
Cambidge University Press, 1995) 148; Dom Roger Udleston, o.s.b., ed., *Revelations
of Divine Love Shewed to a Devout Ankress by Name Julian of Norwich* (London: Orchard
Books, 1927) 175; Bradley, *Julian's Way* 200–201.

Julian's use of the word "substance" seems more like Augustine's (he uses "substance" as a synonym for existence),[24] or like the Scholastic term *substantia*, which means that of which a thing consists, the being or essence of something, the contents or material matter.[25] Aquinas clarifies this when he describes the human being as "a compound whose substance is both spiritual and corporeal."[26] He delineates what substance contains:

> For as it belongs to the very conception of "this human being" that there should be this soul, flesh and bone, so it belongs to the very conception of "human being" that there be soul, flesh and bone. For the substance of a species has to contain what ever belongs in general to every one of the individuals comprising that species.[27]

Julian's references to substance reflect this interpretation. Necessarily vague because we can never fully describe the essence of human nature, "substance" includes soul and body, all that human nature is. Substance is the essence of who we are as spiritual/embodied persons *oned* to the Maker. We have being in God in our substance. *Oned* in *substance* in the Trinity, we share in divine life.

Oneing *in the Godly Will*

The result of human beings having *being* in God in substance is that we have the ability to align our wills with the will of God: "And as regards our substance, he made us so noble and so rich that always we achieve his will and his glory" (14:57.290). Julian describes this as our *godly will*.[28] Unlike some of the *showings* that Julian cannot understand

---

[24] See Nuth, *Wisdom's Daughter* 109, and Denise Nowakowski Baker, *Julian of Norwich's Showings: From Vision to Book* (Princeton: Princeton University Press, 1994) 119.

[25] Charlton T. Lewis, *A Latin Dictionary: Lewis and Short* (Oxford: Clarendon Press, 1984) (= *LD*) 1782.

[26] Davies, *The Thought of Thomas Aquinas* 209.

[27] Ibid. 210.

[28] Colledge and Walsh relate this to 1 John 3:9-10 (*BSAJN* 443 n. 15. They also suggest the source is William of St. Thierry's *Golden Epistle* (*Julian of Norwich Showings*. Translated by Edmund Colledge and James Walsh [New York: Paulist, 1978] 57). Baker points out that this was plausible because of the popularity of the work mistakenly attributed to Bernard of Clairvaux. She considers this to be more likely than John Clark's suggestion of *De Natura et Dignitate Amoris* as the source. Baker, *From Vision to Book* 76; cf. John P. H. Clark, "'Fiducia' in Julian of Norwich," *The Downside Review* 99 (1981) 218.

as clearly as she would wish, this is a distinctive *showing* in which she sees and understands fully: "For in every soul which will be saved there is a Godly will which never assents to sin and never will . . . so there is a Godly will in the higher part, which will is so good that it cannot ever will any evil, but always good" (13:37.241-242). Julian later repeats this description and explains more fully:

> . . . in each soul which will be saved there is a Godly will which never assented to sin nor ever will, which will is so good that it can [*may*] never will evil, but always constantly it wills good and it does good in the sight of God. Therefore our Lord wants us to know it in our faith and our belief, and particularly and truly that we have all this blessed will whole and safe in our Lord Jesus Christ, because every nature [*kind*] with which heaven will be filled had of necessity and of God's rightfulness to be so joined [*knit*] and united [*oned*] in him that in it a substance was kept which could never and should never be parted from him, and that through his own good will in his endless prescient purpose (14:53.282-283).

Julian gives her teaching authority ("we know in faith and belief"): it is the teaching of Holy Church that we have a *godly will*. *Knit* and *oned* to Christ, inseparable from Christ, the *godly will* is the inviolable goodness of humankind that is kept whole and safe forever in the *oneing* that occurs between human beings and Christ.[29]

Julian also associates the *godly will* with the goodness of God.[30] She observes that "his goodness fills all his creatures and all his blessed works full, and endlessly overflows in them" (1:5.184). We see the connection between the goodness of God and the *godly will* in the text when *godly will* sometimes becomes *goodly will*.[31] This lack of orthographical distinction throughout the manuscript between *godly will* and *goodly will*[32] implies that human beings derive their *godly will* from the goodness of God. Furthermore, although Julian does not make a direct association between the *godly will* and the Holy Spirit she does refer to the mutual enclosure between the *high goodness of* Holy Spirit

---

[29] See Baker, *From Vision to Book* 78.

[30] The relationship of the soul's goodness to the goodness of God has a possible source in Augustine. See *Augustine of Hippo. Selected Writings,* translated by Mary T. Clark (New York: Paulist, 1984), "On the Trinity," 8.3.5 (pp. 317–18). Aquinas has a similar notion. See *Summa theologica* 1, q. 82.1 (p. 413).

[31] Wolfgang Riehle points out (*The English Medieval Mystics* 158) that in Sloane 1 there is no consistent orthographical distinction between *God* and *good*.

[32] ". . . for in him we have this Godly will, whole and safe forever, both in nature and in grace, from his own goodness proper to him" 14:59.296-297.

and humanity. Therefore it is not unreasonable to suggest that the fluidity of Julian's imagery favors an implicit association between the *godly will* and human participation in the goodness of the Trinity through mutual enclosure in the Holy Spirit. Through God's own *good will* human beings are *knit* and *oned* to Christ in such a way that the *godly will* is kept safe in Christ. *Knitting* and *oneing* mean that we have a *godly will* that can never be destroyed.

Julian is convinced that the *godly will* can never be eradicated from the human person. Nevertheless, she still struggles with the problem of sin. Alongside the *godly will* there is "an animal *[beastly]* will in the lower part which cannot will any good *[may will no good]*" (13:37.242).[33] Julian is silent about the source of our *beastly will*, apart from locating it in the "lower part," our sensuality. It is noteworthy that Julian does not directly associate the *beastly will* with lists of sins or equate sensuality with the image of sin. She simply presents the paradox within human nature. Human beings are good and human beings can be evil. Through her concept of the *beastly will* she acknowledges that there is something within human nature that is in contradiction to the goodness of God, something that "may will no good." Significantly, however, Julian does not claim that human beings are intrinsically beastly. Although her use of "may"[34] emphasizes the power or influence the *beastly will* can exhibit, the absence of the word "never" shows that this power has limitations. In contrast, the "godly will . . . may never will evil." We will return to the problem of sin in the next chapter. Mindful that sin intrudes into but never destroys how we have our being in God, we will examine Julian's additional description of the will as the *kindly will*.

Oneing *in the* Kindly Will

The *kindly will* gives a further dimension of human *oneing* in God: "our natural will is to have God, and God's good will is to have us, and we can never stop willing or loving until we possess him in the fullness of joy" (1:6.186). The *kindly will* is the source of our deepest desire for God, which Julian also calls a *kind yearning*. The *kindly will* longs for the fulfillment of our nature in God. The yearning it initiates reflects God's will to have us.

---

[33] I will retain the term *beastly will*, as *beastly* gives more a sense of the depraved than *animal*. See *The Scale of Perfection*, translated by John P. Clark and Rosemary Dorward (New York: Paulist, 1991) 2.13 (p. 214) for a possible source.

[34] The Middle English suggests to be strong, to have power or influence, to prevail over. *NSOED* 1721.

Through her conception of the *godly will* and the *kindly will* Julian shows that there is an inviolable *oneing* between God and humanity that can never be destroyed. There is a unity between God's self-communication in *kind* to us and our dynamic self-transcendence toward the divine. Our most authentic desire is to align our will with the will of God and to return to God. The will enables us to be true to our nature in God and to cooperate with God's deepest desire that we possess God in the fullness of joy. It is highly significant for Julian's soteriology that our ontological *oneing* with God is located in the will. This means that authentic human desire is to be good or Godly, to be true to our *kind*. Our *oneing* in God not only affects our being; it has a direct consequence for our will and actions. The *godly will* and *kindly will* inspire hope that we can respond to divine love.

Within the context of examining Julian's understanding of how humanity has being in God we have concentrated on her interpretation of how we are "knit to God in the making" in the "higher part" of our nature. We have seen that the higher part of our nature is not limited to the soul, but distinguishes who we are. Julian presents multiple images of ontological *oneing*. Made in the image and likeness of the Trinity, humankind is like the Trinity. *Oned* to God in substance, human nature is one with God in the essence of who we are as spiritual-embodied persons. *Oned* to God in the *Godly will* and the *kindly will*, the human will is aligned with the will of God. "Knit to God in the making" creates a sense that "all is well," and "all shall be well." This is the situation of humankind as God intends it to be, with its being in God. Yet this is not the complete story of human existence as we know it. Human beings are "knit to God in the making," but this *oneing* is reciprocal in nature: it occurs through Christ when "God is knit to our kind" in taking flesh. In presenting the reciprocal nature of being *knit* to God Julian shows that an understanding of human existence is grounded not only in the *imago Trinitatis* but also in *imago Christi*. Our gifted origins have a special location in Christ. The Incarnation plays a key role in how we have our being "in the first."

VI. God is Knit to Us

We have seen that from Julian's perspective the whole human person, soul and body, is *knit* and *oned* to the Trinity, Father, Mother, and Holy Spirit in creation. This *oneing* institutes a bond between humankind and the Godhead that can never be destroyed. Unmistakably, this *oneing* occurs in the "higher part" of human nature, in our "substance," where we are knit to God. Just as significant as the *oneing* that occurs in our substance, however, is the *oneing* that reciprocally occurs in the lower part of our nature, our sensuality, through Christ's becoming flesh. We recall: "I saw that our kind is wholly in God . . . and God is knit to our kind, which is the lower part, in taking flesh" (14:57.291). The whole of human nature has being in God. God is knit to our full humanity in the Incarnation. "Knit to our kind" describes the permanent *oneing* between God and humanity. Thus the key to understanding Julian's idea of how we have being in God is to picture human nature in a type of *perichoresis* in the Trinity where we are *knit* to God in our substantial nature. Moreover, we experience "making again" when God is knit to our sensual nature, when Christ becomes flesh. Both locations of *knitting* are integral to how we have being in God.

Oneing *in Sensuality*

When Julian describes how we are one with God in substance she pairs substance with sensuality: "we are double by God's creating, that is to say substantial and sensual" (14:58.294). "Double" suggests that human nature has two essential parts or features, a substantial nature and a sensual nature. Our sensual nature, or sensuality, has a distinctive meaning in Julian's anthropology. As with the word "substance," she never defines the term definitively. The *Middle English Dictionary* delineates sensuality as: "the natural capacity for receiving physical sensation understood as an inferior power of the soul concerned with the body."[35] Julian's use of the term "sensual" far exceeds this definition, however. In Julian's anthropology there is no doubt that sensuality describes the bodily aspect of human nature: "and when our soul is breathed into our body, at which time we are made sensual" (14:55.286). Sensuality describes our humanity, our body and soul, how we exist in the world. Yet Julian stresses that sensuality is not simply our body when she says: "as regards our substance, it can rightly be called our soul, and as regards our sensuality, it can rightly be called our soul, and that is by the union [*oneing*] which it has in God" (14:56.289). She speci-

---

[35] Hans Kurath, Sherman Kuhn, and Robert Lewis, eds., *Middle English Dictionary* (Ann Arbor: University of Michigan Press, 1954–) 436 (hereafter *MED*). The Oxford Dictionary defines the Middle English meaning of sensuality as the aspect of human nature concerned with the senses as opposed to the intellect or spirit, humanity's animal nature, the source of sensual appetites and desires. It can refer to absorption in temporal things rather than intellectual or spiritual matters (*NSOED* 2777). The understanding of the human person as sensual finds its roots in Augustine. See *The Works of St. Augustine: A Translation for the Twenty-First Century*, translated by Edmund Hill (Brooklyn: New City Press, 1990) 12.3.17 (p. 331). Cf. Thomas Aquinas, *Summa theologica* 1, q. 81.1 (p. 410); *LWHM* 90–91.

fies that sensuality is soul by virtue of its *oneing* in God. Julian presents what she understands about sensuality:

> So I understood that our sensuality is founded in nature [*grounded in kind*], in mercy and in grace, and this foundation enables us to receive gifts which lead us to endless life. For I saw very surely that our substance is in God, and I also saw that God is in our sensuality, for in the same instant and place in which our soul is made sensual, in that same instant and place exists the city of God, ordained for him from without beginning. He comes into this city and will never depart from it, for God is never out of the soul, in which he will dwell blessedly without end (14:55.287).

"I understood" suggests that Julian clearly discerns that sensuality is one in God.[36] "Grounded in kind," in nature, sensuality is *oned* in God because all nature or being comes from God. Sensuality is an aspect of human nature in which divine life is actively present. Sensuality is the dwelling place of mercy and grace, which are the gifts that lead us to endless life. Julian's appreciation that sensuality is grounded in mercy and grace reinforces that she does not simply define sensuality in terms of the body, the flesh, or the senses. Sensuality includes our embodied/spiritual nature. It is where we experience the working of grace through Christ the mother of grace, and through the presence of the Holy Spirit. Julian states clearly: "God is in our sensuality." In the act of creation, when God creates the sensual soul, God immediately makes sensuality the city of God. Sensuality is the dwelling place of God, the locale of *oneing*. Critically, the indwelling of God in sensuality is not an afterthought to God's eternal plan: "in the same instant and place when the soul is made sensual, in the same instant and place exists the city of God." Participation in human sensuality is an integral part of the divine plan of sharing love.

Nevertheless, there is something incomplete about sensuality. It is where we experience the effects of the fall that limit our *oneing* with God: "in our substance we are full and in our sensuality we are lacking [*fail*], and this lack God will restore and fill by the operation of mercy and grace, plentifully flowing into us from his own natural goodness" (14:57.291). *Fail* in Middle English suggests that we are found wanting,

---

[36] Though the exact definition of sensuality is impossible to pin down in the text it is noteworthy that Julian does not say that she finds it difficult to understand. In contrast to the understanding she receives about our substantial nature, which comes from an enigmatic *prevy inwarde syghte,* she understands how sensuality is one in God. She seems to assume that her readers will also understand.

or are lacking in something needed.[37] In our sensuality we experience an impediment in our union with God; we experience the effects of the *beastly will*. Thus in our sensuality we are not full, nor are we fully one with divine love or fully one with our substance that is totally one in God. Momentously, however, in our sensuality, where we are inadequate, we are not separated from divine love, because in our incompleteness God restores and fulfills us through the working of mercy and grace. In keeping with this sense of incompleteness Julian lists feelings that we experience in our sensuality: "for in the lower part there are pains and sufferings, compassions and pities, mercies and forgiveness and other such" (14:52.282). Sensuality is not the image of sin or our sinful nature. Sensuality is where we experience feelings associated with an incompleteness in our union with God. These pains, however, are never isolated from compassion and pity, mercy and forgiveness. Sensuality is how we exist in the world, within the fragmentation in the human condition. Although sensuality is where we experience the effects of incompleteness due to the Fall, more fundamentally sensuality is where we encounter the effects of *oneing*. Sensuality is where we are open to the presence of divine life in human lives through Christ and are drawn into the process of growth or *increasing* until we become fully Christ-like. Sensuality encompasses the whole of human existence that God assumes through Christ's becoming flesh. Therefore we can see sensuality as God intends it to be in the humanity of Christ.

Christ knit to our body in the Incarnation encapsulates Julian's version of sensuality:

> For in the same time that God joined *[knit]* himself to our body in the maiden's womb, he took our soul, which is sensual, and in taking it, having enclosed us all in himself, he united *[oned]* it to our substance. In this union *[oneing]* he was perfect man, for Christ, having joined *[knit]* in himself every man who will be saved, is perfect man (14:57.292).

The image of *knitting* interweaves multiple threads of *oneings* or locations of union with Christ. Interwoven are the *oneings* between Christ and our substance and Christ and our sensuality. In being "knit . . . to our body in the maiden's womb" Christ encloses our sensual soul in himself and *ones* it to our substance. "Enclosure" emphasizes the oneness between Christ's humanity and our sensuality. Sensuality is contained within Christ. "Enclosed" further illuminates the indissolubility of the unity between human beings and Christ. Christ models perfect humanity. He points to the possibility that the growth and perfection of

---

[37] *NSOED* 906.

both substance and sensuality may be completely full, one in being in God. Christ works to achieve this potential in human beings by eliminating all fractures between substance and sensuality through the presence of mercy and grace in sensuality. United to Christ in both substance and sensuality, we are brought to participate in divine reality, to exist fully in a divine relationship that encompasses every part of our being.

Moreover, in the Incarnation when Christ takes a sensual soul he becomes the mother of our sensuality: "the second person, who is our Mother, substantially the same beloved person, has now become our mother sensually, because we are double by God's creating, that is to say substantial and sensual" (14:58.294). Because Christ is our "mother sensually" there is no doubt that we are ontologically one in our sensuality in Christ:

> . . . our substance is in our Father, God almighty, and our substance is
> in our Mother, God all wisdom, and our substance is in our Lord God,
> the Holy Spirit, all goodness, for our substance is whole in each person
> of the Trinity, who is one God. And our sensuality is only in the second
> person, Christ Jesus, in whom is the Father and the Holy Spirit (14:58.295).

Our substance is whole in each person of the Trinity—Father, Mother, and Holy Spirit—but our sensuality is only in the second person, Jesus Christ.[38] In other words it is the second person of the Trinity who as Mother is one with our substance, becomes flesh, and is *knit* to our sensuality. Consequently, through Christ being knit to our sensuality, we become the *imago Christi*. Christ, the perfect human being, incorporates both substance and sensuality in himself in a perfect unity.

What is remarkable about Julian's understanding of how human beings have being in God is that this *oneing* embraces all aspects of human existence, including sensuality. Our substance has being in the Trinity. Our sensuality has being in the Trinity because Christ includes our sensual soul in himself in becoming human. This *oneing* is foundational for Julian's soteriology. Salvation does not require a process of denying or suppressing sensuality. Salvation involves becoming fully sensual, *oneing* substance and sensuality, making both substance and sensuality full, just as they are in Christ. "In the first we have our being" means that in principle, in spite of the incomplete nature of sensuality, in both substance and sensuality our being is in God. This *oneing* in the Trinity in substance and sensuality ensures that we will return to the Trinity.

---

[38] This still has a trinitarian dimension because the persons of the Trinity are in Christ.

Salvation is inaugurated in the act of creation when God creates human nature with being in God. This first movement in the *exitus reditus*, where all things have being in God, is foundational for Julian's soteriology. Our origins are gifted because in the first we have being in God. The images of the hazelnut and God in a point illustrate that it is not only human beings, but all things, that have being in God. Julian envisages human nature within this inclusive perspective. In the higher part of human nature, our substance, we are *knit* to God in the making. Reciprocally, God is knit to us in the lower part of our nature, our sensuality. There are multiple images of ontological *oneing*s in the essence of who we are in the *imago Dei*, the *godly will*, and the *kindly will*. Furthermore, in the Incarnation, in being "knit . . . to our body in the maiden's womb," Christ designates our deepest humanity as the dwelling-place of God. The exegesis confirms that for Julian the whole of human nature, both substance and sensuality, irrevocably has being in God. In the next chapter we will see how Christ *increases* our sensuality, making it full and *one* with God through his Passion, death, and resurrection.

Part Four

In the Second We
Have Our Increasing

. . . in the second we have our increasing (14:58.294).

5

Oneing Through the Crucifixion

Here saw I a great oneing between Christ and us (8:18.210).

In the Incarnation Christ becomes the perfect human being who *ones* our substance and sensuality in himself. In this act of *knitting* and *oneing* God confronts the problem of the incompletion of our sensuality and the fragmentation of our existence because human nature is not fully one with Christ, not fully the *imago Christi*. Though we have being in God there is need for change and transformation, for *increasing* or growth. The aim of this chapter is to see how Christ enables our *increasing* through the cross by drawing creation into the meaning of Christ's suffering, death, and resurrection. Julian's theology of the cross focuses intensely on suffering. It is an expression of the truth of which Jürgen Moltmann reminds us: "The Cross is the form of the coming, redeeming kingdom."[1] The *exitus reditus* is cruciform. Yet the suffering of Christ never becomes an end in itself. Julian's concentrated attention on Christ's death leads to a theology of the paschal mystery presented as *oneing* in suffering, *oneing* in love, and *oneing* in joy. Julian's theology of the cross is a theology of glory.

I. IN THE SECOND

We recall Julian's trinitarian formula that describes the pattern of *oneing* that occurs between the Trinity and humanity in the *exitus reditus*: "In the first we have our being, and in the second we have our increasing, and in the third we have our fulfillment. The first is nature, the

---

[1] Jürgen Moltmann, *The Crucified God: The Cross of Christ as the Foundation and Criticism of Christian Theology* (London: SCM, 1974) 185.

second is mercy, the third is grace" (14:58.294). We have seen that at creation God establishes for all time that humanity will participate in the life of God or have *being in God*. There is a series of ontological *one-ings* between God and humanity that cannot be destroyed. But this is not the complete picture of human existence as we know it. In our sensuality we experience the effects of sin and the incompleteness of the human condition that together prevent our substance and sensuality from being fully one in Christ. There is need for redemption. Julian describes this transformation as "in the second we have our increasing."

Julian uses the phrase "in the second" in two ways, without otherwise defining it. "In the second" points to the role of the second person of the Trinity. It identifies the second period in the history of salvation or continual creation when God's self-communication achieves an absolute and irrevocable concrete historical manifestation in Christ's becoming flesh. Beginning with the Incarnation, the expression "in the second" draws together Christ's saving work on the cross and his ongoing continual presence as servant and mother in history. "In the second" refers to what Julian calls "making again" or re-creation through Christ: ". . . our Creator wished us to be like Jesus Christ our savior in heaven forever, through the power of our making again" (2:10.195). When Christ becomes human he draws us into the process of being re-created. A critical point to notice is that re-creation does not occur only once. "Making again" has the dynamic of continual "increasing." It occurs again and again. "In the second" Christ engages us in a process of continual *oneing*.

In popular usage "increasing" suggests making something greater or more numerous. It specifies growth.[2] The way Julian uses the word "increasing" gives it an energy that conveys the dynamic, renewing relationship that Christ sustains. She bestows a specifically theological meaning through relating "increasing" to Christ's work of *oneing*: "in our Mother Christ we profit and increase, and in mercy he reforms and restores us, and by the power of his Passion, his death and his Resurrection he unites us to our substance" (14:58.294). Paired with "profit," increasing benefits humanity by conferring prosperity and fullness of life. Related to mercy, increasing occurs in Christ's Passion, death, and resurrection as Christ reforms and restores all that was lost through the Fall. Increasing, however, is not simply saving creation. There is an evolutionary sense of perfecting creation. Increasing has a transformational, evolutionary outcome that makes the God/human relationship more complete than it was before the fall:

---

[2] Hans Kurath, Sherman Kuhn, and Robert Lewis, eds., *Middle English Dictionary* (Ann Arbor: University of Michigan Press, 1954–) (= MED) 111.

. . . all the gifts which God can give to the creature he has given to his
Son Jesus for us, which gifts he, dwelling in us, has enclosed in him
until the time that we are fully grown our soul together with our body
and our body together with our soul (14:55.287).

All the gifts that God gives us, God gives through Christ. Christ *ones* us
into himself, encloses us in himself, and draws us into the *perichoresis* of
divine loving until we are fully *grown*, fully Christ-like.

Although every dimension of Christ's work increases us, the Passion is the greatest work that brings about increasing: "But to die for
my love so often that the number exceeds human reckoning, that is the
greatest offer that our Lord God could make to man's soul, as I see it"
(9:22.217). The finest gift to humanity is Christ's suffering for love that
draws all creation into the meaning of the cross. On the cross Christ
meets us in suffering, *ones* us to himself, and continues this dynamic
oneing by drawing us into the mystery of divine love and joy. Through
the cross *increasing* occurs at a moment in time for all time. Let us
examine how we experience Christ's "great offer" made through his
Passion, death, and resurrection.

II. A Theology of the Cross

In Christ crucified Julian sees the most powerful expression of the
sharing of divine love that facilitates salvation or increasing. Her interpretation of the Passion, death, and resurrection begins in vivid visual
experience that is confrontingly graphic. What emerges as the revelation unfolds, however, is an intense theology of the cross. Julian interprets how the crucified Christ reveals the meaning of who God is for us
and how God saves through the cross.[3]

Human Need

We have observed that central to Julian's soteriology is the idea of
being saved for relationship with God, saved for fulfillment in God. Related to this movement from God to God, however, is the question of
what we are being saved from. In the previous chapter we saw how
Julian comes to the conclusion in the short text that "sin is nothing."
Years of reflection lead her to move beyond trying to define the being
of sin to concentrate on the consequence of sin: "What is sin? . . . for he
[God] is at the center of everything, and he does everything. And I was
certain that he does no sin; and here I was certain that sin is no deed,

---

[3] See Moltmann, *The Crucified God* 65–75 for an overview of a theology of the
cross.

for in all this sin was not shown to me" (3:11.197-198). Echoing the idea of not seeing presented in the short text, Julian does not see sin. In common speech a deed is an action, performance, or actual fact.[4] Julian uses "deeds" in a similar sense to describe the behavior of humankind:

> For a man regards some deeds as well done and some as evil, and our Lord does not regard them so, for everything which exists in nature is of God's creation, so that everything which is done has the property of being of God's doing. For it is easy to understand that the best of deeds is well done; and the smallest of deeds which is done is as well done as the best and the greatest, and they all have the property and the order ordained for them as our Lord had ordained, without beginning, for no one does but he (3:11.198).

From a human perspective some deeds seem well done and some deeds seem evil. This is not so, however. All things are done by God. Therefore if God does all things, sin is the opposite of God who does all; sin is *no deed*. Sin is the direct opposite to all that God does.

In keeping with this idea of sin as the negation of being and doing, Julian also describes sin as *unkind:* ". . . sin is incomparably worse, more vile and painful than hell. For it is in opposition to our fair nature; for as truly as sin is unclean, so truly is sin unnatural *[unkind]*" (14:63.304). God is *kind unmade,* whereas human beings are *kind made.* The opposite to *kind unmade* and *kind made,* sin is *unkind,* unnatural, in opposition to our fair nature. Sin is inhuman. Sin is so against our humanity that it is "more vile and painful than hell." Sin destroys our humanity by enabling us to deny and reject meaning, truth, goodness, beauty, and love. Sin creates a blindness that makes us unable to recognize the unnaturalness of our ways. Ultimately, sin distorts our nature and we become *unkind* or unnatural.

The First Sin

Consistent with her emphasis on the nonbeing of sin, Julian does not name the original sin that influences the human condition. She refers to original sin as "the first sin," and points to its consequence as *wretchedness:* "Wretchedness is everything which is not good, the spiritual blindness that we fall into by our first sin, and all that follows from that wretchedness, sufferings and pains, spiritual or physical, and everything on earth or elsewhere which is not good" (xxiii:166). Wretchedness is a kind of blindness that creates spiritual or physical pain. In

---

[4] Lesley Brown, ed. *The New Shorter Oxford English Dictionary on Historical Principles.* 2 vols. (Oxford: Clarendon Press, 1993) (= NSOED) 613.

keeping with her understanding, that sin is nothing, wretchedness is the opposite to goodness. Julian also calls the consequence of the first sin the opposition that is within us:

> . . . often we fail to perceive him, and presently we fall back upon [in to] ourselves, and then we find that we feel nothing at all but the opposition that is in ourselves, and that comes from the old root of our first sin, with all that follows from our own persistence (14:47.261).

Julian creates a subtle link between the first sin, the Fall, failure, and the fall into the self. She repeats the idea of the nothingness of sin and associates this with "opposition." Opposition is a feeling of nothingness that opposes our true human nature. The descriptor "old" suggests that the root is deeply buried in the human condition. Julian links this root to existential sin when she suggests that sin occurs when "we fall *in to* our selves." Stemming from the root of original sin, sin haunts our being, creating an absence of peace. This violates the harmonious *oneing* of our being in God, creating an impasse between ourselves and God. Turned in on ourselves, we become blind to the constant presence of divine love.

Two Sicknesses

Julian's emphasis on sin as nothing, *no deed, unkind,* and original sin as influencing all that is not good and creating opposition in ourselves is distinctive for its lack of reference to actual sins. Although Julian mentions Church teaching in regard to "sins that would lead us to endless torment, as Holy Church teaches us," usually referred to as mortal sin, and also with regard to venial sin (14:52.281), she does not develop lists of sins or pursue a distinction between mortal and venial sin. She singles out two weaknesses, impatience and despair, through which she comprehends all sin:

> One is impatience or sloth, because we bear our labor and our pain heavily. The other is despair or doubtful fear, as I shall say afterwards. He showed sin generally, in which all sin is comprehended; but he showed no sins in particular but these two, and it is these two which most belabor and assail us (16:73.322).

Julian identifies these "sicknesses" in her own life, causing "no pleasure in living" (15:64.306). Of these sins, *despair or doubtful dread* is the deadliest. Without making a distinction between the temptation to despair and actual despair, in the short text she associates a stirring to despair with an assault from the devil:

> . . . the devil returned with his heat and his stench, and kept me very
> busy. The stench was vile and painful, and the physical heat was fearful
> and oppressive; and I could also hear in my ears chattering and talking,
> as if between two speakers, and they seemed to be both chattering at
> once, as if they were conducting a confused debate, and it was all low
> muttering. And I did not understand what they said, but all this, it
> seemed, was to move me to despair (xxiii:165).

Although it is difficult to say how literally Julian understood this
devilish assault, she expresses a fear of the devil that permeated her
era. In the long text she distinguishes her depiction of the fiend from
the rest of the *showings* by situating it in her sleep. The affront seems to
be a type of nightmare that tempts her to despair. The gruesome portrayal of the fiend engages all the bodily senses. There is a fearful and
oppressive heat and smell, confused debate and soft muttering. This
links with the nothingness and meaninglessness of sin, for Julian did
not understand what was said. Reminiscent of the confusion that evil
creates in our ability to listen and to understand as illustrated in the
tower of Babel myth (Gen 11:1-9), despair creates an unsettling busy-
ness that distorts understanding and leads us to distrust the constant
presence of divine love.

The sicknesses through which Julian understands all sin, impatience, and despair are inimical to personal and communal hope. They
lead to an interpretation of suffering as evidence that nonbeing is more
powerful than being, that *no deed* is more forceful than deeds, and that
God is not involved in human suffering. These feelings feed off the
nonbeing of sin and overshadow the reality of human *oneing* with the
divine.

For Julian, then, there is something indefinable about sin. It is an
absurdity that seductively creates a distortion in our true humanity in
God. While the exact nature of sin remains elusive, we can see its
effects as it causes destructive existential pain: "I did not see sin, for I
believe that it has no kind of substance, no share in being, nor can it be
recognized except by the pain caused by it" (13:27.225). Because sin has
"no manner of substance" it is not grounded in God, nor does it share
in the life of God. The nonbeing of sin has a devastating existential consequence. It impacts on our lives, inflicting pain: "sin is so vile and so
much to be hated that it can be compared with no pain which is not
itself sin" (13:40.247). Sin creates existential agony.

We may criticize Julian for her lack of concern about violent sins,
such as the violence associated with war and larceny or the inhumanity
that poverty brings. Indirectly we see her concern for violence, however, in her sorrow over the brutality experienced by Christ in the Pas-

sion. She connects sin to this violence by describing the scourges on Christ's body: "I saw the body bleeding copiously in representation of the scourging" (4:12.199). The image of scourging then becomes the descriptor of sin. Sin is the "sharpest scourge" that inflicts pain, so persistently and intrusively that it "belabors man or woman, and breaks a man" (13:39.244). Sin beats and breaks human nature.

Remarkably, as Julian confronts the nonbeing of sin she comes to understand that sin is *necessary [behouelye]*. In the short text (xiii:244) she makes this statement without any qualifications. In the long text she adds a significant qualifier: "Sin is necessary, but all will *[shall]* be well, and all will *[shall]* be well, and every kind of thing will *[shall]* be well" (13:27.225). A closer look at the etymology of the word *behouely* reveals Julian's meaning. *Behouely* evolves from the root word *bihoveth*.[5] It signifies that something is necessary or inescapable with respect to circumstances and destiny. This is not an ontological necessity, however.[6] Rather it suggests that, though the origin of sin is unknown, sin is an inescapable part of human destiny. Paradoxically, however, just as sin is a fact of life, God's eternal plan for salvation is also a fact of life. Despite sin, God will continue to bring this salvific plan to completion. *Behouely* also has roots in *bihoveable*,[7] meaning helpful, useful, and beneficial. The long text makes this apparent. "Sin is *behouely*, (beneficial), but all shall be well. Thus sin is a *felix culpa*.[8] We benefit from the effects of sin through experiencing the presence of divine love forgiving and healing in the midst of sin.

Essentially, in Julian's soteriology, humanity is saved from the meaningless despair and life-denying pain that the nonbeing and nondoing of sin inflict on the human condition. She emphasizes suffering that exists because of sin rather than identifying sins or attributing blame for sin. In light of this approach to sin as the negation of all that is natural and loving, her version of redemption through the cross concentrates on a theology of the presence of divine love revealed through the cross.

[5] *MED* 844. Cf. Denise Nowakowski Baker, *Julian of Norwich's Showings: From Vision to Book* (Princeton, N.J.: Princeton University Press, 1994) 70.

[6] Joan Nuth, *Wisdom's Daughter: The Theology of Julian of Norwich* (New York: Crossroad, 1991) 121.

[7] *MED* 842.

[8] *Felix culpa*, "O happy fault," occurs in the *Exultet*, sung at the Easter vigil celebration in Julian's day. Julian is not presenting a position that suggests that the torment and despair we feel because of sin are necessary for salvation. Rather sin is a *felix culpa*, a happy fault, because it cannot keep Love from continuing to love. This occurs singularly through the cross. Sin is a *felix culpa* because in it we come to understand more fully the all-encompassing love of God.

The cross makes sin nothing by continuing the work of *oneing* humanity to the divine. The cross reveals that in spite of sin *all shall be well:*

> Sin is the cause of all this pain, but all will [*shall*] be well, and every kind of thing will [*shall*] be well. These words were revealed most tenderly, showing no kind of blame to me or to anyone who will be saved. So it would be most unkind of me to blame God or marvel at him on account of my sins, since he does not blame me for sin (13:27.225-226).

In contrast to the pain felt because of sin, Julian feels that "all shall be well," and this is revealed "most tenderly." Although the nonbeing of sin is the cause of the life-denying pain in the universe, the presence of divine love is more powerful than sin. Therefore *all shall be well.* The solution to the problem of sin is not to be found in imputing blame. Salvation is not about attributing blame to human beings or to God for the incomplete nature of the universe and the suffering within the human condition. The love expressed through Christ's redemptive death and resurrection reveals that in spite of sin "all shall be well, and all manner of things shall be well."

III. *Oneing* Through the Cross

Julian *beholds* the full expression of the words "all manner of things shall be well" in the crucified Christ, who meets humanity in suffering and *ones* humanity to himself in love. It is important to note at this stage, however, that while the suffering of Christ reveals how "all shall be well" because it has an effect on the incompleteness of human nature, the ultimate motive for Christ's suffering is love, not sin. Julian sees this *oneing* take place in three manners of *beholding* the cross that arise in her understanding: *beholding* suffering, *beholding* love, and *beholding* joy.

We recall that *beholding* enables Julian to participate in what Christ's Passion signifies, to become one with it, to be transformed by it, and to understand its meaning. She gives this *beholding* authority by associating the insights that emerge with the will of God:

> It is God's will, as I understand it, that we contemplate [*behold*] his blessed Passion in three ways. Firstly, that we contemplate [*behold*] the hard pain he suffered with contrition and compassion[9] [or: behold with

[9] There is some discrepancy in the reference to contrition and compassion that makes a difference to Christ's response in suffering. Even though Sloane 1 has a similar statement to the Paris text (see xxi:753-754.65), Edmund Colledge and James Walsh shift the position of contrition and compassion in their translation so that

contrition and compassion the cruel pain he suffered]; and our Lord revealed that at this time, and gave me strength and grace to see it (8:20.214).

Later Julian continues:

And this I saw as the second way of contemplating [beholding] his blessed Passion. The love which made him suffer it surpasses all his sufferings, as much as heaven is above earth; for the suffering was a noble, precious and honorable deed, performed once in time by the operation of love. And love was without beginning, it is and shall be without end (9:22.217).

Subsequently she adds: "And here I saw the third way of contemplating [beholding] his blessed Passion, that is to say the joy and the bliss which make him take delight in it" (9:23.218). Essentially there are three interrelated experiences of *beholding*. The first *beholding* reveals "the hard pain he suffered." This shows how human beings are one with Christ in suffering. The second *beholding*, of "the love which made him suffer," discloses *oneing* in love. The third *beholding*, of "the joy and the bliss which make him take delight in it," imparts *oneing* in joy.

In one sense there is a continuum in suffering, love, and joy. In another sense, however, one experience of *beholding* cannot be isolated from the others. *Oneing* in suffering is never an end in itself; it always includes *oneing* in love and joy. Therefore, although there is the movement of the paschal mystery in the cross, as suffering transfigured through love becomes joy, Julian's theology of the cross is exceptional in its ability to express paradox. In *beholding* Christ suffering Julian does not simply attach the resurrection to the Passion and view it as another event in addition to the death of Christ. For her the death of Christ begins in the Incarnation. ". . . he died in our humanity, beginning at the sweet Incarnation and lasting until his blessed Resurrection on Easter morning" (9:23.219). Without collapsing the resurrection into the death of Jesus, or passing over the death in favor of the resurrection, Julian shows that Incarnation and suffering for love form a single

---

contrition and compassion describe how human beings should behold the Passion. The confusion seems to have arisen because it is not usual in our contemporary use of the word to associate contrition with Christ. The Middle English text is clear, however. It is Christ's contrition and compassion, his sorrow for the incompleteness of humanity that Julian observes in her experience of beholding. *MED* 578 gives an example from *The Book of Margery Kempe*, where Margery associates contrition with a quality of Christ.

context for the breakthrough of the joy of the resurrection. Love and joy are always manifest in suffering, and suffering for love is the underlying dynamic of joy. Though we may criticize Julian for giving no sense of the life and ministry of the Jesus of the gospels, what she does present in these *beholdings* of suffering, love, and joy is a theology of the paschal mystery. She excels at interpreting the meaning of Christ's Passion, death, and resurrection. We will now examine each *beholding* in turn.

Oneing *Through Suffering*

The first *beholding* is "the hard pain he suffered with contrition and compassion." Julian presents a description of Christ's contrition and compassion and shows how these emotions echo throughout the entire cosmos:

> Here I saw a great unity [*oneing*] between Christ and us, as I understand it; for when he was in pain we were in pain, and all creatures able to suffer pain suffered with him. That is to say, all creatures which God has created for our service, the firmament and the earth, failed in their natural functions because of sorrow at the time of Christ's death, for it is their natural characteristic to recognize him as their Lord, in whom all their powers exist. And when he failed, their nature constrained them to fail with him, insofar as they could, because of the sorrow of his sufferings. And so those who were his friends suffered pain because of love, and all creation suffered in general; that is to say, those who did not recognize him suffered because the comfort of all creation failed them, except for God's powerful, secret preservation of them (8:18.210-211).

Consistent with the image of the hazelnut, the cross not only unites Christ with the pain of the human condition, but this *oneing* extends to all creatures, the earth, and the cosmos. Julian sees that human beings are created in Christ. Bound to Christ by nature, we recognize him as Lord. Furthermore, creation in Christ unites humanity to all creation. This bond is such a *great oneing* that as Christ experiences the pain of the Passion it reverberates over the entire cosmos.

In the short text Julian draws out the link between the cross and creation by identifying the suffering of the sun and the moon: ". . . the sun and moon ceased to serve men, and so they were all abandoned in sorrow at that time" (x:143).[10] Possibly echoing apocalyptic imagery

---

[10] It is noteworthy that many illuminations of the Passion have a sun and moon: for example, the "Crucifixion" in the Lapworth Missal (1398), where a distressed

(Matt 27:51b or Mark 13:24), Julian emphasizes the relationship between Christ and all creation by highlighting the withdrawal of light. Her accent is on the profound interrelationship between Christ and creation. Whatever affects the body of Christ affects God. Conversely, whatever affects God affects the body of creation. In the long text Julian extends her reference to this *great oneing*, making the connection with the Passion even more distinctive. She drops her reference to the sun and the moon and speaks of God as the maker of *planets* and *elements.* She presents Pilate, the traditional judge of Christ, and "St. Denis of France, who at that time was a pagan" (8:18.211),[11] as examples revealing that Christ's death influences all people, even nonbelievers:

> Either the world is coming to an end, or else he who is the creator of nature is suffering. Therefore he caused to be written on an altar: This is an altar of the unknown God. God in his goodness, who makes the planets and the elements to function according to their natures *[kind]* for the man who is blessed and the man who is accursed, in that time withdrew this from both. So it was that they who did not recognize him were in sorrow at that time. So was our Lord Jesus afflicted for us; and we all stand in this way of suffering with him, and shall till we come to his bliss, as I shall afterwards say (8:18.211).

Following tradition by interlacing her ideas with passages from Scripture, Julian links together a number of images from Acts 17, where Paul has a discussion with Epicurean and Stoic philosophers about Christ's suffering, death, and resurrection and the presence of God in creation. She makes direct reference to Acts 17:23-24. Through these comments placed in the mouths of nonbelievers Julian makes some significant theological points about the meaning of Christ's death. It is not

---

sun and moon are sketched into the gold background of the painting. The whole miniature is a merging of observed reality with decorative forms to convey the suffering of Christ and the consequent suffering of all creation. Kathleen L. Scott, *A Survey of Manuscripts Illuminated in the British Isles,* edited by J.J.G. Alexander (London: Harvey Miller Publishers, 1996) Plate 4.

[11] Known today as Pseudo-Dionysius, St. Denis was originally thought to be Paul's convert Dionysius the Areopagite, mentioned in Acts 17:34. Edmund Colledge and James Walsh, eds., *A Book of Showings to the Anchoress Julian of Norwich.* 2 vols. (Toronto: Pontifical Institute of Mediaeval Studies, 1978) (= *BSAJN*) 368 n. 27. This theology was popular in England in her day and is the major source of the *Cloud of Unknowing.* Central to Pseudo-Dionysian theology is the transcendent unknowability of God. For this reason he is the perfect person to connect the unknown God to the suffering Christ. I am grateful to Andrew Louth for pointing out to me that in Letter 7 Dionysius records an experience in Egypt of the eclipse that Julian could be referring to.

simply the humanity of Christ that suffers, but the second person of the Trinity, the *maker of kinds,* is the one who suffers. This union between the suffering of the Creator and the suffering of creation confirms both ontological and existential *oneing* between God and creation. The relationship between Christ's Passion and "an altar to the unknown god" (Acts 17:23) suggests that in Christ we see the suffering of God. At another time, however, Julian points out that it is only Christ the second person of the Trinity who suffers, not the whole Trinity: "All the Trinity worked in Christ's Passion, administering abundant virtues and plentiful grace to us by him; but only the virgin's Son suffered" (9:23.219). Thus the imagery maintains paradox. From the point of view of God's transcendence, suffering cannot touch the being of God. From the point of view of God's immanence, God through Christ is present in suffering, feels what the cosmos suffers and suffers with the cosmos. In preserving both these perspectives Julian can retain the Trinity's personal relationship with creation in suffering without the Trinity being limited to this relationship. As an altar to "the unknown god," Christ's suffering makes the transcendent God immanent in the suffering of the cross. Moreover, the suffering of Christ is oriented to the future. It continues in time in human experience as Christ was afflicted for us, and we all stand in this suffering with him. Human beings and creation remain in relationship with the suffering of the cross until all is transfigured, transformed, and *increased* in the relationship of *oneing* and shall "come to his bliss." The cross of Christ stands out as the *great oneing* that embraces the suffering of creation.

Oneing *Through Love*

Within the context of Christ's being one with all creation in suffering, Julian concentrates on humanity. The second *beholding* reveals ". . . the love that made him suffer." Although this love permeates each scene of the crucifixion, the most significant vision Julian describes is Christ's wounded body and broken heart. Though Julian does not name it as such, this is a spirtual insight. She uses concrete imagery, but there is something ethereal and intangible about the vision. In the short text Julian places this icon of love in the center, in the thirteenth of twenty-five chapters, so that it is the heart of the *Showings*. In the long text, although she continues to give the vision prominence, she draws our attention more to a theology of joy.

The vision leads Julian's understanding into the body of Christ:

> . . . our good Lord looked into his side, and he gazed with joy, and with his sweet regard he drew his creature's understanding into his

side by the same wound; and there he revealed a fair and delectable place, large enough for all mankind that will be saved and will rest in peace and in love (10:24.220).

At first this vision seems like a "bodily sight" of a painting of Christ's dying body hanging on a "tree" with a wound in his side.[12] Though graphic, the imagery is not at all realistic. It reflects the contemplative imagination. In the vision Christ looks into his side and leads Julian's understanding into his side "by the same wound." Julian's understanding enters the body of Christ. In this moment of insight she becomes one with Christ in suffering, and gains deeper understanding. She explains what comes to her mind in this *beholding* that she identifies as "sweet":

> . . . he brought to mind the dear and precious blood and water which he suffered to be shed for love. And in this sweet sight he showed his blessed heart split in two, and as he rejoiced he showed to my understanding a part of his blessed divinity, as much as was his will at that time, strengthening my poor soul to understand what can be said, that is the endless love which was without beginning and is and always shall be (10:24.220-221).

First she thinks of Christ's blood and water poured out for love. Then she sees his "blessed heart split in two." The concrete images of blood, water, and a broken heart become catalysts for deeper understanding. The cross reveals the endless love that was without beginning, is, and always shall be. In this contemplative moment when Christ led Julian's understanding through his open wound Julian understands that the cross reveals eternal love. The scene continues in a dreamlike manner. The body of the wounded Christ is a "fair and delectable place," a home for humankind. Significantly this is not a home for a select few. It is large enough for all. Love draws all humanity into the body of God through the wound of Christ and makes the heart of Christ the home for all to rest in, in peace and love.

---

[12] In the Lapworth Missal "Crucifixion" there is a wound in Christ's ribs near his heart. The wound in Christ's side that leads to his heart illustrates the Johannine Passion scene (John 19:34) and the Last Supper discourse, especially John 14:2 and John 15:4. It also reflects Bernard of Clairvaux's (1090–1153) allegorical exposition on the Song of Songs that connected the wounds of Christ to the clefts in the rock that become the home of the dove (Song 2:14), and the clefts or wounds that proved to Thomas that Christ was risen (John 20:27). See Bernard of Clairvaux, *St. Bernard on the Song of Songs: Sermones in Cantica Canticorum,* translated and edited by A Religious of C.S.M.V. (London: A. R. Mowbray & Co. Limited, 1952) 194.

The outpouring of blood and the broken heart reveal that the body of Christ is the home of all peoples. The images impart something of the mystery of eternity. Karl Rahner's explanation of the word "heart" helps illuminate how the image extends Julian's understanding of divine love:

> But there are human words which, because they mean human things, can properly be said only in a human way. And if they mean something human which belongs eternally to God himself, then such human words are words of eternity which men can never cease to utter, either here or in eternity. And to these words of earthly beginning and eternal ending belongs the word which God will still say to us men in all eternity: 'Behold this heart, which has so loved men.'[13]

The images unambiguously reveal that divine love is present to humanity in Christ, yet paradoxically these earthly images not only reveal the present reality of divine love active in human lives: they are words of eternity. They reveal eternal love. The images hold within them an eternity of divine loving and show how those who love as Julian loves Christ know something of eternity. The imagery reveals how suffering human beings are made one with Christ in woundedness, and consequently are drawn beyond suffering into the eternity of God. Christ's flowing blood and broken heart express the dynamic unity of "charity unmade, charity made, and charity given." They embody the fact that love is our beginning, love is our present, and love is our end.

When Julian articulates her theology of the cross from the perspective of love she expands her understanding of the salvific task of *oneing* humanity to the divine. Although we may criticize Julian's romantic description of the imagery, she makes some significant points that add to her interpretation of salvation through the cross. First, the portrait of Christ's open side and broken heart gives an excellent example of the sharing of uncreated charity, created charity, and given charity. The scene is an archetype of given charity through the cross. The imagery reveals the extremes to which divine love will go to in order to share love. Second, the image of Christ's body wounded and yet a place of comfort for all humankind reflects the totality of meaning found only in divine love. The imagery embraces the paradox expressed in the cross: that through being wounded Christ draws us beyond woundedness into the heart of God. Third, the imagery draws emphasis away from the suffering of the Passion as merely a response to human sin.

---

[13] Karl Rahner, "'Behold This Heart'! Preliminaries to a Theology of Devotion to the Sacred Heart," *Theological Investigations* 3, translated by Karl-Heinz and Boniface Kruger (London: Darton Longman and Todd, 1967) 330.

The imagery presents the cross unequivocally as being about *oneing* in love.

Oneing *in Joy*

The love revealed in Christ's broken heart interrelates with the third *beholding:* "the joy and bliss which makes him like it" (9:23.218). Christ's death, as the dramatic pictures of Christ dying lead us to expect, is a scene of joy:

> . . . suddenly, as I looked at the same cross, he changed to an appearance of joy [*blessedful cheer*]. The change in his blessed appearance changed mine, and I was as glad and joyful as I could possibly be. And then cheerfully our Lord suggested to my mind: Where is there now any instant of your pain or of your grief? And I was very joyful (9:21.214-215).

Beholding reveals that it is the resurrected Christ still on "the same cross." This suggests that the cross is intrinsically part of the resurrection. Christ is not dead but joyously alive with a countenance of *blessedful cheer*. The variety of spellings, *blisful cheer* and *blessefull chere*, *blessydfulle cheer* or *glad cheer*, in both the Paris and Sloane 1 manuscripts, gives a sense of the meaning of this expression for Julian. Her use of the adjective *blessydfulle* describes the supreme enjoyment of Christ. *Cheer* points to the demeanor of Christ's face, the attitude expressed, which communicates his intention for humanity. Thus *beholding blessydfulle cheer* discloses the joyfulness of Christ who suffered for love. This face-to-face recognition makes Julian "very joyful."

Continued contemplation of this cheer informs Julian's understanding:

> . . . we are now on his cross with him in our pains, and in our sufferings we are dying, and with his help and his grace we willingly endure on that same cross until the last moment of life. Suddenly he will change his appearance for us, and we shall be with him in heaven. Between the one and the other all will be a single era; and then all will be brought into joy (9:21.215).

With startling clarity Julian expresses her understanding of why Christ radiates joy: "we are now on his cross with him." Completely drawn into Christ's *meaning*, we not only share in Christ's suffering "in our pains and in our suffering"; we also share in his joy. Julian points to the timeless nature of this sharing in joy describing this as a single era. The cross places the eternal nature of God in time and draws time and eternity together in a single moment. This encounter with Christ's joy informs Julian that we already participate in Christ's joy and yet, as Nietzsche suggests, "every enjoyment seeks to be eternal."[14]

There is no doubt that Julian's theology of the cross is Christocentric. *Beholding* joy reveals conclusively, however, that the cross is "our salvation which is in the blessed Trinity" (9:23.219). The self-giving of Christ in suffering, love, and joy is the self-giving of the Trinity. As Julian continues to describe the joy revealed in the Trinity her language becomes more mystical:

> . . . my understanding was lifted up into heaven, and there I saw three heavens; and at this sight I was greatly astonished, and I thought: I see three heavens, and all are of the blessed humanity of Christ. And none is greater, none is less, none is higher, none is lower, but all are equal in their joy (9:22.216).

Julian characterizes the revelation of the Trinity in the humanity of Christ as three heavens,"[15] which directly identifies Christ's humanity with the three divine persons. The word "heavens" emphasizes the divine nature of the Trinity. It points to the absolute unity of the Trinity, as "none is greater, none is less. . . ." The imagery also identifies Christ's humanity with the joy of heaven, for Julian describes heaven as the joy that is to come.

Subsequently Julian shows how the three heavens relate to each person of the Trinity:

> And in these three sayings: It is a joy, a bliss and an endless delight to me, there were shown to me three heavens, and in this way. By "joy" I understood that the Father was pleased, and by "bliss" that the Son was honored, and by "endless delight" the Holy Spirit. The Father is pleased, the Son is honored, the Holy Spirit takes delight. And here I saw the third way of contemplating his blessed Passion, that is to say the joy and the bliss which make him take delight in it (9:23.218).

The *oneing* of the cross gives "joy, bliss, and endless delight" to the Trinity. The scene reveals that there is in reality no gulf between humanity and God, suffering and joy, earth and heaven. The joy ex-

---

[14] Dermot A. Lane, *Keeping Hope Alive: Stirrings in Christian Theology* (Dublin: Gill and Macmillan, 1996) 16.

[15] Traditionally "heavens" describes the abode of God, regarded as beyond the sky. It identifies the state or condition of living with God after death. Medieval astronomers divided the celestial spheres into regions of space ranging from seven to eleven (*NSOED* 1208). Three seems to be a deliberate association with the Trinity.

pressed by the Trinity of three heavens reinforces the eternal nature of joy. Joy is not limited by the constraints of temporal existence. Joy embraces the present and the future, this world and the transformation of creation in eternity.

Julian reaches a climax in *beholding* joy when she presents an imageless vision of the glorified Christ:

> . . . he appeared to me more glorified than I had seen him before, in which I was taught that our soul will never have rest till it comes into him, acknowledging that he is full of joy, familiar and courteous and blissful and true life. Again and again our Lord said: I am he, I am he, I am he who is highest. I am he whom you love. I am he in whom you delight. I am he whom you serve. I am he for whom you long. I am he whom you desire. I am he whom you intend. I am he who is all. I am he whom Holy Church preaches and teaches to you (12:26.223).

In this mystical description of Christ in his glory Julian reveals conclusively that the theology of the cross is in essence not a theology of suffering but a theology of joy, trinitarian joy. We can see the significance she gives to joy when we compare this ineffable vision with the painting of the resurrected Christ, created around 1381, which was a panel in the retable at St. Luke's altar at Norwich Cathedral in Julian's day.[16] In this painting a solemn, triumphant Christ arises from his tomb, clad in a regal red cloak. He clasps a flag in his left hand while making a sign of victory with his right. There is an aura of fear in the picture: two soldiers tumble to the ground in terror. A third soldier peers in amazement. The victorious Christ, oblivious to the suffering of the soldiers, places his foot on the neck of the soldier on the right. Though Christ has a crown of thorns on his head and the marks of the Passion on his feet and hands he dispassionately gives no sign that he has suffered for love. Rather there is an air of violent triumphalism and callous indifference. This is not Julian's understanding of love or joy; in fact it is quite the opposite. In absolute contrast to this portrait of the resurrection, Julian's mystical vision of the glorified Christ gives no hint of triump or indifference. For Julian the resurrected Christ who imparts joy is the transcendent and immanent: "I am he who is all."

When Julian describes the resurrection she attempts to portray its meaning beyond the partiality of visual imagery. Christ proclaims: "I am he." He then repeats "I am he" twelve times in the locution.[17] "I am he" is an obvious allusion to the words of God to Moses in the story of

---

[16] See Monica Furlong, *The Wisdom of Julian of Norwich* (Oxford: Lion Publishing, 1996) 27.

[17] *BSAJN* 402 n. 7.

the burning bush (Exod 3:14) and to the "I am" passages from John's gospel. This identifies Christ with the great ineffable name of God and designates Christ as the subject of all that is. Christ is the only true reality for human beings. The litany of attributes that describes Christ echoes the unity of the Trinity described in the three heavens, placing the reality of Christ not only in the present but in eternity. This reveals that Christ is the complete revelation of God. Christ is our true reality, all that we desire and long for, and all that will give meaning to our existence. Ultimately Christ is *all*.

All echoes Julian's earlier images of God in "all things" and her refrain, "all shall be well." It contains an allusion to Eph 4:6, where the author identifies the divine as "one God and Father of all, who is above all and through all and in all." For Julian the resurrected Christ communicates how trinitarian love permeates all reality. Through the cross Christ is simultaneously above all, through all, and in all. "I am he who is highest" reminds us that in one sense Christ is more than *all*, transcends *all*. At the same time Christ is *through all* in the teaching and preaching of Holy Church. He is in *all* as he compassionately shares in human suffering and draws us into the meaning of the cross. In the resurrection Julian sees *all* in relation to Christ. Because Christ is *all*, the *alpha* and *omega* of all reality, the fullness of reality is directed to Christ. Awareness of this *allness* imparts joy.

Therefore for Julian the joy of the Trinity, which the crucified and risen Christ imparts, is not a momentary facile pleasure or happiness, or an optimism that is a kind of presumption that ignores the realities of pain, suffering, and evil. Joy manifests a harmony that comes through struggling with the ambiguity of existence so powerfully reflected in the cross and knowing that the presence of divine love through Christ transcends all reality. Through this joy darkness and light, tragedy and transformation, death and glory unite in a single moment in Christ. Joy, then, is not the opposite of suffering. Joy encompasses the deep darkness of the cross. Julian's understanding of joy resonates with what Paul Tillich described centuries later: "joy is the expression of our essential and central fulfillment."[18] In Julian's understanding we experience this essential and central fulfillment in Christ through his Passion, death, and resurrection. Joy is a sense of deep well-being that human beings attain to when they know the love of Christ. Joy results when we see that all things come together in Christ, when, through Christ, we are united to all that is. Joy proliferates in the awareness that all creation exists in relation to the divine through Christ, who is *all*. Christ draws us into the eternity of trinitarian joy.

[18] Paul Tillich, *The New Being* (London: SCM, 1963) 149.

When Julian articulates her theology of the cross from the perspective of *beholding joy* the salvific task that increases human *oneing* to the divine becomes complete in joy. It reveals that salvation embraces the joy of Christ, the joy of the Trinity, and the joy of humanity. The notion of joy completes Julian's theology of the cross and adds important aspects to her soteriology. First, *beholding joy* heals the insurmountable division between the suffering of the Passion on one hand and the resurrection on the other. It balances Julian's preoccupation with suffering and shows how joy reveals that suffering is not more powerful than the presence of divine love. Second, the language Julian uses in her description of the resurrection indicates that she does not speculate about the reality of the resurrection event or the nature of the empty tomb or resurrected body. Her only interest is in the salvific power and presence of the risen Christ. Third, Julian's consistent emphasis on the joy of Christ and the joy and bliss of the Trinity suggests that the work for human salvation is not a joyless task that an obedient Christ must endure. It presents human salvation as a joyous event that fulfills trinitarian desire and ultimately gives glory to the Trinity. Fourth, joy extends our understanding of resurrection beyond an experience that happened to Christ and defines it in terms of an ongoing process that draws human beings into the life of trinitarian joy. Finally, we see that Julian's reflection on the Passion, death, and resurrection is not a strange preoccupation with suffering. *Beholding* Christ's suffering, love, and joy creates the ground for hope in eschatological fulfillment for individuals and the world. The joy of Christ at the heart of all reality inspires hope.

IV. A GLORIOUS ASSETH

Thus Julian's theology of the cross is a theology of glory, a *glorious asseth*, literally translated "glorious satisfaction." *Glorious asseth* summarizes all the aspects of *oneing* that are the glory of the cross.[19] Julian invites her readers to

---

[19] Although the translation of glorious *asseth* (satisfaction) resonates with the satisfaction theology made famous by Anselm of Canterbury, Julian differs from Anselm in her understanding of *asseth* making. Anselm argues that in the Fall sin disturbed the order of the universe and offended God's honor. Because God is merciful and just, God must take into account the divine reality, the nature of creation, and the essence of sin, and do justice to all three. He argues: "Human nature alone could not do this, nor could it be reconciled without the satisfaction of a debt, nor could the justice of God pass over the disorder of sin in his kingdom. The goodness of God came to help, and the Son of God assumed manhood in his own person, so that God and man should be one and the same person. He had what is above all

> . . . contemplate *[behold]* the glorious atonement *[asseth]*, for this aton-
> ing is more pleasing to the blessed divinity and more honorable for
> man's salvation, without comparison, than ever Adam's sin was harm-
> ful. So then this is our blessed Lord's intention, and in this teaching we
> should pay heed to this: For since I have set right the greatest of harms,
> then it is my will that you should know through this that I shall set
> right everything which is less (13:29.228).

We must engage the hermenuetic of *beholding* to understand the
meaning of the *glorious asseth*. Julian states her teaching firmly: *asseth
making* is more glorious than ever sin was harmful, and is honorable for
humanity's salvation. Although Julian never specifically defines *asseth*,
her reference to the term gives it a dense theological meaning. It summarizes her interpretation of salvation through the cross. Her use of the
qualifying term *glorious* suggests that *asseth making* includes her whole
theology of the cross: suffering, love, and joy. Because it is *glorious*,
asseth is eschatological. *Glorious asseth* sums up the whole of Christ's experience of incarnation, death, and resurrection. It reveals that Christ is
present now in a new way, increasing and fulfilling. *Asseth making* embraces transfiguration, exaltation, glorification, eschatological fullness
and completion through the one who said: "I am he who is all."
In the *glorious asseth* Christ draws us into this meaning with him into
the fullness of glory. The *glorious asseth* makes well all that is less. The
glorious asseth makes hope for salvation real.

Scholars disagree about the interpretation of *asseth*. Edmund Colledge and James Walsh translate *asseth* as *atonement* (as above), but this
translation causes problems in interpretation. We recall Brant Pelphry's

---

beings that are other than God, and he took on himself all the debt that sinners
ought to pay, and this when he himself owed nothing, so that he could pay the debt
for the others who owed it and could not pay." Anselm of Canterbury, "Meditation
on Human Redemption" in Benedicta Ward, editor and translator, *The Prayers and
Meditations of St. Anselm* (Harmondsworth: Penguin, 1973) 103–11, 233. It is impossible to determine whether Julian was directly familiar with the source of Anselm of
Canterbury's theory of satisfaction. Scholars generally agree, however, that the terminology was so embedded in the religious vocabulary of fourteenth-century England that Julian would be familiar with the theology expressed by the specific
words. Cf. *BSAJN* 412 n. 1; Ritamary Bradley, "Julian of Norwich: Everyone's Mystic," in William Pollard and Robert Boenig, eds., *Mysticism and Spirituality in Medieval England* (Cambridge: D. S. Brewer, 1997) 139–58, at 149; *LWHM* 142; Lillian
Bozak-DeLeo, "The Soteriology of Julian of Norwich," in John Apczynski, ed., *Theology and the University*. The Annual Publication of the College Theology Society
1987. Vol. 33 (Maryland: University Press of America, Inc. 1990) 37–46, and Joan
Nuth, "Two Medieval Soteriologies: Anselm of Canterbury and Julian of Norwich,"
Theological Studies 53 (1992) 611–45.

reservations. Atonement includes too many connotations of humanity separated from Christ. Furthermore, "the various 'theories' of atonement . . . are as different from one another as they are exclusive in their claims to be correct."[20] Mona Logarbo translates *asseth* literally as "that which makes sufficient" in the sense of making up for something that is lacking.[21] This concurs with Ronan Crampton's translation of *asseth* as reparation.[22] Ritamary Bradley in contrast refers to *asseth* as satisfaction.[23] This aligns with the scribbling of the word "satisfaction" in the margin of the Sloane 1 and Cressy editions of the *Showings*,[24] but because Julian's emphasis on *asseth making* has its own theological consequences and the translation "satisfaction" indirectly places Julian's soteriology within Anselm's framework of vicarious satisfaction, I will maintain the term *asseth*.[25] Julian's interpretation of *asseth making* emphasizes the work of *oneing* humanity to the Trinity in suffering, love, and joy. *Asseth making* increases humanity. It encompasses all the aspects of *oneing* that are the glory of the cross.

Julian gives a clear indication of the purpose of *asseth making* in a dialogue she has with the resurrected Christ still on the cross:

> . . . our good Lord put a question to me: Are you well satisfied that I suffered for you? I said: Yes, good Lord, all my thanks to you; yes, good Lord, blessed may you be. Then Jesus our good Lord said: If you are satisfied [*apayde*], I am satisfied [*apayde*]. It is a joy, a bliss, an endless delight to me that ever I suffered my Passion for you; and if I could suffer more, I should suffer more (9:22.216).

There is no sense in which this is a corporeal sight, yet the words have clear expression. Christ, through Julian, addresses an unanticipated question to all humanity: "Are you well satisfied [*apayd*] that I suffered for you?" This is not God being *paid* or *satisfied* through the cross. The payment is directed at humanity. Salvation revealed on the cross is a mutual exchange between Christ and humanity. The *oneing* between Christ and humanity is so great that if we are satisfied Christ is *apayde*.

---

[20] Brant Pelphrey, *Love Was His Meaning: The Theology and Mysticism of Julian of Norwich* (Salzburg: Institüt für Anglistik und Amerikanistik, 1982) (= *LWHM*) 133.

[21] Mona Logarbo, "Salvation Theology in Julian of Norwich: Sin, Forgiveness, and Redemption in the Revelations," *Thought* 61 (1986) 370–80, at 374.

[22] Georgia Ronan Crampton, ed., *The Shewings of Julian of Norwich*. Teams Middle English Texts Series (Kalamazoo: Medieval Institute Publications, 1994) 74.

[23] Bradley, "Everyone's Mystic," 145.

[24] *BSAJN* 412 n. 1.

[25] The word still features in the Oxford Dictionary. See *NSOED* 134.

As far as I can ascertain, Julian's association of payment with humanity makes her soteriology unique.

If we translate *apayde* as "satisfied" we experience the same problems of interpretation described above. Although *apayde* has its roots in the Latin *pacare,* to appease, to pacify, to satisfy, to please or to gratify, and *pac, pax,* to give peace,[26] Julian gives this term a particular theological direction toward humanity. Before she asks the question "are you well *apayd*?" she explains that the reason Christ suffers is so that "we be made heirs with him of his joy" (9:21.215). She goes on to explain: "and for this little pain which we suffer here we shall have an exalted and eternal knowledge in God which we could never have without it" (9:21.215). *Apayde* incorporates bringing pleasure and peace but it also includes eschatological glory for humanity. Thus a more nuanced translation of *apayd* would integrate Julian's emphasis on the present and the eternal, the eternity of joy found in suffering. I would argue that *at peace* could capture the various nuances reasonably accurately. If human beings find peace through the *oneing* of the cross, Christ feels joy, bliss, and endless delight in what he accomplishes for humanity through the cross. In keeping with Julian's use of paradox, however, the pleasure that comes from the joy that Christ initiates through the cross is not an absence of suffering, but peace found in recognizing Christ's presence in the midst of suffering.

We gain further knowledge of how Julian uses the language of payment through the way she adopts the term "buying again":

> And despite [*not withstanding*] this rightful joining [*knitting*] and this endless uniting [*oneing*], still the redemption and the buying-back of mankind is needful and profitable in everything, as it is done with the same intention and for the same end as Holy Church teaches us in our faith (14:53.283).

The phrase *not withstanding* is convoluted. It makes interpretation difficult. In Middle English *not withstanding* suggests not standing in the way of, or not impeding.[27] Julian's meaning becomes clearer if the term is stated positively, as supporting, sustaining, or upholding. "The redemption and the buying-back" *sustain* the "rightful knitting and this endless oneing." Redemption or buying back is integral to the process of *oneing*. Redemption does not mean that Christ buys humanity or pays a price for humanity; redemption is the process of "this rightful joining [*knitting*] and this endless uniting [*oneing*]" that Christ achieves through the cross. Julian's alignment of herself with the teach-

---

[26] Ibid. 2129.
[27] Ibid. 3706.

ing of the Church on this matter gives her statement more authority. The language of buying relates directly to Christ's work of *knitting* and *oneing*.

Further reference to the *glorious asseth* affirms this interpretation:

> He gave understanding of two portions. One portion is our savior and our salvation. This blessed portion is open, clear, fair and bright and plentiful, for all men who are of good will are comprehended in this portion. We are bound to this by God, and drawn and counseled and taught, inwardly by the Holy Spirit, and outwardly through the same grace by Holy Church. Our Lord wants us to be occupied in this, rejoicing in him, for he rejoices in us. And the more plentifully we accept from this with reverence and humility, the more do we deserve thanks from him, and the more profit do we win for ourselves. And so we may see and rejoice that our portion is our Lord (13:30.228).

Although one part remains hidden, one part is open. Significantly, in the open part we are "bound by God." "Bound" interacts with the image of being *knit* to Christ, *oned* to Christ. Julian notes that it is by the will of Christ that we enjoy being bound to God and that God enjoys being bound to us. A teaching becomes clear: "our portion is our Lord." The body of Christ and the body of humanity are one and the same. Redemption is not a joyless task directed toward a remote God, or reparation for sin, or a victory over death. It is a glorious, joyous *oneing* that makes the human part Christ's part.

Towards the end of the *Showings* Julian concludes:

> We know in our faith that God alone took our nature, and no one but he, and, furthermore, that Christ alone performed all the great works which belong to our salvation, and no one but he; and just so, he alone acts now in the last end, that is to say he dwells here in us, and rules us, and cares for us in this life, and brings us to his bliss. And so he will [shall] do as long as any soul is on earth who will come to heaven; and so much so that if there were no such soul on earth except one, he would be with it, all alone, until he had brought it up into his bliss (16:80.335-336).

Christ is gloriously risen and present. He dwells in us, drawing us to bliss. He *shall* do this as long as we are on earth. The *oneing* will continue until he has brought us into his bliss and we have become one with him in glory.

We can see from all this how *in the second we have our increasing* through Christ's suffering, death, and resurrection. The three *beholdings* of the Passion that Julian distinguishes should be viewed within the context of the problem of sin and the human need for redemption. The *beholdings* reveal how Christ draws us into the dynamic "increasing" of a *perichoresis* of love, *oneing* us in suffering, love, and joy. There is no doubt that for Julian the cross marks the way of the joy that is to come. The *exitus reditus* is cruciform, yet suffering is not an end in itself. Julian's theology of the cross is a theology of the paschal mystery, a theology of glory, a *glorious asseth*. Through the cross Christ draws us into his experience of glory. We will now examine how Christ continues this dynamic *oneing* that increases us and draws us into trinitarian joy through his identity with us and his work as servant.

6

Oneing Through the Servant

Jesus is in all who will be saved, and all who will be saved are in Jesus (14:51.276).

The parable of the lord and the servant gives Julian deeper understanding of how "all shall be well." Composed as an allegory, the story illustrates significant components of God's response to suffering humanity that Julian was unable to distinguish before. A condensation of the whole story of salvation, a vignette of the *exitus reditus*, it becomes the key that unlocks her most complex understanding of the nature of salvation. We must now examine the key soteriological elements of how our *being*, our *increasing*, and our *fulfilling* occur through the servant. We see how *oneing* takes place through the servant in the experience of the Fall, the relationship of the lord to the servant during the Fall, the bestowal of grace, and the fulfillment of eternal *oneing* in the Trinity.

Julian adds the parable to the long text after twenty years' reflection on the meaning of the revelations. She identifies the parable as "a wonderful example," an exemplum that presents theological insights in the form of an allegorical narrative that unlocks the meaning of the revelations. The teaching is revealed within Julian's being, "whereby I may have some understanding of our Lord's meaning, for the mysteries of the revelation are hidden in it, even though all the showings are full of mysteries" (14:51.276). She distinguishes the parable from the bodily and ghostly sights of the rest of the *showings*, emphasizing that she sees doubly: "one part was shown spiritually in bodily likeness, the other more spiritually without bodily likeness." Although the parable is mysterious and mystical it gives Julian perception into the significant aspects of salvation in three interrelated ways: the instruction that she

understands immediately as she receives the vision, the inward learning that she gradually comes to after the event, and the condensation of
the meaning of the whole revelation in the example. Julian notes that
these are not separate levels of meaning, but interrelate and ultimately
produce one meaning. The integration of these three levels occurs as
Julian presents the example of a description in bodily likeness, recapitulates her immediate response to the images, and adds her subsequent
interpretation. She receives instruction "to take heed to all the attributes,
divine and human, which were revealed in the example" (14:51.270).
Each detail in the parable conveys insight into the meaning of salvation
expressed in the *Showings* as a whole.

I. A SUMMARY OF THE PARABLE

The narrative unfolds in phases.[1] On a literal level Julian describes
the vision as she sees it in the present tense. The parable features two
characters described in bodily likeness, a courteous and dignified lord
and a beloved servant, who dwell peacefully together in respectful intimacy. The lord sends the servant on a mission. In his eagerness to ac-
complish the lord's will the servant falls into a dell, suffers grave injury
(a metaphor for sin) and becomes powerless to fulfill the lord's wishes.
His injuries are so severe that he cannot get himself out of the dell. The
greatest pain is his inability to recognize the love of the lord. The lord
watches this event with tender regard, assigning no blame to the servant for this unfortunate situation.

Toward the middle of the parable Julian identifies the lord as God
and the servant as Adam, the representative of humankind. Consequently she turns her attention to the lord. She receives a teaching
about how God looks on humanity in sin: "I understood that the lord
who sat in state in rest and peace is God. I understood that the servant
who stood before him was shown for Adam" (14:51.270). She sees that
the consequence of sin creates pain that does its own blaming and punishing, whereas the lord is kindly and loving, longing to bring us to
bliss. The dignified lord clothed in luxurious azure blue waits patiently
with loving regard for the servant because he wants to make the servant's soul his dwelling place.

Meanwhile, toil in the dell wears the servant's clothes. Subsequently Julian observes "a treasure in the earth which the lord loved"
(14:51.273). The servant becomes a gardener who labors tirelessly to

---

[1] 14:51.2-331,513-545. The text of the parable is too long to be included here. The
summary presents significant aspects of the story that will aid comprehension of
the theology.

find the treasure that will become food for the lord. This leads Julian to understand the servant as human nature, both Adam and Christ. Adam falls into the dell and experiences sin in the Fall. Christ, because of eternal union with us, willingly falls into the womb of the maiden. The eternal union between Adam and Christ is so much one that "Jesus is in all who will be saved, and all who will be saved are in Jesus" (14:51.276).

The parable closes as the scene transposes to a beatific vision of heaven. The lord is God the Father, the servant God the Son, and the joyous delight that exudes from the relationship is the Holy Spirit. Because of this generous labor the lord does not sit alone on the ground, nor does the servant stand before the lord partially clothed. To the delight of all in heaven, the lord has a precious crown that Julian identifies as humankind: "we are his crown, which crown is the Father's joy" (14:51.278). Now the servant sits joyfully at the lord's right hand.

With an overview of the parable in mind, and an awareness of the three levels of meaning in the parable, we are now in a position to follow Julian and "to take heed to all the attributes, divine and human, which were revealed in the example" and to see how the parable unlocks the mysteries of salvation.

II. THE FALL

We saw in the previous chapter that as Julian *beholds* the suffering of the cross she confronts the problem of sin. When she tries to reduce the question of sin to the question of how sin can occur in a world governed by the saving power of God she finds no solution. She simply observes that "sin is nothing" (viii:137), "sin is no deed," (3:11.198), "sin is unnatural *[unkind]*" (14:63.304). In the parable Julian points to the nebulous yet destructive character of sin through the image of a slade, a bare open area of grassland or marsh between banks or woods that creates a valley or a dell.[2] The slade forms a dangerous chasm that the servant is unable to see. Julian does not describe the slade itself in the parable, however. She concentrates on the painful effects that the fall in the slade have on the servant. She does not ask why the slade existed, why God allowed the fall to occur, or why human suffering exists, nor does she distinguish between suffering that results from sin and other suffering. While we can only speculate about why Julian does not address these questions, the parable reveals a primary concern to ground insights about God's relationship with us in human experience.

[2] Lesley Brown, ed. *The New Shorter Oxford English Dictionary on Historical Principles.* 2 vols. (Oxford: Clarendon Press, 1993) (= *NSOED*) 2889.

In Julian's allegory of the fall of humankind the motive that leads
to the fall is significant: "Not only does the servant go, but he dashes
off and runs at great speed, loving to do his lord's will" (14:51.267). The
fall occurs in spite of the servant's loving desire to do the will of the
lord. The parable presents a poignant illustration of the pain that ensues when the fall in the slade interrupts the servant's deepest longing
to do the will of the lord:

> And soon he falls into a dell and is greatly injured; and then he groans
> and moans and tosses about and writhes, but he cannot rise or help
> himself in any way. And of all this, the greatest hurt which I saw him in
> was lack of consolation, for he could not turn his face to look on his lov-
> ing lord, who was very close to him, in whom is all consolation; but like
> a man who was for the time extremely feeble and foolish, he paid heed
> to his feelings and his continuing distress, in which distress he suffered
> seven great pains (14:51.267).

We note how an aura of great sorrow permeates life in the slade.
The servant "groans and moans and tosses about and writhes." Overcome by woe, he becomes unwise and blind to the comforting presence
of the lord. Moreover, he is powerless to change the situation by turning to the lord, the only one who could change the situation. Further *beholding* reveals seven specific ways in which the servant suffered:

> The first was the severe bruising which he took in his fall, which gave
> him great pain. The second was the clumsiness of his body. The third
> was the weakness which followed these two. The fourth was that he
> was blinded in his reason and perplexed in his mind, so much so that
> he had almost forgotten his own love. The fifth was that he could not
> rise. The sixth was the pain most astonishing to me, and that was that
> he lay alone. I looked all around and searched, and far and near, high
> and low, I saw no help for him. The seventh was that the place in which
> he lay was narrow and comfortless and distressful (14:51.267-268).

Although the seven capital vices that give rise to sin (pride, avarice,
lust, anger, envy, sloth, and gluttony) dominated medieval culture, Julian
in contrast concentrates on the seven specific dimensions of the servant's
suffering that emerge: severe bruising, clumsiness of body, weakness,
blindness in reason, an inability to rise from the slade, and an awareness that the place is narrow, comfortless, and distressful. Most aston-
ishing to Julian was "that he lay alone." Julian identifies both bodily
and spiritual pains that indicate the effect the perceived isolation from
the lord has on both the bodily and spiritual aspects of the human
being. Because he is isolated and trapped in self pity, blindness be-

comes pervasive, preventing the servant from recognizing his *godly will*, which, made in the image of God, cannot be eradicated from human beings.

Julian's shift from a willful act of disobedience by the servant to a fall in the slade has significant implications for her soteriology. It distinguishes the fall as an accident and emphasizes the essential goodwill of the servant. Rather than stress the one act that condemned all humankind she accentuates the great pains the servant experiences after the fall. Her perspective has biblical precedent in Rom 7:15, "I do not understand my own actions. For I do not do what I want, but I do the very thing I hate." She creates a confronting depiction of the suffering caused by sin, which leaves human beings prone to doing the very things they do not wish to do. Disoriented by sin, human beings forget their natural love for God and become blind to the experience of divine love.

III. The Courteous Lord

Julian then turns her attention to the lord who, in the suffering that ensues in the slade, embodies how God is with human beings. The lord never abandons the servant. He experiences heartfelt compassion while waiting patiently for the servant to complete his task. He reacts to the sense of isolation the servant experiences when he falls, and chooses to reward such faithfulness in wanting to do his will: "Is it not reasonable that I should reward him for his fright and his fear, his hurt and his injuries and all his woe?" (14:51.268). Subsequently Julian receives a spiritual insight about the lord's meaning:

> that his beloved servant, whom he loved so much, should be highly and blessedly rewarded forever, above what he would have been if he had not fallen, yes, and so much that his falling and all the woe that he received from it will be turned into high, surpassing honor and endless bliss (14:51.269).

The fall in the dell does not limit the love the lord has for the servant. Rather it initiates a loving response that exposes the endless patience, endless concern, and endless resourcefulness of the lord, who gladly and generously showers plentiful grace that can restore the servant to more glory than he received before the fall. It becomes clear that "only pain blames and punishes, and our courteous Lord comforts and succours, and always he is kindly disposed to the soul, loving and longing to bring us to his bliss" (14:51.271). The experience of sin creates its own punishment. Therefore in contrast to sin that can create only suffering, the lord who is all goodness never attributes blame for sin, but constantly offers healing love. The lord is a courteous lord exhibiting all the traditional qualities of graceful politeness and consideration toward others. Moreover, as we saw in Chapter 3, courtesy characterizes love that is both majestic and noble, tender and intimate. The lord sits beside the servant, courteously inviting a loving relationship, leaving the servant free to respond to his offer of strength, comfort, and hope. The courteous lord bestows grace that can help the servant bear the consequences of sin and fend off despair. The lord affirms love where wrath was expected and offers the hope of a better future.

Julian's choice of verbs, "comforts" and "succours," does not mean that God eliminates all pain; rather it reflects *con-forto* (from *fors, fortis*),[3] meaning to strengthen greatly by standing beside those who need strength, enabling humanity to participate freely, responsibly, and meaningfully in life, confident of God's providential presence in life, death, and destiny. The awareness of the courteous nature of the Father touches Julian deeply, as she has previously noted: "the greatest abundance of joy which we shall have, as I see it, is this wonderful courtesy and familiarity *[homliness]* of our Father" (1:7.189).

Intrinsic to the courteous nature of the lord are the qualities of *ruth, pity, mercy, joy,* and *bliss:*

> The compassion and the pity of the Father were for Adam, who is his most beloved creature. The joy and the bliss were for the falling of his dearly beloved Son, who is equal with the Father. The merciful regard of his lovely countenance filled all the earth, and went down with Adam into hell, and by this continuing pity Adam was kept from endless death. And this mercy and pity abides with mankind until the time that we come up to heaven (14:51.271-272).

It is noteworthy that these qualities reflect those Julian saw on the crucified Christ in her *beholding* of suffering, love, and joy. As in the *showings* of the Passion, the qualities of *ruth, pity,* and *mercy* reaffirm the comforting presence of God as human beings labor through life.[4] The semantics and etymology of *compassion* lead back to the Hebrew *rahamin* (trembling womb),[5] the Greek *oiktirmos* (the feeling of compas-

---

[3] Charlton T. Lewis, *A Latin Dictionary: Lewis and Short.* Founded on Andrew's Edition of Freund's Latin Dictionary Revised, Enlarged and in Great Part Rewritten (Oxford: Clarendon Press, 1984) (= LD) 416.

[4] Palliser, *Christ, Our Mother of Mercy,* 167, points out that Julian uses this statement of God's *ruth* and *pity* nineteen times in connection with the parable.

[5] Phylis Trible, *God and the Rhetoric of Sexuality* (Philadelphia: Fortress, 1978), 31–59.

sion) and *splanchna* (the bowels or seat of the emotions),[6] and the Latin *compassio* (suffering with, feeling sympathy and agreement).[7] In Middle English compassion *(ruth)* conveys a sharing of suffering with another, sympathy and a feeling of sorrow for another's troubles, and involvement in an affliction as in 1 Cor 12:26, "If one member suffers, all suffer together with it."[8] Like compassion, *pity* expresses the tenderness or concern aroused by the misfortune of others.[9] *Mercy* and *pity* denote the forbearance and tolerance shown to powerless people who expect a severe response.[10] Julian defines mercy as "a compassionate property, which belongs to motherhood in tender love. . . . Mercy works, protecting, enduring, vivifying and healing, and it is all of the tenderness of love" (14:48.262). *Ruth, pity,* and *mercy* all imply elements of tenderness, graciousness, pathos, steadfastness, and faithful love. They communicate the love metaphorically felt in the womb or the belly of God that becomes tangible in acts of grace that comfort us in the midst of pain.

The greatest act of compassion, the sending of the Son, brings *joy* and *bliss* to the Father. Julian's description of the joy and bliss of the Father is consistent with her earlier descriptions of joy. As we observed in Chapter 5, joy for Julian is not a momentary facile pleasure or happiness, or an optimism that is a kind of presumption that ignores the realities of pain, suffering, and evil, especially the vulnerability of human beings. Joy manifests a harmony that transpires through struggling with the ambiguity of existence and knowing the presence of divine love that transcends all reality. Joy embodies darkness and light, tragedy and transformation, death and glory. It expresses hope for eternity in God. Thus the joy and bliss the Father radiates come from knowledge that divine love is present to humanity, transforming suffering and drawing it into eternal bliss that exceeds all that has been lost through the Fall.

During the time of transformation that occurs through the sending of the Son, the lord waits alone in the wilderness for the beloved servant to complete his task: "The place which the lord sat on was unadorned, on the ground, barren and waste, alone in the wilderness" (14:51.271).

[6] Margaret Ann Palliser, o.p., *Christ Our Mother of Mercy: Divine Mercy and Compassion in the Theology of the Shewings of Julian of Norwich* (Berlin and New York: Walter de Gruyter, 1992) 212.

[7] *LD* 387.

[8] Hans Kurath, Sherman Kuhn, and Robert Lewis, eds., *Middle English Dictionary* (Ann Arbor: University of Michigan Press, 1954–) (= *MED*) 460.

[9] *NSOED* 2228.

[10] *NSOED* 1746.

The solitude of the lord and the barrenness of the wilderness bear a striking resemblance to the solitary servant in a lonely, grievous place. The lord experiences the same pains as the fallen servant. Julian then elucidates these inhospitable images:

> But his sitting on the ground, barren and waste, signifies this: He made man's soul to be his own city and his dwelling place, which is the most pleasing to him of all his works. And when man had fallen into sorrow and pain, he was not wholly proper to serve in that noble office, and therefore our kind Father did not wish to prepare any other place, but sat upon the ground, awaiting human nature, which is mixed with earth, until the time when by his grace his beloved Son had brought back[11] his city into its noble place of beauty by his hard labor (14:51.272).

Julian summarizes the Father's salvific plan. The Father created humankind, the most pleasing of all his works, to be his city and dwelling place. When human beings fell they were unable to fulfill this noble office. Consequently, a detailed image of the Father emerges from the misty desert panorama and we are made to understand that this is a kind Father who does not wish to choose another dwelling place. He sits on the earth, waiting for humankind who are "mixed with earth." The association with Julian's version of Gen 2:7, that God fashioned human beings from the slime of the earth, ("When God was to make man's body, he took the slime of the earth," 14:53.284) seems apparent. This is not a distant Father who waits enthroned in heaven for the Son to complete his task. This is a Father who freely chooses earth to be his waiting place, earth that is a constituent of human nature. Though the Fall has interrupted the Father's greatest longing, to make humankind his dwelling place, in reality the Father has never separated himself from creation. Surrounded by desert that will only become fertile through union with human beings, he waits for the Son to bring the city (humankind) again into fairness worthy of the Father. Vulnerable to human experience in the desert, the Father waits patiently for the Son to complete his task.

Subsequently Julian gives further details about the meaning of the Father's sitting: "The sitting of the Father symbolizes the divinity, that is to say to reveal rest and peace, for in the divinity there can be no labor" (51:14.276). In contrast to the servant who "groans and moans and tosses about and writhes" in the dell, "digging and ditching, sweating and turning the soil over," and the continuous travail of the servant as gardener, the Father presents the fullness of rest and peace of the Godhead. This suggests that in the Father we find natural repose and

---

[11] li.1920,105, says *bowte ageyn*.

relief from a life of toil, freedom from distress and trouble, love, unity, and support on which human beings can rely. Moreover, the word travail or travel in the Sloane 1 manuscript has a double meaning in Middle English. While "travel" suggests going from one place to another, travail describes distress, affliction, weariness, or even an instrument of torture.[12] Thus in this context Edmund Colledge and James Walsh's translation, "labor," seems to be misleading, as it presents an image of an authoritative lord totally uninvolved in the experience of the servant. The point here is not that the Father does not labor or work. Consistent with her emphasis on the compassion of the Father, Julian suggests that in the Father we see nothing that would afflict, distress, or blame people. The rest and peace of the Godhead emanate from the Father. The image creates a dialectic between God who is all rest and peace and God who works tirelessly to restore a union that is greater than before the Fall. The two are not mutually exclusive; both are true. This image keeps before us that ultimately God is true rest and peace.

Julian is unwavering in her presentation of the lord as compassionate. As her understanding continues "into the lord" she sees "in a touch" that even the physical details of the Father's clothing denote the consistency of his loving presence and his compassion:

> The blueness of the clothing signifies his steadfastness; the brownness of his fair face with the lovely blackness of the eyes was most suitable to indicate his holy solemnity; the amplitude, billowing splendidly all about him, signifies that he has enclosed within himself all heavens and all endless joy and bliss; and this was shown in a brief moment, when I perceived that my understanding was directed to the lord. In this I saw him greatly rejoice over the honorable restoration to which he wants to bring and will bring his servant by his great and plentiful grace (14:51.272).

This is not a portrait of an impassible God uninvolved in human affairs, but of a courteous God of pathos who is steadfast in love, sincere, and empathetic, intimately involved in the restoration of human beings after the Fall. The Father is joyful as he sees that human beings will become his dwelling place. The Father communicates endless joy and bliss in what the Son achieves through the abundance of grace.

IV. The Role of the Servant

While the lord waits in the desert, the servant dressed for labor tills the garden:

[12] *NSOED* 3377.

He was to be a gardener, digging and ditching and sweating and turning the soil over and over, and to dig deep down, and to water the
plants at the proper time. And he was to persevere in his work, and
make sweet streams to run, and fine and plenteous fruit to grow, which
he was to bring before the lord and serve him with to his liking. And he
was never to come back again until he had made all this food ready as
he knew was pleasing to the lord; and then he was to take this food, and
drink, and carry it most reverently before the lord (14:51.273-274).

On a literal level the servant is a gardener who carries out the task
assigned to Adam (Gen 3:22) to till the soil. Although this work involves
arduous labor there is also a sense that it is pleasurable because the
servant loves the earth. He devotedly tends it so that it may bear fruit.
The earthiness of the gardener's labor speaks of the goodness of creation especially prevalent in the creation myth of Genesis 1, the garden
of paradise in Genesis 2, and the holy ground in Exod 3:5. The gardener
exemplifies the fact that the story of salvation is ultimately about giving life and nourishment to creation. It is not about the violation of
creation.

Julian notes: "There was a treasure in the earth which the lord loved"
(14:51.273). As she wonders what the treasure in the earth might be, in
her understanding she perceives: "It is a food which is delicious and
pleasing to the lord" (14:51.273). The treasure in the earth is solid food
and nourishment, the most significant meal for the lord. Metaphorically, Julian points out, the treasure describes human nature mixed
with earth (14:51.272), which God's grace will restore through the
Incarnation. Although it has been suggested that the treasure hidden
in the earth is eternal life,[13] the context seems more to intimate that it
is humankind fallen in the dell. The metaphor speaks of something
absolute within humankind and creation that can unite with the divine, as the ground the servant cultivates represents human sensuality.
The treasure is the human soul "that was founded in the lord in a marvellous depth of endless love" (14:51.274).[14] The treasure of love in the
earth is humankind made in the image of God and at one with God.
Grace, operative in Christ, enables human beings to be touched by
Christ's ground of love and to come to know themselves as created in
the image and likeness of God. The effort and pain of this labor in the

[13] Ritamary Bradley, *Julian's Way: A Practical Commentary on Julian of Norwich*
(London: Harper Collins, 1992) 125.

[14] This metaphor of the human person as a garden has many biblical precedents,
such as Isa 5:7, "the vineyard of the lord of hosts is the house of Israel," and Song
4:12, "You are an enclosed garden, my sister, my bride." The theme is repeated after
the narrative part of the parable.

garden and the holiness of this life's toil have their reward in the uncovering of the treasure. The servant acts as caretaker of the human soul, which is like a garden. He enables humankind to cooperate in the work of creation and continue God's labor of crafting creation into God.

The gardener is tenacious in his efforts to uncover the treasure in the earth. He penetrates the soil, into the deepest darkness: "for then he went down into hell; and when he was there, he raised up the great root out of the deep depth, which rightly was joined [knit] to him in heaven" (14:51.277). The context of the image in the parable suggests that the root is union with Christ, "knit to him in heaven," which, even if it is hidden in the deepest darkness through the Fall, can never be destroyed.[15] Though Julian does not identify it as such, this image relates to the idea of the *godly will*. The image of the root, pregnant with the promise of growth and life, presents a challenging picture revealing that the cultivation of the garden includes even the depths of hell. It hints at universal salvation for humanity through the gardener who tends and gives life to all in the garden of redemption.

After reflecting on the servant as garden dweller Julian explains that "I did not understand everything which this example meant. And therefore I wondered where the servant came from" (14:51.274). Julian goes to some length to point to the unity of wills between the lord and the servant. Outwardly Julian's servant looks like a laborer ready to perform a service:

> Outwardly he was simply dressed like a laborer prepared to work, and he stood very close to the lord, not immediately in front of him but a little to one side, and that on the left; his clothing was a white tunic, scanty, old and all worn, dyed with the sweat of his body, tight fitting and short, as it were a hand's breadth below his knee, looking threadbare as if it would soon be worn out, ready to go to rags and to tear (14:51.272-273).

Inwardly, however, the servant reveals a bond of love:

> And, inwardly, there was shown in him a foundation of love, the love which he had for the lord, which was equal to the love which the lord had for him. The wisdom of the servant saw inwardly that there was one thing to do which would pay honor to the lord; and the servant, for love, having no regard for himself or for anything which might happen to him, went off in great haste and ran when his lord sent him, to do the thing which was his will and to his honor (14:51.273).

[15] Cf. Karl Tamburr, "Mystic Transformation: Julian's Version of the Harrowing of Hell," *Mystics Quarterly* 20 (1994) 60–67.

The "foundation of love" the servant has, "equal to the love which the lord had for him," indicates that love is the origin and source of divine life, the foundation of the trinitarian relationship. Love links the servant to the lord in such a way that there is a unity of wills between the two. This union in love manifests itself as divine wisdom. The wisdom of the servant intrinsically knows what to do to bring pleasure and honor to the lord. Thus the bond of love that results in the union of wills for the servant reflects the eternal will of God enacted as love. The servant is the eternal Son of God, wisdom of God made flesh, who knows the divine plan for salvation. He enacts this by carrying out the work of crafting creation into God. There is a union of wills between the lord and the servant. This tempers any possibility that the lord sends the servant on a mission or the Father sends the Son to complete a task in which the Father is uninvolved. It erases any implication that the Father is aloof and untouched by the suffering of the Son.

Julian blurs the boundaries between Christ and humankind: "In the servant is comprehended the second person of the Trinity, and in the servant is comprehended Adam, that is to say all men" (14:51.274). She emphasizes the ontological union between Christ and humanity. This implies that Christ does not merely represent humanity: he is humanity. Yet Julian seems to struggle with this *oneing* between Christ and humanity as we see from her comment that "I did not understand what the example meant." She continues to ponder "from where the servant came" by returning to the theme of the Fall that began the parable. She concentrates on the theological perspective that makes the Fall central to the story of salvation:

> When Adam fell, God's Son fell; because of the true union [*oneing*] which was made in heaven, God's Son could not be separated from Adam, for by Adam I understand all mankind. Adam fell from life to death, into the valley of this wretched world, and after that into hell. God's Son fell with Adam, into the valley of the womb of the maiden who was the fairest daughter of Adam, and that was to excuse Adam from blame in heaven and on earth; and powerfully he brought him out of hell (14:51.274-275).

Julian's repetition of the word "fell" creates an echo that resounds throughout the text and confronts her refrain *all shall be well*. While at first glance the multiple images of the Fall present us with the opposite of the hope that "all shall be well," as "Adam fell from life to death into the valley of this wretched world, and after that in to hell," there is a paradoxical counteracting image of the Fall: "God's son fell with Adam, into the valley of the womb of the maiden . . . and . . . he brought him out of hell." In the first image humanity feels estrangement in the fall into the valley. Although the phrase "Adam fell from life to death" could suggest an ontological separation or distancing between humanity and God in the fall,[16] Julian falls short of establishing such a profound separation. When she concentrates on the Fall the darkest image she envisages of the separation between God and humanity is the root that, though in hell, is *knit* to Christ in heaven, and thus is never ontologically separate from the divine.

Furthermore, the *oneing* between Christ and humanity is so complete that when human beings fall Christ falls. Julian uses powerful imagery to emphasize the life-denying pain experienced in the human condition in the valley. Christ falls into "the valley of the maiden's womb" in his birth and takes on "our foul mortal flesh" (14:51.278).[17] His flesh falls in the pain of the Passion: "the flesh was torn from the skull, falling in pieces until when the bleeding stopped" (14:51.277). Yet this scene of the complete humbling of Christ in the Fall, where his flesh literally falls to pieces, paradoxically becomes an experience of glory:

> Adam's old tunic, tight-fitting, threadbare and short, was then made lovely by our savior, new, white and bright and forever clean, wide and ample, fairer and richer than the clothing which I saw on the Father. For that clothing was blue, and Christ's clothing is now of a fair and seemly mixture, which is so marvellous that I cannot describe it, for it is all of true glory (14:51.278).

Time and eternity coalesce as the Fall that brings death confronts the fall that brings life, and Adam's old, dirty, tattered garment becomes "new, white and bright, forever clean, even richer than the clothing of the Father." While Julian has told us that "the blewness of his clothing speaks of Christ's steadfastness," Christ clothes humanity in a garment even more steadfast or firmly fixed than the Father's. This implies that human transformation brought about through Christ's fall into the womb of the maiden can never be annulled.

Although I have argued that Julian's predominant understanding of the motive for the Incarnation is love, in this passage she considers the Incarnation from the perspective of the Fall. Interpretation is difficult because the expression "for the true *oneing* which was made in heaven, God's Son could not be separated from Adam" is ambiguous.

---

[16] See Denise Nowakowski Baker, *Julian of Norwich's Showings: From Vision to Book* (Princeton, N.J.: Princeton University Press, 1994) 94.

[17] Julian is not intimating here that all flesh is evil. *Foul flesh* suggests that Christ took on all in humanity that causes demise, all that is life-denying.

Denise Baker interprets this to mean that the predestination of humanity in the second person of the Trinity from all eternity necessitates the
Incarnation of Christ when Adam falls from union with God into the
region of unlikeness.[18] Thus the emphasis is on Christ's becoming
human as a response to the Fall. I would argue, however, that Julian is
not fully convinced of this theological perspective, and that the reference connects to her comments about Christ *knit* to humanity at creation. It is Christ the second person of the Trinity who becomes the
concrete expression of divine love in the history he shaped and formed
as preexistent within the Trinity. In this theological perspective human
nature was always intended for the Son, irrespective of the Fall. This
maintains the perspective that the Incarnation was always part of the
divine plan. When the Fall occurs, Christ, eternally one with human
nature, must remain one with human nature even in the experience of
the Fall.

Nevertheless, Julian's ensuing comments maintain the ambiguity:

> So he was the servant before he came on earth, standing ready in pur-
> pose before the Father until the time when he would send him to do the
> glorious deed by which mankind was brought back to heaven. That is
> to say, even though he is God, equal with the Father as regards his
> divinity, but with his prescient purpose that he would become man to
> save mankind in fulfillment of the will of his Father, so he stood before
> his Father as a servant, willingly taking upon him all our charge. And
> then he rushed off very readily at the Father's bidding, and soon he fell
> very low into the maiden's womb, having no regard for himself or for
> his cruel pains (14:51.275).

Julian maintains the perspective that human nature was always
intended for the Son in her comment: "so he was the servant before he
came on earth," but the following statement "that he would become
man to save mankind in fulfillment of the will of his Father" places
emphasis on the fact that the Fall instigates the Incarnation. It also emphasizes the humiliation of Christ in becoming human. Christ fulfills the
will of the Father and takes upon himself all human blame. But Julian
also emphasizes our ontological *oneing* with Christ. Because Christ is in
union with human beings, in looking at humanity God sees Christ:
"our Father may not, does not wish to assign more blame to us than to
his own beloved Son Jesus Christ" (14:51.275). Human beings are not
blameworthy, and the Father will not assign blame to us because he
makes no distinction between humanity and Christ.

[18] Baker, *From Vision to Book* 97.

Julian then leaves aside her concentration on the Fall and focuses on the *oneing* between Christ and humanity. Echoing imagery from Col 1:15-19, she indicates that Christ is the one who communicates both the transcendence and relationality of God by conflating two significant Pauline images of Christ as "the wisdom of the Father" (1 Cor 1:30a) and Christ as head of the mystical body: "he is the head, and we are his members" (14:51.276). The wisdom motif verifies that there is no separation between creation and redemption. Christ, the Incarnation of the wisdom of God, manifests how creation and Incarnation are intrinsically connected in the one divine plan. Paradoxically, just as in 1 Cor 1:24-25, the falling of Christ reveals the wisdom of God.

The metaphor of the mystical body then reveals how the wisdom of God becomes embedded in humankind in the movement of creation and re-creation. With Christ as the head, humankind participates in the life of Christ so that the body of Christ becomes the body of the community.[19] The union is so complete that "Jesus is in all that shall be saved, and all that shall be saved are in Jesus." These metaphors of Christ as the wisdom of God and the head of the mystical body of all who will be saved affirm for Julian that the whole story of salvation is about love. The love of God makes no distinction between Christ and humanity.

V. Eternal Oneing in the Trinity

The parable concludes with a beatific vision. In a tableau reminiscent of an image of the Trinity from a Breviary or Book of Hours, where Christ sits to the right of the Father and the Holy Spirit in the form of a dove unites them, the saved servant reflects an ambience of glory. Cloaked in splendor, he is adorned with a precious crown that he shares with the Father.[20] Julian describes the crown: "For it was revealed that we are his crown, which crown is the Father's joy, the Son's honor, the Holy Spirit's delight, and endless marvellous bliss to all who are in heaven" (14:51.278). The crown of humankind founded in love rewards Christ for all the pain he endured in his labor of love. The image affirms that we are necessary for the joy, honor, and delight of God.

The final scene of the parable presents hope for salvation. Reminiscent of the Canticle of Canticles, the image of the soul as a garden and Christ as the gardener is transposed: "Now the spouse, God's Son, is at

---

[19] Cf. 1 Corinthians 12; Gal 3:28.

[20] See 267, Initial B, Introducing the Votive Mass of the Trinity, The Carmelite Missal, in Richard Marks and Nigel Morgan, *The Golden Age of English Manuscript Painting 1200–1500* (New York: George Braziller, 1981) 91.

peace with his beloved wife, who is the fair maiden of endless joy" (14:51.278). Julian uses bridal imagery to show how the love of Christ enables us to approach final union with the divine. The exchange of love between Christ and human souls is a spiritual marriage between the heavenly bridegroom and human brides. Christ takes us as his bride and, being one with Christ, we experience God's promise of final transformation. In the embrace of divine love we become one in joy.

The whole process of salvation rehearsed in the parable bears witness to the Father, Son, and Holy Spirit. "Now the Son, true God and true man, sits in his city in rest and in peace, which his Father has prepared for him by his endless purpose, and the Father in the Son, and the Holy Spirit in the Father and in the Son" (14:51.278). For union to be complete, the whole person and the triune God become one. The entire work of creation and redemption is the work of the triune God.

The parable teaches Julian that God's providential care will not cease. The imagery unveils the pain of the fall into blindness and the longing of believers finally to see and to be open to experience God's love. Paradoxically, the experience of falling becomes an experience of grace. Human woundedness, occasioned by the Fall, reveals the transforming power of God's healing love made tangible through the labor of Christ. In the parable the pain of weariness of life disconnected from God gives way to a deep joy of being always in the presence of the merciful love of the triune God who is ever renewing and recreating human life in Christ. The example discloses that, although believers know sorrow and suffering, it is now experienced as part of the living out of the truth of being one with Christ. Sustained by this union with Christ we can wait peacefully and live in hope-filled expectation that the union depicted in the parable is partially possible in a life centered on Christ and is a foretaste of the joy of heaven. Immediately after the parable Julian's understanding reaches its climax in her christology of Christ the deep wisdom of the Trinity, our mother.

7

Oneing Through Christ the Deep Wisdom of the Trinity Our Mother

> *We are all bound to god by nature, and we are bound to god by grace* (14:62.303).

Julian's soteriology climaxes in the idea that "the deep wisdom of the Trinity is our mother." The unfolding character of the continuum of Christ's dynamic role within the Trinity, his Incarnation, death, and resurrection, and his ongoing existential presence and care within history take on new meaning. The last two chapters looked at the christological/ soteriological models that emerge from the saving work of Christ through the cross and his role as servant. This chapter sets out to explore how the insight that "the deep wisdom of the Trinity is our mother" reveals that the redemptive nature of Christ's work cannot be found in any one event separated from the others. Only reflection on the meaning of the whole experience of the deep wisdom of the Trinity as our mother will reveal the fullness of the salvific reality that occurs through Christ. The christology communicated in this statement draws together the ontological and existential dimensions of our being in God and our *again making* or re-creation in Christ. It places these experiences of *oneing* in dialectical relationship. The christology expresses that Christ draws together creation (our *being*), re-creation (our *increasing*) and fulfillment (our *fulfilling*). Although Christ's role as deep wisdom and mother is a soteriological unity it is necessary to analyze the theology expressed in each aspect of the idea so that the dynamic quality of Julian's soteriology may become clear. Three *beholdings* of Christ's motherhood are integral to our investigation: the motherhood of *kind,* the motherhood of *grace,* and the motherhood of *working.* Christ, deep wisdom and mother, is now present in the Church. In the Church we are bound to God by nature and by grace.

I. THE DEEP WISDOM OF THE TRINITY IS OUR MOTHER

In the long text, after the three *beholdings* of the Passion and the parable of the lord and the servant, Julian makes a consequential soteriological statement:

> For the almighty truth of the Trinity is our Father, for he made us and keeps us in him. And the deep wisdom of the Trinity is our Mother, in whom we are enclosed. And the high goodness of the Trinity is our Lord, and in him we are enclosed and he in us. We are enclosed in the Father, and we are enclosed in the Son, and we are enclosed in the Holy Spirit. And the Father is enclosed in us, the Son is enclosed in us, and the Holy Spirit is enclosed in us, almighty, all wisdom and all goodness, one God, one Lord (14:54.285).

Embedded in a passage about the Trinity that emphasizes inter- and intra-trinitarian relationship, the statement "the deep wisdom of the Trinity is our Mother, in whom we are enclosed" signals that salvation occurs within this trinitarian *perichoresis*. Christ plays a vital role in creating an indissoluble unity between human beings and the Trinity because he belongs to the depth of the Trinity and yet humanity is enclosed in him and he in humanity. The imagery of "deep wisdom" and "mother" enables Julian to locate *perichoresis* not only in the inner life of the Trinity but also in the mystery of the one communion of love between the divine and the human. Each word in Julian's statement reveals how Christ maintains the one communion of love. "Deep wisdom" and "mother" form a dialectic that struggles to condense the essence of how human beings experience ontological and existential *oneing* in Christ in the Trinity. Significantly, Julian never polarizes these perspectives by associating wisdom with the Godhead and motherhood with Christ's humanity. Rather, she utilizes the dynamic of this imagery to expose a dialectical tension that unites both aspects of how we are ontologically and existentially one in Christ. Many authors note the significance of the theme of Christ's motherhood.[1] As we can see from the passage, however, it is important to remember that it is not simply Christ's role as mother that characterizes the christology that informs Julian's soteriology. It is the dialectical unity created between

---

[1] Brant Pelphrey, *Love Was His Meaning: The Theology and Mysticism of Julian of Norwich* (Salzburg: Institüt für Anglistik und Amerikanistik, 1982) (= *LWHM*) 186; Joan Nuth, *Wisdom's Daughter: The Theology of Julian of Norwich* (New York: Crossroad, 1991) 65; Palliser, *Christ Our Mother of Mercy: Divine Mercy and Compassion in the Theology of the Shewings of Julian of Norwich* (Berlin and New York: Walter de Gruyter, 1992) 110.

Christ's role as deep wisdom of the Trinity *and* mother and the reciprocal enclosure between us and each person of the Trinity that make Julian's soteriology so distinctive and unique.

Deep Wisdom

Julian's theologically dense reference to Christ as "deep wisdom" discloses how salvation is assured, because human beings experience ontological *oneing* in Christ. "Deep wisdom" echoes the image of the crucified Christ that "contained and specified the blessed Trinity." The qualifying term *deep* places Christ within the unfathomable abyss of the Trinity. It accentuates how profoundly Christ belongs to the Trinity and marks the centrality of his role within the Trinity. It expounds how Christ reveals trinitarian love. *Deep* creates a sense of the incomprehensibility of the mystery of the Trinity. This protects the transcendence of the Trinity, the mysterious holy otherness of God. *Deep* points to the eternal nature of the Trinity, identifying Christ's role as the *alpha* and *omega,* the beginning and end of all things. Through his function as deep wisdom Christ brings all things together in the unfathomable depth of the Trinity, and at the same time plays a dynamic role in creating an ontological *oneing* between the Trinity and human beings.

Within the idea of *deep wisdom* there are possible allusions to Wisdom literature and *logos* theology, which describe the role wisdom plays in creation.[2] The reference hooks into and brings to a climax allusions to wisdom throughout the text. In the short text Julian points to "the endless providence of God's wisdom" (viii:137). In the long text this becomes "the forseeing wisdom of God" (3:11.337). Both designate God's providential care that leads humanity "to the best end." We recall that Julian also presents the motif of divine wisdom in the parable of the lord and the servant, where she attributes the quality of wisdom to Christ. The wisdom of the servant knows how to bring honor to the lord. Identified as the wisdom of the Father, he is the Incarnation of the wisdom of God. The wisdom of the servant knows and does the Father's will. Wisdom makes God's hopes real.

After the parable Julian identifies Christ, the wisdom of the Father, with the role of mother: "in our true Mother Jesus our life is founded in his own prescient wisdom from without beginning, with the great power of the Father and the supreme goodness of the Holy Spirit"

---

[2] Cf. Ritamary Bradley, *Julian's Way: A Practical Commentary on Julian of Norwich* (London: Harper Collins, 1992) 135–37; Nuth, *Wisdom's Daughter* 65–66; Denise Nowakowski Baker, *Julian of Norwich's Showings: From Vision to Book* (Princeton, N.J.: Princeton University Press, 1994) 122–23.

(14:63.304). Mother Christ, the life of humanity, is grounded in his own wisdom eternally in a trinitarian unity. In the strength of this connection Julian comes into her own. Edmund Colledge and James Walsh express this well: "the tradition shows a persistent reluctance to make the connection which is Julian's audacious starting-point."[3] The tradition has identified Christ with wisdom. It has described the care of Christ as being like a mother's.[4] Julian's great contribution is that she links both these ideas together. Julian interrelates the wisdom and mother themes so that the roles they identify are fluid. In referring to Christ as mother grounded in the wisdom of himself eternally she points to an ontological union between Christ's identity as wisdom and his role as mother. This creates a dialectic between our ontological *oneing* in Christ and *oneing* through his ongoing existential care. The juxtaposition of images of wisdom and mother shifts emphasis away from the gender of Christ. It accentuates Christ's all-encompassing humanity. This makes Christ's salvific role absolutely inclusive.[5] All distinctions between male and female are annulled.

The Lovely Word "Mother"

In some ways Julian uses the image of the mother in a traditional way. We see this when she interprets Christ's role as savior in his giving birth to humanity: ". . . our savior is our true Mother, in whom we are

---

[3] Edmund Colledge and James Walsh, *A Book of Showings to the Anchoress Julian of Norwich*. 2 vols. (Toronto: Pontifical Institute of Mediaeval Studies, 1978) (= *BSAJN*) 154. The idea of Christ as mother occurs in both Eastern and Western traditions. Cf. Ritamary Bradley, "The Motherhood Theme in Julian of Norwich," *Fourteenth Century English Mystics News Letter* 2 (1976) 25–38; eadem, "Patristic Background of the Motherhood Similitude in Julian of Norwich," *Christian Scholars Review* 8 (1978) 101–13; Jennifer P. Heimmel, *God is Our Mother: Julian of Norwich and the Medieval Image of Christian Feminine Divinity* (Salzburg: Institüt für Anglistik und Amerikanistik, 1982) 1–33; Patricia Mary Vinje, *An Understanding of Love According to the Anchoress Julian of Norwich* (Salzburg: Institüt für Anglistik und Amerikanistik, 1983) 153; Ritamary Bradley, "Mysticism in the Motherhood Similitude of Julian of Norwich," *Studia Mystica* 8 (1985) 4–14; Valery M. Lagorio, "Variations on the Theme of God's Motherhood in Medieval English Mystical and Devotional Writings," *Studia Mystica* 8 (1985) 15–37.

[4] See Kerrie Hide, "The Deep Wisdom of the Trinity Our Mother: Echoes in Augustine and Julian of Norwich," *The Australasian Catholic Record* 4 (1997) 432–44.

[5] Although it is impossible to say whether Julian was directly familiar with a plethora of texts that refer to Christ as wisdom or mother, she certainly would have known scriptural references such as Wis 7:11-12; Sir 24:19-29; Isa 49:15; Matt 11:19b. Christ as mother hen in Matt 23:37 would also be commonplace. Cf. Sister Mary

endlessly born and out of whom we shall never come" (14:57.292). This is a unique birthing, however, because we are endlessly born. Christ continually re-creates us. Eternally enclosed in the body of Christ, we never leave it. Julian further associates Christ's giving birth to us to the pain of his death on the cross:

> . . . our true Mother Jesus, he alone bears us for joy and for endless life, blessed may he be. So he carries us within him in love and travail, until the full time when he wanted to suffer the sharpest thorns and cruel pains that ever were or will be, and at the last he died. And when he had finished, and had borne us so for bliss, still all this could not satisfy his wonderful love (14:60.298).

In the Passion Christ *ones* us to himself. We are drawn into the body of Christ, and so he carries us in "love and travail." But the dying is for life. Christ's pain becomes labor pangs that give birth to us. Through Christ's Passion we are born into bliss.

The image of the mother not only reflects traditional imagery of giving birth and nurturing. Julian also defines the word theologically:

> This fair lovely word "mother" is so sweet and so kind in itself that it cannot truly be said of anyone or to anyone except of him and to him who is the true Mother of life and of all things. To the property of motherhood belong nature, (kind) love, wisdom and knowledge, and this is God (14:60.298-299).

The word "mother" is so sweet and natural that Christ is the only one who truly deserves the title. The properties of motherhood, nature *[kind]*, love, wisdom, and knowledge, are properties that extend from the being of God. We recall that *kind* has a number of associations that Julian integrates into her use of the word. In this context *kind* denotes authentic nature as well as distinguishing the quality of love *(kind love)*. To say that *kind* is a property of motherhood is to say that God is kind or good while also being the Mother or source of all nature. The property of *kind* creates a bond in nature between the Godhead and humankind.[6]

Along with *kind*, love also denotes the being of God and the sharing of love through grace. Love reminds us of the nature of the Godhead as

---

Francis Smith, *Wisdom and the Personification of Wisdom Occurring in Middle English Literature Before 1500*, Ph.D. diss. Catholic University of America, 1935, and Rita-mary Bradley, "Mysticism in the Motherhood Similitude of Julian of Norwich," *Studia Mystica* 8 (1985) 4–14.

[6] Even though the Sloane 1 text leaves out the comma and has *kind love*, this integration of kindness, love, and nature could still apply. See lx:2516.124.

charity unmade, charity made, and *charity given.* Related to *kind* and love, "wisdom" refers to the deep wisdom of the Trinity. We have noted that wisdom designates the divine foresight that is eternally involved in the providential care of creation. Knowledge *[knowing]* then completes the list of properties. Julian specifically associates *knowing* with a gift received through the power of the Holy Spirit. These four properties, *kind,* love, wisdom, and *knowing* identify the *oneing* in nature and grace that is effected by Christ's being our mother. At the end of the explanation Julian summarizes her definition: motherhood *is God.* Motherhood describes who God is and how God relates. Therefore while Julian's definition of "mother" includes giving birth and nurturing, she does not limit mothering to a traditional parental role. Motherhood incorporates properties that belong to the trinitarian unity of the Godhead.

This definition of "mother," which associates motherhood with the Godhead, seems clear enough in the Paris manuscript. A discrepancy in Sloane 1 makes interpretation more problematic. The Sloane 1 manuscript waters down the association of motherhood with the Godhead:

> This fair word full of love, mother, it is so sweet and so kind and comes from the self so that it may not in truth be said but only of him, and of her who is true mother of him and of all. The property of true motherhood is kind love, wisdom and knowing, and it is good (60:121-122).

Though it is possible that the words "it is good" are simply the result of a lack of orthographical distinction between God and good, or a scribal error, there are theological ramifications in the change—if it is deliberate—because the direct association of motherhood with the Trinity is lessened. This is in marked contrast to the Paris text, which asserts that motherhood describes who God is: "and it is God." Sloane 1, as this example indicates, places more emphasis on Christ's motherhood as occurring in Christ through the Incarnation. It gives more attention to the role of Mary ("and of her who is true mother of him and of all"). Theologically, if motherhood relates to the Godhead and is not simply a role limited to Jesus' humanity, the role of mothering has profound theological value. The roles of mother and father have equal theological status. The implications are that both masculine and feminine images are essential in describing who God is in relation to creatures. Although Julian does not argue her point systematically, the statement "and it is God" undoubtedly raises the status of feminine images of God. Indirectly this validates the position of women and their experience of God.

I suggest that the less controversial image, limiting motherhood to Christ's humanity, in the Sloane 1 text is consistent with that manuscript's failure to develop the theme of the body as a purse. This is more evidence that suggests that the scribe of the Sloane 1 manuscript tried to restrain Julian's theology within conventional bounds.[7] But in spite of the possibility that a scribe played down the theological implications of relating motherhood to the Godhead in the Sloane 1 manuscript we can be assured that the motherhood of the Godhead revealed in Christ is a key soteriological principle for Julian.

"The deep wisdom of the Trinity is our mother" is a theologically rich statement that defines Christ's salvific role. As a theological précis it holds together the underlying trinitarian unity in the desire for human salvation and the specific revelation of divine love occurring through Christ. The interface between the imagery of *deep wisdom* and *mother* creates a dialectic between ontological *oneing* with the Trinity through Christ and his providential care that continues the task of *oneing*. The idea consolidates Christ's role in creation and redemption. Remembering that the christology contained in the whole expression "the deep wisdom of the Trinity is our mother" is central to Julian's soteriology, we are now ready to examine the three *beholdings* of motherhood in God.

II. THREE WAYS OF BEHOLDING MOTHERHOOD IN GOD

As with the three manners of *beholding* the Passion, Julian differentiates: three ways of contemplating *[beholding]* motherhood in God. The first is the foundation of our nature's creation (our *kind making*); the second is his taking of our nature *[kind]*, where the motherhood of grace begins; the third is motherhood at work. "And in that, by the same grace, everything is penetrated, in length and in breadth, in height and in depth without end; and it is all one love" (14:59.297).

We recall that *beholding* is a way of contemplative seeing. It is the expression of the inner eye of the soul with its ability to see spiritually. *Beholding* is seeing with a felt understanding of love. Thus *beholding* the motherhood in God expresses contemplative insight that extends Julian's understanding of salvation. *Beholding* reveals that, although motherhood occurs in God, we see the full expression of divine motherhood in and through Christ. The three ways of *beholding* motherhood draw together the complex christological dimension of Julian's soteriology of *oneing*. The first *beholding* distinguishes the *oneing* that occurs through Christ's being our mother of *kind*, the second points to *oneing*

[7] It is noteworthy that Christ's motherhood does not appear in the Westminster florilegium.

through Christ the mother of grace, while the third reveals *oneing* through Christ the mother of working.

Mother of Kind

In the first *beholding* of the motherhood in God, the foundation of "our *kind*'s creation," Julian emphasizes the significance of the beginning of the God/human relationship. We recall the *oneing* that distinguishes how "in the first we have our being." At creation God is the Father and Mother of humankind or nature: "And so in our making, God almighty is our loving *[kindly]* Father, and God all wisdom is our loving *[kindly]* Mother, with the love and the goodness of the Holy Spirit, which is all one God, one Lord" (14:58.293). God is the mother of *kinds*. The locus of this familial relationship is specifically in Christ: ". . . the mediator wanted to be the foundation and the head of this fair nature, out of whom we have all come, in whom we are all enclosed, into whom we shall all go" (14:53.283). The unique role that Christ plays as the ground and head of human nature is grounded in the Incarnation:

> Our Mother in nature, our Mother in grace, because he wanted altogether to become our Mother in all things, made the foundation of his work most humbly and most mildly in the maiden's womb. And he revealed that in the first revelation, when he brought that meek maiden before the eye of my understanding in the simple stature which she had when she conceived; that is to say that our great God, the supreme wisdom of all things, arrayed and prepared himself in this humble place, all ready in our poor flesh, himself to do the service and the office of motherhood in everything (14:60.297).

Observing with the eye of her understanding, Julian sees that in the Incarnation Christ is both our mother of *kind* and our mother of grace. The reference to his desire to become our Mother "in all things" relates to Julian's image of all things having being through the love of God in the vision of the hazelnut, and to the resurrected Christ who says "I am he who is all."[8] A significant aspect of sovereign wisdom's becoming the mother of all things occurs when he takes the ground of his being into the womb of the maiden. In the Incarnation Christ not only becomes our mother in substance (who we essentially are in God),

---

[8] Christ as the ground and head of all things echoes the doctrine of recapitulation elaborated by Irenaeus (130–202). Cf. Col 1:13-20 and Eph 1:10. This found its way into monastic theology in the work of Richard of St. Victor (ca. 1173). See *BSAJN* 557 n. 32.

but also our mother in sensuality (in the more bodily aspect of our existence): "the second person, who is our Mother, substantially the same beloved person, has now become our mother sensually, because we are double by God's creating, that is to say substantial and sensual" (14:58.294). Thus in taking our *kind* Christ becomes our "sensual mother." Through this image of Christ as mother of our substance and sensuality Julian shows how we are ontologically one with Christ in both substance and sensuality. She maintains that God through Christ is intimately present in the flesh and spirit of humanity, choosing flesh as a personal reality.

This idea of Christ's becoming our mother substantially and sensually links with the assertion that ". . . our Creator wished us to be like Jesus Christ our savior in heaven forever, through the power of our making again" (2:10.195). Because Christ is our mother not only in substance but also in sensuality we are "double by God's creating." We experience "making again *[geyn]*." *Geyn* in Middle English means "another time," "once more," "repeated."[9] In Julian's theological usage "making again" refers to the Incarnation, when Christ assumes sensuality. When God through Christ becomes human, human nature is made again or re-created. Significantly, re-creation does not occur only once. "Making again" occurs over and over. "Making again" involves continual *oneing*. Endlessly born and created again through Christ, the mother of *kind*, all humanity both male and female is drawn into continual *oneing* until we are the same *kind* as mother Christ, authentically human.[10] Furthermore, when the deep wisdom of the Trinity our Mother chooses sensuality, grace begins to work and Christ, the mother of *kind*, becomes our mother of grace.

Mother of Grace

The second *beholding* of motherhood that Julian points to is the "taking of our nature *[kind]*, where the motherhood of grace begins" (14:59.297). The *beholding* of Christ as the mother of grace reveals that

---

[9] Lesley Brown, ed. *The New Shorter Oxford English Dictionary on Historical Principles*. 2 vols. (Oxford: Clarendon Press, 1993) (= *NSOED*) 38.

[10] Though Julian does not use the term, this idea relates to the doctrine of divinization based on Gal 2:19-20; 2 Pet 1:4; 1 John 3:2. This was articulated by Cyril of Alexandria: "God became human that we humans might become divine." It was expressed in various forms by Irenaeus, Athanasius, Gregory of Nazianzus, Gregory of Nyssa, Augustine, Leo the Great, and many others. Because of its popularity it could easily have been familiar to Julian. See Michael Downey, ed., *New Dictionary of Catholic Spirituality* (Collegeville: The Liturgical Press, 1993) 285–86.

grace is God's self-communication to humankind. Grace is instanta-neously present when Christ assumes our sensual nature in the Incar-nation, by which we become one with Christ not only in nature but also in grace. Christ's words make the connection between nature and grace lucid: "I am he, the power and goodness of fatherhood; I am he, the wisdom and the lovingness of motherhood; I am he, the light and the grace which is all blessed love" (14:59.295-296). Grace is God's presence in our humanity in Christ that is "all blessed love," or "charity given." It is important to remember, however, that while Christ is mother of grace in assuming our sensuality there is an underlying trinitarian in-volvement in this sharing of the uncreated love that is the essence of the Trinity. Thus grace flows from the uncreated love of the Trinity with a specific locus of revelation in Christ. The wisdom and kindness of Mother Christ communicate the tangible, personal response of divine love in history. Significantly, *beholding* the motherhood of grace reveals that grace is not an additional gift external to human nature, added to assist salvation. Grace is a constituent of nature that begins to work when Christ "takes our *kind*." In assuming our *kind* Christ places grace within human nature.

Earlier in the text Julian has described grace in insights that emerge from *beholding*:

> For I contemplated [*beheld*] the property of mercy, and I contemplated [*beheld*] the property of grace, which have two ways of operating in one love. Mercy is a compassionate property, which belongs to motherhood in tender love; and grace is an honorable property, which belongs to royal dominion in the same love. Mercy works, protecting, enduring, vivifying and healing, and it is all of the tenderness of love; and grace works with mercy, raising, rewarding, endlessly exceeding what our love and labor deserve, distributing and displaying the vast plenty and generosity of God's royal dominion in his wonderful courtesy. And this is from the abundance of love, for grace transforms our dreadful failing into plentiful and endless solace; and grace transforms our shameful falling into high and honorable rising; and grace transforms our sor-rowful dying into holy, blessed life (14:48.262-263).

When Julian *beholds* the property of grace she also *beholds* the property of mercy. This suggests that grace is intrinsically related to Christ's mercy. Mercy and grace are two properties, with two manners of work-ing, in one love. Grace is the "abundance of love," the life within love that communicates love. Julian's identification of grace as an "honor-able property" recognizes the distinctive nature of grace. Grace is iden-tified with the sovereignty of God expressed in courteous love that is majestic and yet intimate. Linking with Julian's other descriptions of courteous love, grace is abundantly transformational, transfiguring "failing" into "plentiful and endless solace," "falling" into rising, and "dying" into "holy blessed life."

Mother of Mercy

Although Julian does not distinguish mercy in her *beholdings* of motherhood, she refers to Christ as the mother of mercy. The gracious working of the mother of mercy supports the work of Christ as mother of grace. Christ becomes the mother of mercy when he assumes human sensuality in the Incarnation:

> . . . the second person of the Trinity is our Mother in nature in our substantial creation, in whom we are founded and rooted, and he is our Mother of mercy in taking our sensuality. And so our Mother is working on us in various ways, in whom our parts are kept undivided; for in our Mother Christ we profit and increase, and in mercy he reforms and restores us, and by the power of his Passion, his death and his Resurrection he unites us to our substance (14:58.294).

Mercy is the active quality of love, which has "a pitiful property." It expresses the tender love of divine motherhood. The work of mercy is protecting, enduring, vivifying, and healing, responding to the condition of sin that caused a rift between substance and sensuality. Mercy is perpetually embedded in love; its source is love and its work is to keep us in love. Ultimately mercy is "all love in love." In mercy Christ restores us through his Passion, death, and resurrection and *ones* our sensual nature to our substance.

Julian also pictures human beings in relationship with the mother of mercy as being like a crying child hurt from falling over:

> The mother may sometimes suffer the child to fall and to be distressed in various ways, for its own benefit, but she can never suffer any kind of peril to come to her child, because of her love. And though our earthly mother may suffer her child to perish, our heavenly Mother Jesus may never suffer us who are his children to perish, for he is almighty, all wisdom and all love, and so is none but he, blessed may he be (14:61.300-301).

The picture conveys a tension between security and abandonment. Though it seems on a human level that the fallen child, like the fallen servant in the parable, could perish, the heavenly mother will never allow that to happen. Julian seems to try to solve the tension between human freedom and response to grace by suggesting that human beings need to take initiative when God reveals the need for grace. At the same time, however, there is a strange innocence about the child, who seems incapable of committing serious sin. Moreover, she places no emphasis on the readiness of the child, its preparation for grace, or moral responsibility. Leaving the problem of human freedom and capacity for denial of the mother's love unresolved, Julian creates a picture of a distressed child running to its mother and crying for help. From one perspective the idea of mother Jesus who is almighty, all wisdom, and all love does not limit human freedom by preventing human beings from experiencing pain and distress caused by their choice to sin. Nevertheless the mother, always in control, offers a free and unmerited gift. In the tradition that sin is necessary, human wretchedness becomes a *felix culpa* because the mother transforms suffering children through this experience of frailty. The scene encourages an attitude of trust:

> But often when our falling and our wretchedness are shown to us, we are so much afraid and so greatly ashamed of ourselves that we scarcely know where we can put ourselves. But then our courteous Mother does not wish us to flee away, for nothing would be less pleasing to him; but he then wants us to behave like a child. For when it is distressed and frightened, it runs quickly to its mother; and if it can do no more, it calls to the mother for help with all its might. So he wants us to act as a meek child, saying: My kind Mother, my gracious Mother, my beloved Mother, have mercy on me (14:61.301).

When we see our wretchedness clearly by the sweet light of grace and feel shame and disgrace the merciful mother wishes that we take on the condition of a child and flee to the arms of the mother, trusting in tender love and asking the mother to have mercy. Always consistent in love, the heavenly Mother gradually enables human beings to mature or *increase*, though often they make mistakes and feel reproach. Instead of a withdrawal of motherly tenderness and love, sinners receive more virtue and grace. In spite of sin, the Mother of mercy and grace ceaselessly works in human sensuality. This presence of mercy and grace in mother Christ, enabling us to see our wretchedness and ask for forgiveness, places mercy and grace in the midst of human sinfulness. When we encounter mother Christ in our sinfulness we encounter a spiritual birth in our sensuality that heals us of sin and guilt until we become one with our substance. Through the careful responsive nurturing of mother Christ we experience the sanctifying and divinizing effect of grace. Paradoxically then, rather than being wretched, childhood is a holy state:

> And I understood no greater stature in this life than childhood, with its feebleness and lack of power and intelligence, until the time that our

gracious Mother has brought us up into our Father's bliss. And there it will truly be made known to us what he means in the sweet words when he says: All will be well and you will see it yourself, that every kind of thing will be well. And then will the bliss of our motherhood in Christ be to begin anew in the joys of our Father, God, which new beginning will last, newly beginning without end (14:63.305).

There is no higher state in this life than childhood. In the feebleness and failing of our childhood we come to know that "all shall be well." The response of mother Christ to our wretchedness means that we will see ourselves, in our personal lives, that "all manner of things shall be well." The motherhood of Christ creates a new beginning or "making again" in the joy of God that will last eternally.

Through *beholding* the motherhood in God assuming our *kind* and becoming the mother of grace Julian extends the christological dimension of her soteriology of *oneing*. We are one with Christ our mother of *kind* and are drawn into a relationship of further *oneing* through the work of mercy and grace. Within human nature mercy and grace work to respond to the effects of sin, transforming the experience of feebleness and failing in childhood into an experience of grace.

Mother of Working

The third *beholding* that Julian distinguishes is the "motherhood in working," which informs the other two *beholdings* by describing how grace continues the work of *oneing*. "Working," we recall, designates the action of sharing ecstatic love within the Trinity. The working of grace brings to completion what human beings are by nature. The predominant task of the working of grace is to return us to God, to enable the *reditus* to come to fulfilment. Through grace "everything is penetrated, in length and in breadth, in height and in depth without end; and it is all one love." The penetration of grace occurs personally in a bodily and spiritual sense and communally through the presence of mother Christ in the sacraments, and in "Holy Church."

Julian explains how the mother of mercy and grace works to return us to God:

> I should say a little more about this penetration, as I understood our Lord to mean: How we are brought back *[again]* by the motherhood of mercy and grace into our natural place, in which we were created by the motherhood of love, a mother's love which never leaves us (14:60.297).

The phrase "I understood our Lord to mean" gives weight to Julian's interpretation, since it indicates that she is stating what she believes Christ wishes to communicate. Explicit theological interpretation of the following phrase is complicated, however, by inconsistencies in the Paris and Sloane 1 manuscripts. The Paris manuscript identifies this work as "how that we be brought again."[11] Sloane 1 reads "how that we be *[bowte agen]*."[12] The Paris text conveys a sense of human beings returning to their natural place *oned* in our kindly mother. The Sloane 1 text in contrast draws on the soteriological concept of "buying back." Although Julian describes redemption as "buying again" in the Paris manuscript, it is more to qualify the significance of *knitting* and *oneing*.[13] "Buying" does not become a major concept in the soteriology of the Paris text.[14] In contrast, the Sloane 1 text's emphasis on "buying again" draws on Anselm's theory of redemption, which stresses the need for Christ to buy or pay a price to redeem humanity. I suggest that the Paris text, "we are brought again by the motherhood of mercy and grace," is more consistent with the image of a mother bearing or nurturing a child. Nevertheless, even if we accept "bought again" as Julian's original phrase, both "brought again" and "bought again" convey a salvific sense of the constant presence of grace, penetrating every aspect of human existence until human beings return to their home in Christ.

The result of the sharing of grace is to return humanity to our *kindly* place, our natural home in Christ. We are brought to birth so that we may return to our home in Christ both physically and spiritually: "For though it may be so that our bodily bringing to birth is only little, humble and simple in comparison with our spiritual bringing to birth, still it is he who does it in the creatures by whom it is done" (14:60.299). Our "bodily bringing to birth" must be considered in light of Julian's

[11] In Middle English *brought* means to come from, into, out of, to a state or condition, to cause to become (*NSOED* 284).

[12] lx:2480.123. *Bought* includes connotations of paying a price for something. It is noteworthy that John Skinner has translated *bowte* as brought in *Julian of Norwich: A Revelation of Love. Newly translated from Middle English* (Evesham: Arthur James, 1996) 120; cf. *NSOED* 309. Georgia Ronan Crampton, ed., *The Shewings of Julian of Norwich* (Kalamazoo: Medieval Institute Publications, 1994) 213, translates *bowte* as "bought, purchased, redeemed." It is noteworthy however that Grace Warrack, *Revelations of Divine Love Recorded by Julian Anchoress at Norwich Anno Domini, 1373* (London: Methuen & Company, 1901) 149, translates *how that we be bowte agen* as "how that we be brought again."

[13] See 14:53.283.

[14] See Ritamary Bradley, "Julian of Norwich: Everyone's Mystic," in William Pollard and Robert Boenig, eds., *Mysticism and Spirituality in Medieval England* (Cambridge: D. S. Brewer, 1997) 139–58, at 145–46.

anthropology, which emphasizes the importance of the whole human person, substance and sensuality becoming one in Christ. Christ's work involves our "bodily bringing to birth" or the *oneing* of our sensuality, the more bodily aspect of our existence, into its natural home in Christ. Julian then portrays the "spiritual bringing to birth" in some detail:

> . . . in our spiritual bringing to birth he uses more tenderness, without any comparison, in protecting us. By so much as our soul is more precious [*pryce*] in his sight, he kindles our understanding, he prepares our ways, he eases our conscience, he comforts our soul, he illumines our heart and gives us partial knowledge and love of his blessed divinity, with gracious memory of his sweet humanity and his blessed Passion, with courteous wonder over his great surpassing goodness, and makes us to love everything which he loves for love of him, and to be well satisfied [*apayde*] with him and with all his works (14:61.299-300).

Spiritual bringing to birth deepens our participation in the being of God. Distinguished by tenderness, it is "keeping" that involves Christ's "gracious touch": "when we fall, quickly he raises us up with his loving embrace and his gracious touch. And when we are strengthened by his sweet working, then we willingly choose him by his grace, that we shall be his servants and his lovers, constantly and forever" (14:61.299-300). "Touching," we recall, describes the physical and spiritual engagement between God and humanity, the common ground where understanding can be deepened. Describing it as a "sweet working" suggests that Christ's involvement with us is delightful. He touches every aspect of our being, our understanding, our actions, our conscience, our soul, and our heart. This "gracious touching" gives us "partial knowledge and love" of Christ's divinity and a "gracious memory" of his humanity. Ultimately the work of "bringing to birth" makes us "love everything that Christ loves for love of him." When we fall he graciously raises us and strengthens us until we willfully choose Christ. Thus grace is not something we can earn. Grace is always present and active within us. Furthermore, grace is not something that helps us act well where our acting is our own. Rather the presence of grace means that God is involved in all that we do. Grace is Christ's work within us that enables us to be in harmony with our Christ-like nature, to align ourselves with Christ, to choose freely to fulfill our natural potential to be one in our natural place in mother Christ.

It is noteworthy that Julian integrates the language of payment in her reference to grace. "Our soul is of more precious [*pryce*] in his sight. Again she uses this imagery in her own way. "Price" alludes to levels of soteriological meaning. In Middle English *price* designates a sum of money or goods for which a thing may be bought or sold. It can also designate value, worth, honorableness, or virtue.[15] Associated with *prize*, it can represent a reward as a symbol of victory in a contest or competition.[16] Also related to *praise*, it can be the expression of adulation and the ascription of glory as an act of worship.[17] The translation *precious* conveys something of this meaning. In terms of other images in the *Showings*, however, *price* links with the final scene in the parable of the lord and the servant where humankind is described as Christ's crown and his reward. This word emphasizes what inestimable value humankind has for Christ. Julian's ability to give the language of satisfaction her own meaning continues when she points out that Christ's bringing to birth is directed at humanity, which is "to be well *apayde* with him and with all his works." The language reinforces Christ's words on the cross: "If you are *apayde*, I am *apayde*" (9:22.216). Salvation revealed on the cross and through Christ's work as mother is a mutual exchange between Christ and humanity. Therefore through Christ's identity as mother and his work as mother humanity finds pleasure or peace and is drawn into eschatological glory.

Julian's imagery, which describes the motherhood of *kind*, the motherhood of grace, and the motherhood of working, is extravagant. It specifically links nature and grace to the *oneing* that occurs between Christ and humanity. The three *beholdings* reinforce the identity between Christ and humanity that Julian distinguished in the parable of the lord and the servant. Julian pushes the distinction between the otherness of Christ and the working of grace so far that the differentiation between Christ and humanity is almost dissolved. We may criticize Julian's christology for its inability to maintain the distinction between who Christ is and the divinization of humanity that occurs through Christ. There seems to be no room for human resistance or even rebellion against the process of *oneing* that occurs through Christ. On the opposite side, however, this christology negates any concept of God as not intimately involved in human experience. The principle that Christ, the deep wisdom of the Trinity our mother, is mother of *kind*, mother of grace, and mother in working reinforces hope. It describes how the *exitus reditus* pattern is continuous. God loves humanity into existence, joins us in the Incarnation, surrounds us with love, and therefore grace, to consummate and culminate what was already set in motion in and through the gift of creation.

---

[15] *NSOED* 2349–2350.
[16] Ibid. 2360.
[17] Ibid. 2319.

III. MOTHER CHRIST IN MOTHER CHURCH

This salvific *increasing* through Christ has a specific locus in the Church. Mother Christ continues to be present and active in the Church through the sacraments:

> The mother can give her child to suck of her milk, but our precious Mother Jesus can feed us with himself, and does, most courteously and most tenderly, with the blessed sacrament, which is the precious food of true life; and with all the sweet sacraments he sustains us most mercifully and graciously, and so he meant in these blessed words, where he said: I am he whom Holy Church preaches and teaches to you. That is to say: All the health and the life of the sacraments, all the power and the grace of my word, all the goodness which is ordained in Holy Church for you, I am he (14:60.298).

Though Julian does not develop an extensive sacramental theology, the importance of the sacraments seems to be something she takes for granted in the text.[18] Earlier in Chapter 57 she refers to the seven sacraments: "in our faith come the seven sacraments, one following another in the order God has ordained them in for us" (14:57.292). In referring to Christ as mother she singles out "the blessed sacrament" (Eucharist) as the locale of the ongoing presence of Christ as mother in the Church.[19] She creates a picture of a Mother feeding a child at her breast and presents a comparison between the nourishment of breast milk and the food that mother Jesus feeds us, which is "precious food of true life." This meal that Jesus shares expresses the present reality of spiritual nourishment and the future hope of the feasting experienced in the beatific vision. In contrast to earthly mothers, Jesus "feeds us with himself" and we become one body with Christ. While this passage gives no indication that Julian is referring to communion under both species, earlier in the text she remarks: "We pray to God for his holy flesh and for his precious blood" (1:6.185). In this passage she makes the point that in feeding us with himself Christ becomes the life and salvation of human beings. The image places Christ at the center of the sacramental life of the Church.

---

[18] This contrasts with the emphasis on the Eucharist in European mystics of the same period. See André Vauchez, "Eucharistic Devotion and Mystical Union in Late-Medieval Female Saints," in idem, *The Laity in the Middle Ages: Religious Beliefs and Devotional Practices,* edited by Daniel E. Bornstein; translated by Margery J. Schneider (Notre Dame: University of Notre Dame Press, 1993) 237–42.

[19] *Ancrene Wisse* advises the anchoress "to take communion as often as our lay-brothers do, fifteen times in twelve months." It suggests suitable feast days. *AW* 199.

In one sense Julian's description of being fed by the blessed sacrament emphasizes personal salvation enabled by the Eucharist. But her direct association of the sacrament with "Holy Church" suggests that it is not just individuals who are nourished by Christ, but the entire body of the Church. Her threefold statement, which integrates "the health and the life of the sacraments, the power and the grace of my word" and "the goodness which is ordained in Holy Church for you," emphasizes the relationship between the sacraments, Christ's word, and the Church. Julian maintains a profound identification between Christ and the Church as she has made perfectly clear earlier in both the short and long texts:

> God showed the very great delight that he has in all men and women who accept, firmly and wisely, the preaching and teaching of Holy Church, for he is that Holy Church. He is the foundation, he is the substance, he is the teacher, he is the end, he is the reward for which every loving soul labors; and this is known and will be known to every soul to whom the Holy Spirit declares this (13:34.235-236).

We note how "I am he whom Holy Church preaches and teaches to you" (12:26.223) summarizes Julian's statement that Christ is the foundation, substance, teacher, end, and reward. Because the Church is grounded in the substance of Christ, the body of Christ, Christ's labor for salvation is worked out in the Church. Thus the motherhood of Christ ontologically extends to "our mother Holy Church":

> . . . he wants us to commit ourselves fervently to the faith of Holy Church, and find there our beloved Mother in consolation and true understanding, with all the company of the blessed [all the blessed common]. For one single person may often be broken, as it seems to him, but the entire body of Holy Church was never broken, nor ever will be without end. And therefore it is a certain thing, and good and gracious to will, meekly and fervently, to be fastened and united [oned] to our mother Holy Church, who is Christ Jesus (14:61.301-302).

The Church, ontologically grounded in Christ, now carries out Christ's office of motherhood toward humanity. In the Church the faithful can find Christ "our beloved Mother in consolation and true understanding." Julian's image of the Church as *all the blessed common,* translated as "company of the blessed," is an inclusive term that creates a sense of members of the Church in blessed communion with the Trinity and in a shared relationship with each other. The image may draw on the idea of a common, the area of land held jointly by all members of a community. In this sense it emphasizes the sharing of all persons and

things, the sharing of ground that gives life and nourishes human beings. Though it could be argued that *common* refers to the common,
ordinary people, Julian uses the phrase *all the blessed common* in the context of describing "the entire *[hole]* body of Holy Church." The qualifying terms *all* and *blessed* emphasize the *hole body* and the sacredness
of this body. Furthermore, *all the blessed common* resonates with her
other term, *even Christians* (1:8.319), which accentuates equality and
connectedness within the communion of believers.

In a time of much upheaval in the Church it is remarkable that
Julian's only allusion to official Church office is her reference to the
clerical person, possibly a secular priest,[20] who brings the crucifix to her
bedside when she is ill. She identifies him as *the parson, my curette*
(ii:208) in the short text, and as *my curate* (1:3.290) in the long text, and
as a *religious person* (xxi:266; 16:66.632) who comes later on the same
day to ask how she is. There is no mention of Church hierarchy or dis-
cord in the Church. The only inkling she gives about dissension in the
Church is her saying "one single person may often be broken," which
she passes over quickly. Ultimately she believes that the whole body of
holy Church, which is Christ's body, will never be broken.

Julian's ecclesiology is intensely christocentric. Significantly, the
union between Christ and the Church does not occur *through* Christ or
in Christ. The Church *is* Christ. There is a fundamental ontological
identity between Christ and the Church:

> Here we can see that we are all bound to God by nature *[kind]*, and we
> are bound to God by grace. Here we can see that we do not need to seek
> far afield so as to know various natures, but to go to Holy Church, into
> our Mother's breast, that is to say into our own soul, where our Lord
> dwells. And there we should find everything, now in faith and under-
> standing, and afterwards truly, in himself, clearly, in bliss. But let no
> man or woman apply this particularly to himself, because it is not so. It
> is general, because it is our precious Mother Christ (14:62.303).

Within the Church we are bound to God in nature and grace. Julian's
statement that we are "bound" presents another facet of her concept of
oneing. In common Middle English usage *bound* has a variety of associations that emphasize union. *Bound* signifies tying or fastening a knot,
attaching or binding in knitting. *Bound* can mean to encircle. It also
draws on the image of healing, putting dressings on a wound, winding
cloth or bandages on a wound. *Bound* can further denote being united
in marriage. *Bound* can specify a state of being obliged by covenant or

[20] *BSAJN* 208 n. 23.

contract, being compelled by legal authority or subject to legal contract.[21] Therefore within Julian's text it is possible that the image has
links with her concept of *knitting* and *oneing*. The word *bound* acts like a
connecting thread that joins together multiple images of being bound,
such as the image of mutual enclosure between the Trinity and humanity, the idea of Christ healing the wounds of humanity, and the scene
from the parable of the lord and the servant where humanity becomes
the spouse of Christ.

We are bound to God in nature because Christ is the mother of *kind*.
This suggests that it is our natural heritage to be part of the body of
Christ, which is the Church. "Bound to God by grace" draws on Christ's
role as mother of grace and mother of working. This places the presence and working of grace within the Church. From a contemporary
perspective we may criticize Julian because she does not extend the
concept of being bound to Christ in nature and grace beyond the Church.
For Julian in fourteenth-century England, all society is the Church. Yet,
as we have seen, Julian's definition of Church as *all the blessed common*,
Christ's work on the cross for all creation, and her subtle doctrine of
universal salvation, which we will examine in Chapter 9, suggest that
in reality this binding extends beyond the Church. "Bound to God"
describes the unbreakable salvific covenant between the Trinity and
humanity.

Within the Church there is no sense of the priority of nature over
grace or grace over nature. Nature and grace both play significant roles
in salvation. Julian then makes a major leap in her ecclesiology by identifying Holy Church as "our Mother's breast" and equating this with
"our own soul, where our lord dwells." This identity between the body
of mother Christ, the breast of mother Church, and the indwelling of
Christ within individuals creates a dialectic between the indwelling
presence in the individual and the indwelling presence in the communal. Within the Church individuals now experience themselves as
dwelling-places of Christ woven into a mystical whole in the Church
that is also the dwelling-place of Christ.

Julian repeats the idea that we are bound to God by nature and by
grace. The repetition suggests that it is an important concept for her. In
each repetition she develops another aspect of its implications for our
return to our natural home in God. Significantly, being bound to God in
nature and grace affects our condition of sin:

> Here we may see that truly it belongs to our nature *[kind]* to hate sin,
> and truly it belongs to us by grace to hate sin, for nature *[kind]* is all

[21] *NSOED* 229.

good and fair in itself, and grace was sent out to save nature *[kind]* and destroy sin, and bring fair nature *[kind]* back again to the blessed place from which it came, which is God, with more nobility and honor by the powerful operation of grace. For it will be seen before God by all his saints in joy without end that nature *[kind]* has been tried in the fire of tribulation, and that no lack or defect is found in it. So are nature *[kind]* and grace of one accord; for grace is God, as uncreated nature *[kind]* is God. He is two in his manner of operation, and one in love, and neither of these works without the other, and they are not separated (14:63.303-304).

Julian affirms the goodness of nature, since it is natural for human nature to hate sin. Immersed in the fire of tribulation, nature has suffered and found not to be lacking. Grace is sent out to save nature and destroy sin. There is a repetition of the idea of being brought *into* God rather than being bought *for* God ("and bring fair nature *[kind]* back again to the blessed place from which it came, which is God"). *Again* reminds us of Christ's task of *making again*. Julian leaves no doubt about whence we came and where we will return, that is, *God*. In her theology of grace the relationship between Christ our mother of *kind* and our mother of grace means that there is no dichotomy between nature and grace. Nature and grace are not two separate and seldom interacting ways in which divine love shares itself. Mother Christ intrinsically relates nature to grace, "neither of these works without the other." They are never contrasted. Julian avoids two extremes in her theology of grace when she concludes: "so are kind and grace of one accord; for grace is God, as uncreated kind is God." Without equating nature with grace or viewing nature as independent of grace she presents nature and grace as of one accord in Christ. Nature and grace both ensure that what comes from God returns to God.

Julian summarizes her understanding of salvation achieved through nature and grace: "So I understood that all his blessed children who have come out of him by nature *[kind]* ought to be brought back into him by grace" (15:64.305). In the Paris manuscript this occurs at the beginning of Chapter 64, where Julian suspends theologizing and returns to the experience of her illness. In the Sloane 1 manuscript the scribe places the statement at the end of Chapter 63 (LXIII:2658-2660,129) as a summary of all that has gone before. We have seen in the *beholdings* of the motherhood in God that in being the ground of our kind and in taking our kind "all his blessed children have come out of him through nature." Grace also begins to work in the Incarnation when Christ assumes human sensuality so that humanity should "be brought again in to him by grace," or as Sloane 1 states "shall be *bowte ageyn* into Him by grace" (LXIII:2658-2660,129). *Should,* like shall, emphasizes the promise, assurance, and necessity that this return will occur.[22] There is no sense in which grace is something imposed on human nature. Through mother Christ we naturally live the life of grace. Our nature is such that fulfillment of our potential for divine life with Christ naturally comes through grace. In spite of the discrepancy in the manuscripts as to whether grace returns us to Christ or buys our return to Christ, the final result is clear: human beings come from Christ in nature and will return to Christ through grace. Grace fulfills nature. *Oneing* in nature and grace ensure that what comes from God returns to God.

The christology expressed in the idea that "the deep wisdom of the Trinity is our mother" draws Julian's soteriology to a climax. The fluid dialectical unity between Christ's identity as deep wisdom of the Trinity and mother expresses how he undertakes a continuous role of *oneing* through nature and grace. This *oneing* that occurs through the mother of *kind*, the mother of grace, and the mother of working ensures that we will be true to the potential of our nature and return to our source in God. Now Christ continues this task in the Church, so that in the Church we are bound to God by nature and bound to God by grace. Julian summarizes the soteriology expressed in this christology. All children who come out of Christ by nature will return to Christ by grace. The Holy Spirit also plays a dominant role in this return by grace. The continual working of grace in human lives that continues through the Holy Spirit must now be addressed in the next chapter.

[22] See Chapter 8.

Part Five

In the Third We Have Our Fulfillment

. . . in the third we have our fulfilling (14:58.294).

8

Oneing Through the Holy Spirit

. . . he draws us to him by love (14:43.36-37,479).

Central to Julian's soteriology is the belief that human beings originate with God and will return to God. Love from the Godhead, conveyed in Christ through the power of the Holy Spirit, creates a divine
presence in human lives, fulfills human beings, and substantiates
God's salvific promise that "all shall be well." The next two chapters
examine how Julian creates a balance between the transcendence of
God that leads to hope for final fulfillment in the eschaton and the immanence of God that gives her eschatology a this-world orientation. Julian unites these elements of the transcendence and immanence of God
in her pneumatology. She shows how the Holy Spirit is present to us as
"charity given," encloses us in love, renews us, and leads us to God. In
Julian's understanding, fundamental to the partially realized experience of our fulfilling is the Holy Spirit's engagement with us. The Spirit
inspires three manners of knowing: of God, of ourselves in nature and
grace, and of ourselves as against sin. The Holy Spirit orients us to the
presence of divine love and invites a response through prayer.

I. JULIAN'S THEOLOGY OF THE HOLY SPIRIT

Though Julian has difficulty in defining the reality meant by the
Holy Spirit, she grounds her understanding of the Spirit in the triune
symbol of God and identifies the Holy Spirit with the love within the
Trinity. Apart from the title "Our Lord" she never conceives of the
Spirit in concrete symbols.[1] Most consistently she associates the Holy

---

[1] It is noteworthy that in a text that has such concentrated visual imagery there
is no reference to a visual description of the Holy Spirit. There is no mention of the

Spirit with love. In the tradition of the doctrine of appropriations, while maintaining that the Trinity is love she also designates love as appropriate to the Holy Spirit:

> Truth sees God, and wisdom contemplates God, and of these two comes the third, and that is a marvellous delight in God, which is love. Where truth and wisdom are, truly there is love, truly coming from them both, and all are of God's making. For God is endless supreme truth, endless supreme wisdom, endless supreme love uncreated (14:44.256).

The third person of the Trinity is love coming forth from the truth and wisdom of the Godhead. Julian distinguishes this divine love as "the marvelous delight in God." In the tradition of the *filioque* clause, which says that the Holy Spirit proceeds from the Father and the Son,[2] the Holy Spirt is "love, coming of them both." Although this is similar to the Augustinian doctrine whereby the Holy Spirit originates from the love between the Father and the Son,[3] there is a subtle shift in Julian's understanding that emphasizes the one love of the Father, Son, and Holy Spirit. The Spirit is not a passive product of the Father and the Son. Rather, in communion with the Father and the Son, the Spirit dynamically expresses the action of uncreated love. This is the same love we saw in the image of the hazelnut, where God is identified as the maker, the keeper, and the lover.

Julian's identification of the Holy Spirit with love reaches its high point when she concentrates on the activity of the Holy Spirit as *given charity*. We recall that "given charity is virtue, and that is a gift of grace in deeds, in which we love God for himself, and ourselves in God, and all that God loves for God" (16:84.341). *Given charity* is the free gift of the very self of God within human nature, drawing humanity into the life of trinitarian love. The freedom in giving love emphasizes the Spirit's desire to be oriented toward human beings. *Given charity* is the "touching of grace" (14:52.279), which is characterized as "sweet" (14:52.281). It is dynamic, personal, relational, and intimate. *Given charity* is "virtue," the gift of the theological virtues of faith, hope, and love

---

symbol of a dove common in paintings of the Trinity, nor is there a reference to Pentecost or the title of Paraclete.

[2] *Filioque* means literally "and from the Son." This is the traditional Latin formula that designates how the Holy Spirit proceeds from the Father and from the Son as a single principle. It was added to the Nicene-Constantinopolitan creed at the end of the seventh century. See Jaroslav Pelikan, *The Christian Tradition: A History of the Development of Doctrine. The Spirit of Eastern Christendom (600–1700)* (Chicago: University of Chicago Press, 1974) 2:183–98.

[3] See Augustine, *De trinitate* 15.17.27-31,491-96.

that enable human beings to respond to grace. The specific role of the Holy Spirit is to renew these virtues: "For the same virtues which we have received from our substance, given to us in nature by the goodness of God, the same virtues by the operation of mercy are given to us in grace, renewed through the Holy Spirit" (14:57.292). The Spirit takes part in *making again* by revitalizing the theological virtues and spiritually renewing us. The Spirit participates in God's redemptive activity through a personal, free presence that enables us to respond in love. The Spirit is the saving action of love given.

Julian presents the love of the Holy Spirit as ontologically grounded in the uncreated love of the Trinity flowing from both the Father and the Son. The Holy Spirit is also the Spirit of Christ. Though she never directly explains the association between the risen Christ, the sending of the Holy Spirit, Christ the mother of grace, and the working of grace through the Holy Spirit, there is an implicit connection between Christ's motherhood of grace and the grace of the Holy Spirit. Both the grace of Christ and the grace of the Holy Spirit work within us: "for Christ is mercifully working in us, and we are by grace according with him, through the gift and the power of the Holy Spirit. This working makes it so that we are Christ's children and live Christian lives" (14:55.286). There is a flexible interplay between Christ's work and the sanctifying function of the Holy Spirit. Christ mercifully works within us. The Spirit, also working within us, accords us to Christ. Julian does not make a genuine theological distinction between Christ and the Spirit. Their roles are fluid. We see an example of this flexibility expressed in the words "good Lord," which she uses for Christ and also for the Spirit.[4] Christ and the Spirit in communion express two integrated ways in which the Trinity accomplishes salvation through the presence of grace.

Humanity's participation in trinitarian indwelling in the Holy Spirit mirrors our reciprocal enclosure in Christ. We recall the references to the Holy Spirit in Julian's image of trinitarian enclosure: "the high goodness of the Trinity is our Lord, and in him we are enclosed and he in us . . . we are enclosed in the Holy Spirit . . . the Holy Spirit is enclosed in us . . . all goodness, one God, one Lord" (14:54.285).[5] The Holy Spirit is identified with high goodness, all goodness, or the ultimate good. The Holy Spirit is engaged in mutual enclosure, *perichoresis*, a permanent exchange of goodness that freely flows between the persons of the Trinity and creatures. Thus mutual enclosure in the goodness of the Holy Spirit enables us to participate in the goodness of the Trinity.

---

[4] E.g., in 1:5.183 "our good Lord" refers to Christ.

[5] I have highlighted the sections that relate to the Holy Spirit to emphasize the Spirit's role.

Julian further portrays this indwelling presence as endless life dwelling in the soul:

> . . . our good Lord the Holy Spirit, who is endless life dwelling in our soul, protects us most faithfully and produces in the soul a peace, and brings it to ease through grace, and makes it obedient and reconciles it to God. And this is the mercy and the way on which our good Lord constantly leads us, so long as we are in this changeable life (14:48.261-262).

The "good Lord," the Holy Spirit is the permanent presence of divine love within us, the "endless life dwelling in our soul." This indwelling ensures our *oneing* in the eternal life of the Trinity. The endless life of the Spirit keeps us, works a peace in us, creates ease, makes us obedient, and reconciles us to God. The Spirit continues to lead us "as long as we are in this changeable life." Although there is an implicit consequence, that the indwelling presence of the Spirit means that the Spirit is present in the Church, Julian does not give the Spirit a major role in her ecclesiology. As we have seen, she develops an extensive ecclesiology based on the presence of the risen Christ in the Church.

The Holy Spirit plays an ubiquitous role in expressing trinitarian joy in Christ's work for salvation: "This gift and operation is joy to the Father and bliss to the Son and delight [*liking*] to the Holy Spirit, and of everything which is our duty, it is the greatest delight to our Lord that we rejoice in this joy which the blessed Trinity has over our salvation" (14:55.286). Along with the joy of the Father and the bliss of the Son, the Holy Spirit expresses *delight*. This delight in being part of the "blessed Trinity of our salvation" designates the great pleasure the Spirit has in beloved humanity's being saved. The Spirit plays a significant role in enabling humanity to participate in trinitarian joy.

II. In the Third

The primary work of the Holy Spirit is the bestowal of grace to fulfill humanity: "through the rewards and the gifts of grace of the Holy Spirit we are fulfilled" (14:58.295). *Fulfilling* brings the process of *oneing* to completion. We recall Julian's trinitarian formula: "In the first we have our being, and in the second we have our increasing, and in the third we have our fulfilling. The first is nature, the second is mercy, the third is grace" (14:58.294). Without directly defining what she means by the phrase "in the third we have our fulfilling," Julian associates *fulfilling* with the third person of the Trinity, the Holy Spirit. "In the third" further identifies the third moment in creation, which establishes a link between origin in God and ending in God by grounding the present reality in eternity. Another expression of her trinitarian formula presents this linkage between past, present, and future:

> These are our foundations, in which we have our being, our increase and our fulfillment. For in nature we have our life and our being, and in mercy and grace we have our increase and our fulfillment. This is three properties in one goodness, and where one operates all operate in the things which now pertain to us (14:56.290).

What Julian makes clear in this version of the formula is that being, increase, and fulfilling are "three properties in one goodness." Therefore where one works, all work. This suggests that salvation has more than a future dimension. Our being, our increasing, and our fulfilling work "in the things which now pertain to us." Human *fulfilling* is not just a future hope; it exists now.

Julian's use of the word *fulfilling* reinforces this view. When used in a secular context in Middle English, *fulfill* means to provide fully with what is wished for, to satisfy the appetite or desire. It can also designate bringing to an end, finishing, or completing.[6] Julian gives *fulfilling* a specifically theological meaning by associating it with the work of grace ("the third is grace"). There is some interplay between the secular and theological usage, because *fulfilling* refers to the action carried out by the Holy Spirit that completes the *exitus reditus* and satisfies the human desire for God. But Julian's theological meaning is more intricate. Her preference for the participle *fulfilling* creates an interplay between present and future. *Fulfilling* blurs the distinction between historical time and eternity. *Fulfilling* relates to the partially fulfilled and yet to be fulfilled sense of "all shall be well." Like *fulfilling, shall, shalle* or *shal* emphasizes the present and future dimensions of salvation. Unfortunately our contemporary use of "shall" does not adequately represent the Middle English *shal*, which indicates obligation or necessity more than futurity. Alexander Barratt suggests that a more accurate translation would be: "all things must inevitably come to good."[7] Unlike sin, which has no ontological grounding in God, the idea that "all shall be well" is thus ontologically grounded. "All shall be well" expresses God's desire, which is being fulfilled and will inevitably be ful-

---

[6] Lesley Brown, ed., *The New Shorter Oxford English Dictionary on Historical Principles*. 2 vols. (Oxford: Clarendon Press, 1993) (= *NSOED*) 1039.

[7] Alexander Barratt, "How Many Children Had Julian of Norwich?" in Anne Clark Bartlett, ed., with Thomas Bestul, Janet Goebel, and William F. Pollard, *Vox Mystica: Essays on Medieval Mysticism in Honour of Professor Valery M. Lagorio* (Cambridge: D. S. Brewer, 1995) 36. Cf. *NSOED* 2808.

filled. Thus the statement "all shall be well" does not simply reflect hope for the future. "All shall be well" is already partially realized in our present experience of divine love. In some ways all *is* well, for we know the fullness of joy in the resurrected Christ and in the presence of God in all things: "I should not be glad because of any special thing or be greatly distressed by anything at all, for all shall be well; for the fulness of joy is to contemplate God in everything" (13:35.237). Nevertheless, in other ways all is yet to be well. We are blocked to the presence of God in all things and the fullness of joy is not complete. For Julian, then, while *fulfillment* will only be completed in eternal life, *fulfilling* is the ongoing work of the Holy Spirit in us that makes salvation both a realized and at the same time a future reality, as *charity given* progressively *ones* us into God. Theologically, *fulfilling* draws together the partially realized and not yet complete experience of salvation.

Julian's understanding of past and future expressed in the present anticipates the theology of Paul Tillich, with his concept of the "eternal now" where past and future meet in the present. "In this way," Tillich argues, "the eschaton becomes a matter of present experience without losing its futuristic dimension: we stand now in the face of the eternal."[8] For Julian we experience facets of the eternal in the presence of the Holy Spirit in our lives. The experience of our being, our increase, and our fulfilling in the things that now pertain to us give proleptic access to the eternal in the present, a sense of the "eternal now."

In light of Julian's doctrine of the Holy Spirit, which describes the Spirit as *given charity* engaged in both the present and future realization of divine love, I now turn to the three manners of knowing the Spirit inspires.

III. THREE MANNERS OF KNOWING

The Holy Spirit inspires three manners of knowing:

> The first is that we know our Lord God. The second is that we know ourselves, what we are through him in nature *[kind]* and in grace. The third is that we know humbly that our self is opposed to our sin and to our weakness. And all this revelation was made, as I understand it, for these three (16:72.321).

We recall that knowing for Julian is not discursive knowing but knowledge that comes through reason, memory, love, nature, and grace. It is knowing that transpires from seeing with the love of the

---

[8] Paul Tillich, "The Eternal Now" in idem, *The Eternal Now: Sermons* (London: SCM, 1963) 103–111.

Holy Spirit. This emphasis on knowing reinforces the relationship between our experience of God in this life and the God we hope to be one with in the eschaton. Knowing makes us conscious of who we essentially are in God, in nature and grace. Knowing enables us to come to an awareness that the God we meet after death is not a stranger to us but a God we know in this life. T. S. Eliot's *Little Gidding* expresses the significance of the "knowing" that Julian's theology implies:

> and the end of all our exploration
> will be to arrive
> where we started
> and *know* the place for the first time.[9]

Through knowing God, knowing ourselves (what we are by nature and by grace), and knowing ourselves in respect to sin and weakness we become familiar with what is already ours. All our exploration does not lead us to a distant God, but to a God who is at home in human nature. The God with whom we hope to be one is in a sense already one with us. The work of the Holy Spirit is to help us truly know this *oneing*.

Julian emphasizes the reciprocal nature of knowledge of God and knowledge of self. The idea of such a reciprocal relationship[10] is consistent with Julian's theology of *knitting*, which points to a permanent intertwining of humanity with God that is so subtle it would be impossible to separate the two individual threads, her image of mutual enclosure between the Trinity and humanity and her idea that we are bound to God by nature and by grace. Knowledge of self she equates with knowledge of our soul, our life-giving principle, the life of the whole person in a unity of mind and body grounded in God. Our soul is so deeply grounded in God that it would be easier to know God than it would be to know our soul:

---

[9] T. S. Eliot, "Little Gidding," in *The Oxford Book of Twentieth-Century English Verse*, chosen by Philip Larkin (Oxford: Clarendon Press, 1973) 257. Emphasis supplied.

[10] This idea has its source in Plotinian cosmology. It relates to the theology of *exitus reditus*. Andrew Louth, *The Origins of the Christian Mystical Tradition* (Oxford: Clarendon Press, 1981) 40, summarizes this concept: "As the soul ascends to the One, it enters more and more deeply into itself; to find the One is to find itself. Self-knowledge and knowledge of the ultimate are bound up together, if not identified. Ascent to the One is a process of withdrawal into oneself." Augustine gave the relationship between knowledge of self and knowledge of God a Christian focus that Julian seems to have inherited in some way. Julian differs from Augustine, however, for whom this is a predominantly intellectual journey. Julian's anthropology permits a much broader appreciation of the whole person journeying to God.

> . . . it is quicker for us and easier to come to the knowledge of God
> than it is to know our own soul. For our soul is so deeply grounded in
> God and so endlessly treasured that we cannot come to knowledge of it
> until we first have knowledge of God, who is the Creator to whom it is
> united [oned] (14:56.288).

Because we are *oned* in God, knowledge of God and knowledge of ourselves are inherently related. We exist only in God and we can only
truly know ourselves in relation to God:

> . . . we have, naturally from our fullness, to desire wisely and truly to
> know our own soul, through which we are taught to seek it where it is,
> and that is in God. And so by the leading through grace of the Holy
> Spirit we shall know them both in one; whether we are moved to know
> God or our soul, either motion is good and true (14:56.288).

The gracious leading of the Holy Spirit teaches us to recognize the
intrinsic *oneing* that exists between the soul and God [both in one]. Because of this dialectical *oneing*, knowledge of self or knowledge of God
both lead us to God, because in reality our soul is in God. The words
"we shall know them both in one" emphasize the certainty of the soul
and God's being *one*. Mindful of the reciprocal nature of this knowledge, we will now consider the effects of the salvific personal presence
of the Spirit by examining each manner of knowing in turn.

To Know God

Julian's description of the human heart, which she sees through her
spiritual eye, expresses the idea that self-knowledge received through
contemplation of the human heart can lead us to know God. This appreciation of the indwelling presence of Christ must have been an
understanding Julian came to early in her life, as she presents this
image in the short text (xxii:163-164). In concrete imagery that points
beyond itself she portrays Christ in the midst of her heart:

> I saw the soul as wide as if it were an endless citadel, and also as if it
> were a blessed kingdom, and from the state which I saw in it, I under-
> stood that it is a fine city. In the midst of that city sits our Lord Jesus,
> true God and true man, a handsome person and tall, highest bishop,
> most awesome king, most honorable lord. And I saw him splendidly
> clad in honors. He sits erect there in the soul, in peace and rest, and he
> rules and guards heaven and earth and everything that is. The human-
> ity and the divinity sit at rest, the divinity rules and guards, without
> instrument or effort. And the soul is wholly occupied by the blessed

divinity, sovereign power, sovereign wisdom and sovereign goodness. The place which Jesus takes in our soul he will nevermore vacate, for in us is his home of homes and his everlasting dwelling (16:68.312-313).

We note how the imagery echoes John 15:4, "abide in me as I abide in you," to describe the mystery of the human heart that points beyond itself. She envisages the unfathomable depths of the soul in the human heart as an endless citadel. Significantly, however, Julian made the point in an earlier chapter that the soul that is a city is not simply the spiritual dimension of the person, but the whole person's substance and sensuality. Within the heart, which is the reality of the mystery of our whole personhood, she pictures the soul as an exquisite city where Christ makes a home. It is congruent with her emphasis on the whole human person as the city of God that the soul is not only a home for the humanity of Christ but the home for the union of Christ's humanity and divinity. There is no sense in which Christ is alienated from the soul. One with the soul, "he sits in the soul in rest and peace." In the short text Julian defines what Christ's sitting communicates to her: "for the contemplation of this sitting revealed to me the certainty that he will dwell in us forever" (xxii:164). *Beholding* Christ sitting informs Julian that Christ dwells in the human heart forever. "Rest" and "peace" signify how harmonious this dwelling is in the soul. Portrayed as a bishop, king, and lord of handsome stature, Christ is a just ruler of the city exhibiting qualities of power, wisdom, and goodness. Although "power" could suggest an imposing, demanding might that exercises domination and control, wisdom and goodness balance power. The triad of qualities works as a whole and suggests that Christ's power is suffused with wisdom and goodness. The final remark leaves no doubt as to how Christ rules in the soul: "for in us is his home of homes *[homeliest home]* and his everlasting dwelling." *Homeliest home* relates to the idea of *homely loving*. The soul is the proper home for Christ, who dwells there in intimate, tender love. Thus we can see that Julian, from the experience of being led by the Spirit into her own heart, becomes familiar with the soul in the midst of her heart and so comes to know that Christ is at home in the depth of her being.

To Know Ourselves in Nature and Grace

The second manner of knowing that the Holy Spirit leads us to is "that we know our selves, what we are through him in nature *[kind]* and in grace." We recall that Julian sees that, through Christ the deep wisdom of the Trinity our mother, we are bound to God by nature and by grace. Through Christ this has a specific locus in the Church. A further dimension that knowledge of ourselves in nature and grace reveals is the set of theological virtues that the presence of grace generates:

> . . . through grace we are touched by sweet illuminations of the life of the Spirit, through which we are kept in true faith, hope and love, with contrition and devotion and also with contemplation and every kind of true joys and sweet consolations. The blessed demeanor of our Lord God works this in us through grace (16:71.319).

Through grace the Holy Spirit keeps us in the theological virtues. These virtues are gifts of grace, ways we are enlightened and touched by sweet illuminations. Grounded in God, these dispositions orient us to our origin. They enable us to respond to God's *oneing* in us by facilitating our cooperation with the working of grace. Faith, hope, and love (charity) are means by which we come to God with contrition, devotion, and contemplation, and experience "true joys and sweet consolations." Later in the text Julian describes the relationship between these virtues: "So charity keeps us in faith and in hope. And faith and hope lead us in charity, and in the end everything will be charity" (16:84.340). Love, which always has priority, keeps us in faith and hope, and conversely, faith and hope keep us in love. Faith is "a light, coming in nature from our endless day, which is our Father, God; in which light our Mother, Christ, and our good Lord the Holy Spirit lead us in this passing life" (16:83.340). Faith is the divine disposition that enlightens us. Faith enables our Father, God, our Mother, Christ, and our good Lord, the Holy Spirit to lead us to our home in the Trinity. Hope, as we will see in the next chapter, sustains us as we look forward to the joy that is to come. Through knowing that we possess the virtues of faith, hope, and love we become more like and influenced by what we know. These gifts of grace continue to *one* us in love to the Trinity until at the end "everything will be charity."

Moreover, the *oneing* in love that the presence of grace creates binds us in love to God and to one another:

> It is God's will that I see myself as much bound to him in love as if everything which he has done he had done for me; and so should every soul think with regard to his lover. That is to say, the love of God creates in us such a unity that when it is truly seen, no man can separate himself from another (15:65.308-309).

In this insight that Julian adds to the long text she draws out the innate communion of human beings with one another that is the result of their being bound to Christ in love. This unity of individuality and relationality in Christ resembles what Paul Ricoeur has identified in contemporary terms as a "dialectical tie between selfhood and otherness."[11] In this sense union with Christ implies that our selfhood cannot be conceived of in isolation from all humanity. Self-knowledge implies that to exist means to be in relation, to experience a relationality reaching back to our origins in God, in Christ, through the Holy Spirit. Significantly, Julian's comment that no one can be separated from another does not limit this unity to the Church. The words are inclusive. No one can become detached from the binding in love between humanity and the Trinity. For Julian the prompting of the Spirit to know ourselves in nature and grace is an invitation to center on the transcendent mystery at the core of our being. Human nature is the natural dwelling place for God and the condition for the free communication of God's self in the dialogue of grace.

Nevertheless, although the Holy Spirit engages in the task of fulfilling by encouraging a gradual maturing in self-knowledge, full self-knowledge will finally occur in eternal life:

> But we may never fully know ourselves until the last moment, at which moment this passing life and every kind of woe and pain will have an end. And therefore this belongs to our properties, both by nature and by grace to long and desire with all our powers to know ourselves, in which full knowledge we shall truly and clearly know our God in the fullness of endless joy (14:46.258).

Knowledge of our true self in God is a continual process that reaches completion in the fullness of eternal life. Although our knowledge of the wonder and depth of the God-human relationship is limited by human knowing, we can confidently expect every good from God who promises not to fail us. Knowledge of who we are in nature and grace encourages a trusting surrender to God in Christ and hope that "all shall be well."

The indwelling of the Holy Spirit inspires us to know ourselves and to know what we are by nature and grace. Awareness of the self in nature and grace reveals our essential grounding in God, the presence of Christ in our humanity, and our continual conformation to Christ. As we grow in knowledge of who we are in God, the Holy Spirit exposes the dimensions of the self that are not in harmony with divine love.

---

[11] Paul Ricoeur, *Oneself as Another* (Chicago: The University of Chicago Press, 1992) 317.

To Know Ourselves in Sin and Weakness

Julian concentrates on the work of the Holy Spirit in revealing our true nature grounded in God in Christ, yet she never abandons Church teaching that human beings are sinners. Essential to the journey to fulfillment is knowledge of this sinfulness. For Julian, knowledge of the sinfulness of our nature only occurs in a sin-grace dialectic. In focusing on the person in sin she never isolates the sinner from the presence of the Spirit:

> And this is a supreme friendship of our courteous Lord, that he protects us so tenderly whilst we are in our sins; and furthermore he touches us most secretly, and shows us our sins by the sweet light of mercy and grace. But when we see ourselves so foul, then we believe that God may be angry with us because of our sins. Then we are moved by the Holy Spirit through contrition to prayer, and we desire with all our might an amendment of ourselves to appease God's anger, until the time that we find rest of soul and ease of conscience. And then we hope that God has forgiven us our sin; and this is true. And then our courteous Lord shows himself to the soul, happily and with the gladdest countenance, welcoming it as a friend, as if it had been in pain and in prison saying: My dear darling, I am glad that you have come to me in all your woe. I have always been with you, and now you see me loving, and we are made one in bliss (13:40.246).

In this extended reflection we can see how Julian can make seemingly contradictory statements and yet claim that both are true. We are against sin and we are offensive. The discrepancy arises because the lack of union between sensuality and substance leads to failure in acting out of our true self, our substance that is in God. When we cease to act out of our true nature in God, the Holy Spirit "secretly touches" us and enables us to receive the assistance of mercy and grace so that we may recognize our true union with God and align both substance and sensuality with God. In contemporary terms the Holy Spirit, as the source and animating principle of the human spirit, leads us toward life in God. This occurs through increasing the desire that belongs to our substantial nature to be conscious of ourselves in God. Still, the limitations of our humanness, a dimension of our sensuality that houses our "beastly will," the false self, our projections, false identifications, and illusions, all make it impossible to comprehend what our self is in God. From this perspective we see ourselves as estranged, incomplete, and imprisoned by death. Hampered by such limitations, we see only a glimpse of what the true self is by faith. We can know ourselves from a human perspective that only sees the repugnance of our sinful ways, or we can know ourselves from God's perspective. Through the courteous presence of the Holy Spirit, God always regards human beings as friends. Knowledge of ourselves in nature and grace leads us to the truth that our true self is against sin. It enables us to act out of that truth. Self-knowledge frees us from fear and facilitates trust and movement in the direction of God.

Julian knows how difficult it is to live from the divine source within the true self. When the Holy Spirit deepens the awareness of the sight of our sin and the painful falling short of the bliss that we long for by our nature we imagine ourselves as foul. The limitations of our human perception lead us to think that God would be angry with us because of our sin. Julian describes this human perception:

> . . . he thinks himself that he is not fit for anything but as it were to sink into hell, until contrition seizes him by the inspiration of the Holy Spirit and turns bitterness into hope of God's mercy. And then the wounds begin to heal and the soul to revive, restored to the life of Holy Church. The Holy Spirit leads him to confession, willing to reveal his sins, nakedly and truthfully, with great sorrow and great shame that he has so befouled God's fair image (13:39.244).

An awareness of our sinfulness causes us to lose sight of reality and to think that we might sink into an abyss of meaninglessness and into hell. In such times of despair, however, the Holy Spirit touches us and transforms despair into compunction that causes us to ask for forgiveness. The Spirit then leads contrite sinners to align themselves with the customs of the Church in seeking confession. Although in maturing self-knowledge we become only too aware of shame at the human capacity to tarnish the image of God, from God's point of view the friendship between us causes the Holy Spirit to touch us tenderly. Awareness of sin deepens through the "sweet light of mercy and grace."

When we know our sinfulness through the light of grace we know that sin is not powerful enough to erase the love of God. Grace enables us to perceive God's point of view: that we should not burden ourselves with extensive self-reproach and blame. Grace facilitates a gentle, loving acceptance of the human condition and imparts an awareness of the love of God at work in the anguish of our lives:

> Do not accuse yourself that your tribulation and your woe is all your fault; for I do not want you to be immoderately depressed or sorrowful. For I tell you that whatever you do, you will have woe. And therefore I want you wisely to understand the penance which you are continually in, and to accept that meekly for your penance. And then you will truly see that all your life is profitable penance. This place is prison, this life is penance, and he wants us to rejoice in the remedy. The remedy is that

> our Lord is with us, protecting us and leading us into the fulness of joy (16:77.331).

Rather than producing self-recrimination, knowledge of our sinfulness through the touching of the Holy Spirit produces both solidarity and energy. Such knowledge awakens awareness that we are never isolated from the presence of Christ and the ongoing work of the Holy Spirit. The disclosure of sinfulness, enabled by the gentle touch of mercy and grace, empowers us to make a response and seek forgiveness. The contradiction continues. We hope that our sin will be forgiven, and even fear God's wrath. God, however, has already forgiven us. Furthermore, God's love assigns no blame. Through the presence of the Holy Spirit knowledge of our sinfulness reveals the constant presence of divine love. In this encounter we are only treated as a lover would treat a beloved. Mercy and grace are constantly available to forgive sin and give a foretaste of eternal joy.

The Self in Suffering

When the Holy Spirit inspires human beings to live consciously in the presence of God this consciousness heightens an awareness of the shadow of sin that blinds human knowledge of our grounding in God and the presence of Christ within the human heart. This confrontation with our sinful nature also exposes enormous suffering in the human condition, caused by sin. Julian's theology of suffering echoes her insights about sin. As with sin, so also with suffering: we can only interpret either through the light of mercy and grace.

Julian asserts that all humanity inherits suffering through Adam's sin. She emphasizes the negativity of suffering, the great pain it inflicts on human beings, and the way it impairs the human ability to recognize the love of God for what it is. She points out that God does not want suffering; God works tirelessly to eliminate its hold on human nature by being present to human beings in the midst of suffering. On the one hand Julian admits the absurdity and meaninglessness of suffering, and on the other hand she acknowledges its salvific possibilities. She grapples with the reality of suffering in the world not by clarifying its origins but by trying to find some meaningful coexistence with suffering. In an extended reflection Julian tries to describe what life is like as we progressively grow in knowledge of ourselves in God and of ourselves as sinners, and the suffering that ensues. She presents life as a sin/grace dialectic, a medley of well-being and woe:

> . . . we have in us a marvellous mixture of both well-being and woe. We have in us our risen Lord Jesus Christ, and we have in us the

wretchedness and the harm of Adam's falling. Dying, we are constantly protected by Christ, and by the touching of his grace we are raised to true trust in salvation. And we are so afflicted in our feelings by Adam's falling in various ways, by sin and by different pains, and in this we are made dark and so blind that we can scarcely accept any comfort. But in our intention we wait for God, and trust faithfully to have mercy and grace; and this is his own working in us, and in his goodness he opens the eye of our understanding, by which we have sight, sometimes more and sometimes less, according to the ability God gives us to receive. And now we are raised to the one, and now we are permitted to fall to the other. And so that mixture is so marvellous in us that we scarcely know, about ourselves or about our fellow Christians, what condition we are in, these conflicting feelings are so extraordinary, except for each holy act of assent to God which we make when we feel him, truly willing with all our heart to be with him, and with all our soul and with all our might. And then we hate and despise our evil inclinations, and everything which could be an occasion of spiritual and bodily sin. And even so, when this sweetness is hidden, we fall again into blindness, and so in various ways into woe and tribulation. But then this is our comfort, that we know in our faith that by the power of Christ who is our protector we never assent to that, but we complain about it, and endure in pain and in woe, praying until the time that he shows himself again to us. And so we remain in this mixture all the days of our life (14.52.279-280).

In this long passage Julian encompasses the whole of human life as a medley of "well-being and woe." Though distinct, well-being and woe are incapable of complete separation. They exist in creative tension in what a contemporary theologian describes as: "a nondual reality in which both elements are not two but neither are they one."[12] Julian specifies two essential dynamics that exist in the medley. We exist within the tension and clash of opposites, in the misery of Adam's falling and the joy of the risen Christ. When we view life within the context of Adam's falling we become aware of a brokenness in the human condition that produces a rift between substance and sensuality: the capacity for sin, a tendency to despair, and an inability to receive any comfort. In this context woe seems to have equal standing with well-being. Woe has almost ontological status, as it seems to exist within the essence of who we are. Julian never goes quite this far, however, because of the vigor of her theology of grace. In the face of all this

[12] Paul F. Knitter "Christian Salvation: Its Nature and Uniqueness—An Interreligious Proposal," *New Theology Review* 7 (1994) 34–35, adopts this terminology from the Hindu Advaitic tradition to describe a non-dual, not-two-but-not-one relationship between very different dynamics.

woe, grace enables us to be mindful that we are not grounded in woe. We are grounded in divine love. We are the dwelling-place for the risen Christ, who facilitates the working of mercy and grace within us.

Mercy and grace support and comfort us when woe overwhelms us and human perception limits our awareness of God's presence. In times of such perceived abandonment the Holy Spirit opens the eyes of our understanding so that we may recognize God's love at work in our lives gracing, healing, and transforming us in order that we may live out of this love. In Julian's interpretation of life, God does not wish human beings to suffer but, because God is in all things and does all things, God permits both to happen, the falling and the rising, and so we exist in the medley of a sin/grace dialectic. Significantly, however, in this medley sin is not the centrifuge from which all reality finds meaning. The love of God in Christ, brought to completion in the Spirit, is what gives meaning to existence. In the medley of well-being and woe the Holy Spirit plays a dominant role in enabling a meaningful coexistence with the various forms of suffering. The Spirit draws us through suffering into fulfillment with God.

When Julian focuses on an exemplum of suffering that was obviously important to her she begins by stating her theological premise: "So I understood that all his blessed children who have come out of him by nature ought to be brought back into him by grace" (15:64.305). All creatures born of God should return to God through grace. She then presents the confronting exemplum that she describes as a "blissful contemplation" (15:64.307). The qualifier "blissful" emphasizes the glorious nature of this *beholding*. She presents a frightful portrait: "And in this time I saw a body lying on the earth, which appeared oppressive and fearsome and without shape and form, as it were a devouring pit of stinking mud" (15:64.306). The exemplum presents contrasting pictures, one seen from a human perspective and the other from God's perspective. Julian could well have observed just such a scene from her cell window.[13] It presents multiple forms of suffering. The mood is dark, heavy, and fearful. The body lying in "a devouring pit of stinking mud" represents the wound sin causes in humanity, which results in alienation, disorder, and pain in the human condition. The stress on the physicality of the scene, with its description of sights and smells abhorrent to human beings, conveys the immense physical suffering endured by the body. The scene also communicates spiritual suffering. The shapeless, formless, lifeless body evokes a sense of meaninglessness and absurdity. The image is reminiscent of the Passion scene of Christ's dehy-

---

[13] Brant Pelphrey, *Love Was His Meaning: The Theology and Mysticism of Julian of Norwich* (Salzburg: Institüt für Anglistik und Amerikanistik, 1982) 286.

drated body dying, the hazelnut that looked as if it would disintegrate into nothing, and the servant fallen in the dell. The exemplum communicates a profound sense of the life-denying pain that occurs within history.

Paradoxically, however, as Julian focuses on the milieu of suffering in which human beings exist the scene transposes into a sin/grace dialectic, a medley of well-being and woe. No matter how it might seem on the surface, woe never has the power to destroy the love of God at work in every human situation. The conclusion of the exemplum illustrates the hope for human fulfillment in spite of suffering: ". . . suddenly out of this body there sprang a most beautiful creature, a little child, fully shaped and formed, swift and lively and whiter than the lily, which quickly glided up to heaven" (15:64.306). The contrast between the horror of the pit and the fairness of the child is stark. This is transfiguration: not a stinking body, but "a most beautiful creature." Though Julian does not explain the reference to the lily, traditionally the lily is a symbol of light and can also represent purity, innocence, and virginity.[14] Thus the image communicates the idea that in the lifeless, abandoned body we do not find the absence of God but the presence of divine life transforming the human experience of suffering. The scene is not one of the absence of God in suffering but of divine presence in suffering. The exemplum becomes an icon of resurrection.

Julian then expounds the imagery in the exemplum:

> The pit which was the body signifies the great wretchedness of our mortal [*deadly*] flesh; and the smallness of the child signifies the cleanness and purity of our soul. And I thought: In this body there remains none of this child's beauty, and in this child there remains none of the body's foulness. It is most blessed for man to be taken from pain, more than for pain to be taken from man; for if pain be taken from us, it may return. Therefore this is a supreme comfort and a blessed contemplation for a longing soul, that we shall be taken from pain. For in this promise I saw a merciful compassion which our Lord has for us because of our woe, and a courteous promise of a clean deliverance, for he wants us to be comforted in surpassing joy (15:64.306-307).

It is clear to Julian that the fairness of the child does not exist within the rotten flesh of the body and the foulness of the body does not exist within the child. In order to understand what she is saying here it is important that we look carefully at her language, particularly her use of

---

[14] *The Herder Symbol Dictionary: Symbols from Art, Archaeology, Mythology, Literature, and Religion.* Translated by Boris Matthews (Wilmette, Ill.: Chiron Publications, 1986) 120.

"soul" and "flesh." We have noted that both substance and sensuality can be called soul. "Soul" in Julian's vocabulary is life, the life of the whole person in a unity of mind and body grounded in God. It is not the intellectual or spiritual expression of the human being alone but the whole human being, including the body. We see this in the body of the child fully shaped and formed. "Flesh," then, is not the body as such, nor sexuality. The *deadly flesh*, like the *beastly will*, is the aspect of human beings not in harmony with God. Julian uses *deadly flesh* in a Pauline sense of the life-destroying capacity of human beings alienated from God (Rom 8:1-18). Therefore in Julian's interpretative framework the soul is the whole of human nature created by God, grounded in God. The *deadly flesh* is the aspect of human nature that has become alienated from God.

The exemplum, then, is not about a conflict between body and soul, but is deliberately paradoxical. It reconciles the opposites of well-being and woe. The imagery acknowledges the darker side of the world, a world where Christ was brutally crucified and where pain resulting from illness and pain as a consequence of sin conflict with a view that the world is an image of God. Nevertheless, as the image of the hazelnut signifies, this is a world that only exists through the love of God. This exemplum is an icon of hope. It is *a blissful beholding* that teaches that "we shall be taken from pain." The exemplum testifies that, even in a place saturated by the shapeless non-being of evil, human beings will finally be taken from pain and experience fulfillment through the Holy Spirit.

After the exemplum Julian expounds a long teaching about suffering. She gives weight to this teaching by stressing that "it is God's will that we focus our thought on this blissful contemplation *[beholding]*, as often as we can and for as long as we can continue in it with his grace, for to the soul who is led by God, this contemplation is blissful and greatly to God's glory whilst it lasts" (15:64.307). In order to know how to cope in suffering we must focus on this beholding. Julian outlines the perspective on suffering that evolves from the exemplum: ". . . when we fall back into ourselves, through depression and spiritual blindness and our experience of spiritual and bodily pains, because of our frailty, it is God's will that we know that he has not forgotten us" (15:64.307). At this stage, from a contemporary perspective we may feel frustrated by such passivity. We want to align ourselves with the suffering of the dying child and cry out: "We must do something about such destructive suffering." But when we remember Julian's socialization as a woman who chose to be an anchoress we may have more patience with her perspective. Julian accepts the reality that human beings will fail. We will "fall back into ourselves" and experience "spiritual and bodily pain." We will become disempowered through deadly dread. Rather than allow despair to be the power that guides us Julian advocates hope, encouraged by God's promise: "you will never again have pain of any kind, any kind of sickness, any kind of displeasure, any lack of your will, but always joy and bliss without end" (15:64.307). The concluding rhetorical question is confrontational in its ambiguity: "Why then should it have afflicted you to endure for awhile, since it is my will and to my glory?" (15:64.307). In order to understand what Julian is saying we must recall that she never solves the dilemma of why sin and suffering occur. For Julian, although God does not create the non-being of sin that causes suffering, it must be true that God allows suffering, because nothing can transpire outside of the divine perspective:

> It is God's will that we accept his commands and his consolations as generously and as fully as we are able; and he also wants us to accept our tarrying and our sufferings as lightly as we are able, and to count them as nothing. For the more lightly that we accept them, the less importance we ascribe to them because of our love, the less pain shall we experience from them and the more thanks and reward shall we have for them (15:64.307).

Although the added reflection suggests that God wills suffering and suffering brings honor to God the context of the exemplum leaves room for another interpretation. Julian is not saying that suffering brings pleasure to God. Rather, she is presenting another aspect of her theology of divine presence. God allows suffering, and as we saw in the crucified Christ, God through Christ is one with human beings in suffering until all suffering is transformed into honor. It is the transformation of suffering that brings God honor, not suffering itself. It is God's will that we remember the transformation of the child in the exemplum and that we are one with Christ not only in his suffering but in his resurrection. Therefore, in hopeful expectation that all suffering will be transformed into joy, Julian considers that we should hold suffering lightly. "Lightly" in Middle English can mean with agility, nimbly, quickly, promptly, but it can also suggest without depression, cheerfully, merrily, lightheartedly.[15] In the context of Julian's references to suffering, "lightly" describes a disposition of hope. The more we know the truth contained in the exemplum and the more we view suffering through the lens of resurrection, the less pain we will feel, the more thanks and reward we will experience. This gratitude for all of life's

---

[15] *NSOED* 1586.

experiences is not a glorification of suffering. It is a contemplative stance that enables us always to live in openness to the presence of God in well-being and woe. This attitude enables us to see the whole of our lives, well-being and woe, as gift.

When the Holy Spirit inspires human beings to live consciously in the presence of God this consciousness heightens an awareness of the shadow of sin that blinds human knowing of our grounding in God and the presence of grace. Confrontation with our sinful nature exposes the enormous suffering of the human condition caused by sin. Yet knowledge of our sinfulness need not lead to self-recrimination and guilt, for it reveals the unconditional love of God for humanity. Although God does not wish human beings to suffer, God permits woe and well-being, and so we exist in the medley of well-being and woe. Woe, however, does not have equal status with well-being because we know the transformational experience of resurrection. Knowing ourselves in nature and grace, which are essentially opposed to sin and weakness, inspires hope that we will finally be taken from pain and experience fulfillment through the Holy Spirit.

IV. COOPERATION WITH THE WORK OF *ONEING* THROUGH PRAYER

Throughout our lives, as we exist in the medley of well-being and woe, the three manners of knowing are nourished through prayer. While we wait in joyful expectation that all woe will be eliminated in the joy of heaven, the *oneing* presence of the Holy Spirit invites us to participate in God's desire for our fulfilling through prayer. In prayer we become true to our nature, respond to the working of grace, and realize our oneness with Christ and the truth of the conviction that "all shall be well." In prayer past and future meet in the present, and the joy that is to come becomes part of our conscious reality. In prayer we experience something of the eternal in the present. Although much has been written on Julian's teaching about prayer,[16] I will focus on how praying enables us to cooperate with the work of the Holy Spirit in fulfilling us.

---

[16] Cf. Ritamary Bradley, "Julian of Norwich on Prayer," *Analecta Cartusiana* 106 (1983) 136–54; Gloria Durka, *Praying With Julian of Norwich* (Winona, Minn.: St. Mary's Press, 1989); Robert Llewelyn, *With Pity Not Blame. The Spirituality of Julian of Norwich and the Cloud of Unknowing For Today* (3rd ed. London: Darton, Longman and Todd, 1994), published in the United States as *All Shall be Well: The Spirituality of Julian of Norwich for Today* (New York: Paulist, 1985); Paul Molinari, *Julian of Norwich: The Teaching of a Fourteenth Century Mystic* (London: Longmans, Green, 1958); Brant Pelphrey, *Julian of Norwich: Christ our Mother.* Edited by Noel Dermont O'Donoghue. The Way of the Christian Mystics 7 (Wilmington, Del.: Michael Glazier, 1989).

All the revelations are prayer and teach about prayer. Julian's specific teaching on prayer occurs concisely in Chapter 19 of the short text and Chapters 41 to 43 of the long text. She provides three main teachings about prayer:

> The first is with whom and how our prayer originates. He reveals with whom when he says: I am the ground; and he reveals how by his goodness, because he says: First it is my will. As to the second, in what manner and how we should perform our prayers, that is that our will should be turned, rejoicing, into the will of our Lord. And he means this when he says: I make you to wish it. As to the third, it is that we know the fruit and the end of our prayer, which is to be united *[oned]* and like to our Lord in all things (14:42.250-251).

In essence the teachings on prayer communicate how our life is a journey from God to God. Prayer is the living expression of who we are with our being in God, our increasing in the Son, and our fulfillment through the Holy Spirit.

The Origin of Prayer

Prayer originates in us because of who we are in nature and grace. Prayer arises from Christ, the ground of our being : ". . . our Lord is the ground from which our prayer springs, and also because we do not know that it is given to us by grace from his love" (14:42.251). From this Christ-life in us flows an insatiable desire to become totally one with divine love. Prayer nourishes the process of *oneing* that continues until we finally return to the Trinity and all is love. The desire for God that arises from Christ the ground of our being creates a longing for God that continues all our lives. Julian calls this a *kind yearning*,[17] a natural desire that has an intense passion. She describes this yearning for God in language reminiscent of Augustine: "For until I am substantially united to him, I can never have perfect rest or true happiness, until, that is, I am so attached to him that there can be no created thing between my God and me" (1:5.183).[18] This natural desire for God creates a restlessness and sense of incompleteness that encourages us to come before God

> . . . naked, openly and familiarly. For this is the loving yearning of the soul through the touch of the Holy Spirit, from the understanding

---

[17] The translation "loving yearning" misses the connection between *kind* and nature.

[18] Cf. Augustine, *Confessions* 1.1.1.

> which I have in this revelation: God, of your goodness give me your-
> self, for you are enough for me, and I can ask for nothing which is less
> which can pay you full worship (1:5.184).

The touching of the Holy Spirit naturally present to us creates an
insatiable hunger, an emptiness that longs to be filled. This touching
teaches us to know that only God is our fulfillment, only God is enough.
Significantly, this active request to seek deeper communion affects not
only human beings. It creates a mutual experience of pleasure: "the
soul's constant search pleases God greatly" (2:10.195). Seeking gives
mutual pleasure to Christ and to us. It enables us to experience joy and
delight in each other.

Consequently this insatiable desire for God leads us to ask for what
we need. Julian refers to this as the prayer of *beseeking* or beseeching.
The prefix *be* added to *seeking,* literally "about seeking," reinforces the
idea that this prayer, which arises from our origin in Christ, empowers
our natural yearning to be one with God. All that we ask for in beseeching arises from Christ who reassures us: "I am the ground of your
beseeching. First, it is my will that you should have it, and then I make
you to wish it, and then I make you to beseech it" (14:41.248). Beseeching expresses our fundamental stance before God, arising at the inter-
section between our need and God's desire for our well-being.

Beseeching is "a true and gracious, enduring will of the soul,
united *[oned]* and joined *[fastened]* to our Lord's will by the sweet, secret
operation of the Holy Spirit" (14:41.249). Beseeching is grace working
in us, activating our will to be one and like Christ in all things. It is an
intimate communication between friends by which we ask to live in the
presence of God and surrender our lives to God. In Julian's understanding beseeching is not so much asking in order that God will respond, or trying to change the course of events; rather, beseeching
arises from a response God has already given. Petitions in prayer are
the human face of God's hope for us.

The Manner of Prayer

Julian's second teaching about prayer concentrates on how we
should pray. In prayer "our will should be turned, rejoicing, into the
will of our Lord." Thus prayer is our deliberate choice to conform our
will to the will of God. Significantly, this choice occurs in an ambience
of joy. We see an example of this conversion in the prayer of thanksgiving (14:41.250) that emanates from our inner sense of the presence
and continual work of the Spirit. Through thanking we progressively
become one with God:

Thanksgiving is a true inward acknowledgment, we applying ourselves
with great reverence and loving fear and with all our powers to the
work that our Lord moved us to, rejoicing and giving thanks inwardly.
And sometimes the soul is so full of this that it breaks out in words and
says: Good Lord, great thanks, blessed may you be (14:41.250).

Thanking is both an external expression of praise and a deliberate
act of graciously opening the mind and heart to God in loving awe.
When thanking, Julian views everything as grace. She sees God in all
things. She lives her life as a gift from God and looks upon everything
that happens as a manifestation of that gift. Significantly, Julian not
only describes the prayer of thanking in this more traditional sense of
favorable thought; the prayer of thanking continues throughout times
of woe:

And sometimes the heart is dry and feels nothing, or else, by the temptation of our enemy, reason and grace drive the soul to implore our
Lord with words, recounting his blessed Passion and his great goodness. And so the power of our Lord's word enters the soul and enlivens
the heart and it begins by his grace faithful exercise, and makes the soul
to pray most blessedly, and truly to rejoice in our Lord. This is a most
loving thanksgiving in his sight (14:41.250).

The prayer of thanking has a distinctive nuance. Although we may
turn our will to the will of God in peaceful times to express gratitude, it
is another thing to commit to relationship when we confront dryness.
Thanking is not a superficial gratefulness for peaceful times, but an
attitude that enables us to see the whole of our lives, whether in well-
being or in woe, as gift. Thanking includes our attempts to pray when
our hearts feel dry, barren, or nothing at all. Thanking is a contemplative attitude that enables us to be open to the divine presence in well-
being and in woe.

Though the desire for God is grounded within us, and an attitude
of thanking belongs inherently to our nature, Julian knows how difficult it is to remain faithful to this desire in times of suffering and how
easily this desire can become repressed. In one sense, in Julian's theology of prayer the gift of our desire for God inherited from our being in
God and the presence of grace in our lives mean that this orientation
can never be completely abandoned. In another sense, however, she
knows how easily we can become distracted from our life source. In
times when we experience difficulty in our commitment to turn our
wills to the will of God, Julian gives the following words of encouragement:

> Pray wholeheartedly, though it seems to you that this has no savor for you; still it is profitable enough, though you may not feel that. Pray wholeheartedly, though you may feel nothing, though you may see nothing, yes, though you think that you could not, for in dryness and in barrenness, in sickness and in weakness, then is your prayer most pleasing to me, though you think it almost tasteless to you. And so is all your living prayer in my sight (14:41.249).

Julian knows that commitment to prayer involves pain; prayer includes faithful exercise in dryness and barrenness, in sickness and weakness. She offers encouragement: this prayer is most pleasing to God. She implies that prayer in times of dryness even has purgative elements. Prayer confirms our commitment to relationship. It continues the work of *oneing*, drawing us into deeper participation in Christ. Julian's advice to pray wholeheartedly affirms her belief about life: "all our living is prayer."

The Fruit of Prayer: To Be One With God in All Things

The third teaching about prayer is that we know that "the fruit and the end of our prayer is to be one and like our Lord in all things." In this teaching Julian emphasizes that the reason we pray is to be *one* with Christ, or Christ-like. Although prayer includes times of desolation we also have a consoling experience of *oneing* that gives a foretaste of the eternal *oneing* and joy to come. She refers to this as the prayer of *beholding*.

We have seen that *beholding* is an important concept for Julian. It is through *beholding* that she comes to the insights expressed in the *Showings*. In the specific context of prayer she gives a classic definition of her understanding of the prayer of *beholding*: "But when our courteous Lord of his special grace shows himself to our soul, we have what we desire, and then for that time we do not see what more we should pray for, but all our intention and all our powers are wholly directed to contemplating [*beholding*] him" (14:43.254). We note how Julian includes the reader in this experience. It is not the experience of a select few, for *beholding* is our inheritance as followers of Christ. In essence *beholding* is an experience of grace in which Christ shows himself to our soul. *Beholding* involves contemplative seeing. Julian explains:

> . . . this is an exalted and imperceptible prayer; for the whole reason why we pray is to be united [*oned*] into the vision and contemplation of him to whom we pray, wonderfully rejoicing with reverent fear, and with so much sweetness and delight in him that we cannot pray at all except as he moves us at the time (14:43.254).

Beholding is an experience beyond words by which we respond spontaneously to the presence of Christ, become one with Christ, and experience divine love. The fruits of *beholding* are joy, reverent fear, sweetness, and delight.

Julian attempts, by this description of *beholding*, to portray the mystery of divine presence in our lives. Her discernment suggests that the more nearly we approach God the more the sense of the unknowable mystery of divine love abounds. All we can do is savor and delight in God with reverent fear and great sweetness. Then our response is to pray as the love of God permeates our being and stirs us to pray:

> And when we by his special grace behold him plainly, seeing no other, we then necessarily follow him, and he draws us to him by love. For I saw and felt that his wonderful and total goodness fulfills all our powers; and with that I saw that his continual working in every kind of thing is done so divinely, so wisely and so powerfully that it surpasses all our imagining and everything that we can understand or think. And then we can do no more than contemplate him and rejoice, with a great and compelling desire to be wholly united into him, and attend to his motion and rejoice in his love and delight in his goodness (14:43.254-255).

In prayer the Holy Spirit draws us into the presence of divine love. We become more attentive, turning all our attention to the unlimited reality of Christ. We enjoy and delight in Christ, progressively becoming one with him as he draws us into himself in love, and through the experience of his presence becoming Christ-like. Beholding Christ enables us to surrender trustingly to the mystery of God's plan for salvation and to our own unique call to union with God in Christ through the Holy Spirit.

Consequently, prayer makes the hope for fulfillment a reality: ". . . prayer is a right understanding of that fulness of joy which is to come, with true longing and trust" (14:42.252). Prayer reveals the interrelationship between yearning and trusting: the more we trust in God the more we yearn to become fully one with God. "The savoring or seeing of our bliss, to which we are ordained, by nature makes us to long; true understanding and love, with a sweet recollection in our savor, by grace makes us to trust" (14:42.252). Prayer gives a sense of the eternal in the present, a glimpse of the transcendent mystery, and knowledge that the limitless depths of that mystery are forever being revealed. Ultimately prayer imparts understanding of the fullness of joy.

Julian's pneumatology plays a significant role in distinguishing how salvation is partially realized in the current experience of our fulfilling. It shows how eschatology is grounded in our experience of God in this world. The Holy Spirit, *given charity*, shares divine love through the presence of grace in human lives. The Holy Spirit encloses us in goodness and is reciprocally enclosed in us. The Holy Spirit animates us to enjoy the blessed Trinity of our salvation. Julian demonstrates how inspiring knowledge of God, knowledge of ourselves in nature and grace, and knowledge that our true nature is against sin and weakness enable us to appreciate the medley of well-being and woe. Ultimately, no matter what our experience of woe, we exist in God in nature and grace, drawn into the transformational experience of *oneing*. We experience this *oneing* partially now and look forward to its completion in eternal life. Knowledge of who God is and who we are in this relationship encourages hope that "all is well" and "shall be well." The present reality of this *fulfilling*, brought to consciousness in prayer, gives us strength for our living. It imparts a foretaste of the final joy that is to come in the future. Therefore for Julian hope for eternal *oneing* in God is not based on idle speculation about an unknowable future. Hope for the fullness of salvation flows from grace we experience in the present. She attests to an underlying unity between living and dying and dying and living. We die into God the way we live in God. This leads us to the future dimension of Julian's soteriology, hope for heaven.

9

Oneing in the Eschaton

And there shall we see God face to face, homely and wholly (14:43.255).

Julian presents a theology of hope that has a strong eschatological focus. She expresses this hope as longing for the joy that is to come. All shall finally be well when the Trinity and creatures are one in the eschaton. Nevertheless, each aspect of Julian's soteriology we have examined shows that salvation is not simply a future hope. It is grounded in our being one with God in creation, increased in *oneing* through the cross and the work of Christ as servant, wisdom, and mother, and brought to fulfillment through the work of the Holy Spirit. Julian's eschatology expresses what Karl Rahner observed in this century: "there is a hope that there will be a transposition of present experience of salvation from a mode of beginning into a mode of consummation,"[1] or, as we have said, that the *exitus reditus* will reach fulfillment. We should now examine Julian's eschatology in relation to her soteriology. Although Julian refers to the eschaton as an unknowable reality she voices hope in her famous phrase "all shall be well." This expression of hope rests on a belief in the universal salvific will of God. Julian uses vibrant imagery to describe what it will be like in the eschaton when hope in the joy that is to come reaches fulfillment in the beatific vision.

I. An Unknowable Reality

Julian is not alone in asserting that ultimately the whole realm of eternity is an empirically unknowable reality, a mystery yet to be revealed: "There is a deed which the blessed Trinity will perform on the

---

[1] Karl Rahner, *Foundations of Christian Faith: An Introduction to the Idea of Christianity* (London: Darton, Longman and Todd, 1978) 431.

last day, as I see it, and what the deed will be and how it will be performed is unknown to every creature who is inferior to Christ, and it will be until the deed is done" (13:32.232). Although the deed the blessed Trinity will perform at the end of time is unknowable, it is possible to predict a hopeful future through extrapolation from what we have already experienced. Drawing on her experience of grace, Julian responds to the question of death with hope because she connects our future in God with our present experience of grace. Therefore for Julian hope for eternal *oneing* is not based on speculation about an unknowable future. Hope for the fullness of salvation flows from the grace we experience in the present. She attests to an underlying unity between living and dying and dying and living. We die into God the way we live in God. Thus life in God after death is a fulfillment of this life, a completion.

II. All Shall Be Well

Julian points the way to fulfillment in the eschaton through her famous words "all shall be well." At the end of time as we understand it the blessed will no longer ask the central question of the *Showings:* "Ah, good Lord, how could all things be well, because of the great harm which has come through sin to your creatures?" (13:29.227). We will see with our own eyes the fulfillment of the promise: "it is well" (16:85.341). This affirmation of hope, which identifies the eschaton as the fulfillment of God's intention for the salvation of the world, flows from the deepest level of our beings, from our ontological union with God in nature and grace and our awareness of the constant working of grace in our lives.

Julian never gives a clear description of what it will be like when all is well. The ineffable nature of her language is probably deliberate, as the human experience of well-being in the eschaton can never be fully articulated. The ramifications of the expression "all shall be well" belong to the category Karl Rahner identifies as primordial words:

> Primordial words always remain like the brightly lit house which one must leave behind, "even when it is night." They are always as though filled with the soft music of infinity. No matter what it is they speak of, they always whisper something about everything. If one tries to pace out their boundary, one always becomes lost in the infinite. They are the children of God, who possess something of the luminous darkness of their Father.[2]

---

[2] Karl Rahner, *The Content of Faith: The Best of Karl Rahner's Theological Writings,* edited by Karl Lehmann and Albert Raffelt; translated by Harvey D. Egan (New York: Crossroad, 1993) 161.

The melodic refrain "all shall be well" seizes us before we grasp its meaning. It etches itself in the memory and suggests something about the present and something about eternal life in God. In trying to examine more carefully what Julian means by these words we confront human limitations in describing the infinite. Nevertheless, it is worth trying to probe the various nuances Julian gives to her famous phrase "all shall be well."

There is no doubt that Julian is sensitive to "all the blessed common"; nevertheless, her assurance that "all shall be well" makes her concerns inclusive:

> On one occasion our good Lord said: Every kind of thing *[all manner of things]* will be well; and on another occasion he said: You will see yourself that every kind of thing *[all manner of things]* will be well. And from these two the soul gained different kinds of understanding (13:32.231).

This vague category, "all manner of things," includes all reality down to the smallest things, as the image of the hazelnut conveys. "All manner of" suggests that salvation extends beyond a personal mysticism to encompass social and cosmic realities. Salvation includes "all manner of things," all that is: not only great things, but little, seemingly insignificant things. Julian outlines two meanings she perceives in "all shall be well" and "you will see yourself that all shall be well":

> One was this: that he wants us to know that he takes heed not only of things which are noble and great, but also of those which are little and small, of humble men and simple, of this man and that man *[to one and to the other]*. And this is what he means when he says: Every kind *[all manner]* of thing will be well. For he wants us to know that the smallest thing will not be forgotten. Another understanding is this: that there are many deeds which in our eyes are so evilly done and lead to such great harms that it seems to us impossible that any good result could ever come of them. And we contemplate this and sorrow and mourn for it so that we cannot rest in the blessed contemplation *[beholding]* of God as we ought to do. And the cause is this: that the reason which we use is now so blind, so abject and so stupid that we cannot recognize God's exalted, wonderful wisdom, or the power and the goodness of the blessed Trinity. And this is his intention when he says: You will see yourself that every kind *[all manner]* of thing will be well, as if he said: Accept it now in faith and trust, and in the very end you will see truly, in fullness of joy. And so in the same five words said before: I may make all things well, I understand a powerful comfort from all the works of our Lord God which are still to come (13:32.231-232).

Although Edmund Colledge and James Walsh translate *to one and to the other* as "this man and that man," the phrase really refers to *things*.

Things conveys a sense of the totality of creation. In the second aspect of her interpretation of "all manner of things shall be well" Julian isolates the problem of evil. Although there are many evil deeds that make it impossible to understand how all could be well from a human point of view, "all manner of things shall be well" means that good will come out of even the most evil deeds. The wisdom, might, and goodness of the Trinity will make this so in the time to come. Consequently, "all manner of things" embraces all of creation, even evil.

Well conveys a sense of a dynamic synthesis of all the qualities that give and enhance life. It characterizes a quality and fullness of life, depth, richness of being, health and wholeness, peace, happiness, joy and bliss.[3] In Middle English it conveys a meaning, lost today, of being on terms of intimate friendship or familiarity with a woman.[4] Thus *well* embraces the intimacy of *homely* loving, the experience of *oneing*. Related to Julian's use of the word *well* is her concept of righteousness:

> Righteousness is that which is so good that it cannot be better than it is, for God himself is true righteousness, and all his works are righteously performed, as they are ordained from eternity by his exalted power, his exalted wisdom, his exalted goodness. And what he has ordained for the best he constantly brings to pass in the same way, and directs to the same end. And he is always fully pleased with himself and with all his works (13:35.237).

Righteousness comes from the being of God, flowing from God's might, wisdom, and goodness. It expresses everything that is just, wise, good, genuine, legitimate, desirable, or favorable. Since righteousness by its very nature gives itself and communicates itself, this good will be the end and finality of all things. When all God's works are completed righteously, what God planned in the beginning will be in a state of perfection, reflecting the perfect goodness of God. For Julian, because righteousness arises from God's being it can never be better than it is. When "all is well" everything will be righteous, that is, it will reflect the perfect goodness of God.

III. UNIVERSAL SALVATION

Since "all shall be well" indicates the inclusive nature of God's desire for human well-being when all that God ordained for creation will

---

[3] Note that "will," meaning "pleasure, delight, and joy" is at the root of "well." Lesley Brown, ed., *The New Shorter Oxford English Dictionary on Historical Principles.* 2 vols. (Oxford: Clarendon Press, 1993) (= NSOED) 3686.

[4] *NSOED* 3654.

be righteous, we can situate Julian's soteriology in relation to the concept of *apokatastasis* or universal salvation.[5] The notion of *apokatastasis* is grounded in a belief that the reality of human freedom to commit sin is never powerful enough to overcome the salvific will of God. Yet, as we have seen, Julian does take sin seriously. Her conception of universal salvation is not a pure doctrine of *apokatastasis* that naïvely ignores the reality of sin, trivializes human freedom, and devalues the human struggle to live a good life. On the contrary, for Julian human beings constantly struggle to orient themselves to God in the medley of weal and woe. Nevertheless, human freedom can never be isolated from grace; it is always modified by grace, until the deepest longing of the human heart for union with God and God's longing for union with us converge. In a time when fear of damnation flourished, Julian shifts emphasis away from God as the fierce arbitrator of salvation or damnation toward seeing God as acting to make all things well.

The Work of the Trinity

When Julian first records the expression "all shall be well" in her text it is Christ who communicates this promise of hope. As the *showings* proceed, however, Julian highlights the common operation of the Trinity in making all things well:

> I may make all things well, and I can make all things well, and I shall make all things well, and I will make all things well, and you will see yourself that every kind of thing will be well. When he says "I may," I understand this to apply to the Father; and when he says "I can," I understand it for the Son; and when he says "I will," I understand it for the Holy Spirit; and when he says "I shall," I understand it for the unity of the blessed Trinity, three persons and one truth; and when he says "You will see yourself," I understand it for the union of all men who will be saved in the blessed Trinity (13:31.229).

[5] *Apokatastasis* or universal salvation is the restoration of all creation at the end of time, and its most famous exponent was Origen. It was strongly attacked by Augustine. The doctrine holds that ultimately all free moral creatures, angels, human beings, and even devils will share in eternal happiness and salvation. Although *apokatastasis* was condemned by the provincial Council of Constantinople in 543 it was still accepted to a lesser degree by some of the Church Fathers. In more recent times Friedrich Schleiermacher developed a version of this idea of universalism. Cf. John R. Sachs, s.j., "Apocatastasis in Patristic Theology," *Theological Studies* 54 (1993) 617–40. Julian's universalism is not a pure doctrine of *apokatastasis* because she never discounts Church teaching on the possibility of damnation for sinners and she considers the devil to be eternally damned.

Although it is Christ who discloses the promise of eternal well-being by saying "I may make all things well," the repetition of the word "I" creates a litany with other melodic locutions such as "see, I am God" and "I am he, I am he." "I" not only expresses the essence of Christ and the significant mediating role of Christ in drawing humanity into the eternal well-being of the Trinity; it communicates a promise that Christ will be with us always. Furthermore, the repetition of "I" in relation to each person of the Trinity conveys the reciprocal presence of the divine persons to one another. Julian reformulates the locution within the context of the union between past, present, and future and distinguishes the participation of each person of the Trinity in making all things well. She illustrates how all things are well already because of the continuing action of the Trinity. In another sense all things shall be well because of the faithfulness of the work of the Trinity. She explains that "I may" reveals the involvement of the Father.[6] "I can" designates the role of the Son.[7] "I will" identifies the presence of the Holy Spirit.[8] "I shall" then stresses the unity of the blessed Trinity. The locution gives insight into what Julian means by "all shall be well." "Shall" not only indicates the future, but also discloses the obligation and necessity of the involvement of Father, Son, and Spirit in the unfolding promise of human well-being from the beginning of creation into the present, until its ultimate fulfillment in the Trinity. Finally, "you will see yourself" means that "all that shall be saved" will see themselves at one with the blessed Trinity. In the following chapter she concludes: "For just as the blessed Trinity created all things from nothing, just so will the same blessed Trinity make everything well which is not well" (13:32.233). The whole Trinity is united in realizing our eschatological *oneing*.

In this eschatological statement Julian points to the way our history unfolds in light of the Trinity's universal salvific will to save human beings. Furthermore, because of the Trinity's commitment to making all things well the human choice for salvation cannot be weighed up equally with the potential for eternal damnation.[9] The will of the Trinity

---

[6] The Middle English use of "may" is lost in translation. In Middle English "may" means to be strong, or to have might, power, or influence (NSOED 1721). Therefore it is appropriate that "may" relates to the Father.

[7] "Can" in Middle English means to know, to be acquainted with, or to have learned (*NSOED* 325). In this sense Christ knows what to do for human salvation.

[8] In Middle English "will" expresses desire that exudes pleasure, delight, and joy (*NSOED* 3686). This resonates with Julian's references to the joy and delight of the Holy Spirit.

[9] Here Julian counters the Pelagian belief popular in her time that salvation is a reward for good works and the semi-Pelagian notion that her own effort to do her

for human well-being has the greater power. Nevertheless, the stress on the union of the Trinity in fulfilling its universal salvific will revealed in the words "I shall make all things well" presents a dilemma for Julian. On the one hand she wants to align herself with the teaching of the Church that stressed eternal punishment, and on the other she does not see salvation as simplistically dichotomized into a choice for heaven or hell:

> . . . one article of our faith is that many creatures will be damned, such as the angels who fell out of heaven because of pride, who now are devils, and many men upon earth who die out of the faith of Holy Church, that is to say those who are pagans and many who have received baptism and who live unchristian lives and so die out of God's love. All these will be eternally condemned to hell, as Holy Church teaches me to believe. And all this being so, it seemed to me that it was impossible that every kind of thing should be well, as our Lord revealed at this time (32:13.233).

In reiterating Church teaching that emphasizes the radical potential for human alienation from God, even after God's redemptive activity on our behalf, Julian entertains the possibility that all things can never be well. Christ, however, gives her a response:

> What is impossible to you is not impossible to me. I shall preserve my word in everything, and I shall make everything well. And in this I was taught by the grace of God that I ought to keep myself steadfastly in the faith, as I had understood before, and that at the same time I should stand firm and believe firmly that every kind of thing will be well, as our Lord revealed at that same time (32:13.233).

Christ not only makes a declaration of our worthiness for salvation, but the Trinity through Christ and the Holy Spirit actually performs what looks like an impossibility from a human perspective. "I shall preserve my word in everything" reveals that the *word* of God remains in all things. This *word* is the spoken promise of salvation in that it is the dynamic encounter with the power and dynamism of God's creative and redemptive activity, the efficacious self-communication of the Trinity to all creation that transforms it and makes "all manner of things well." "All shall be well" etches in human memory the fact that the offer of salvation is not selective. The *word* of God remains in all things and is

---

best initiates God's gift of justifying grace. See Denise Nowakowski Baker, *Julian of Norwich's Showings: From Vision to Book* (Princeton: Princeton University Press, 1994) 74.

extended to every human being without exception. No one is excluded *a priori*.

Hell

Nevertheless, Julian does not dismiss the possible contradiction between universal salvation and Church teaching about hell.[10] She places the teaching of the Church beside her own understanding of the salvific will of the Trinity. Both perspectives interact with each other. She asks to see hell and purgatory:

> I desired, so far as I dared, that I might have had some sight of hell and of purgatory; but it was not my intention to make trial of anything which belongs to our faith, for I believed steadfastly that hell and purgatory exist for the same ends as Holy Church teaches. But my intention was to have seen for instruction in everything which belongs to my faith, whereby I could live more to God's glory and to my profit. But for all that I could wish, I could see nothing at all of this except what has already been said in the fifth revelation, where I saw that the devil is reproved by God and endlessly condemned (13:33.234).

Even though Julian asks for a vision of hell[11] and purgatory,[12] she never sees them. If we take into account what seeing means to Julian, namely that it involves *beholding* through a synthesis of all the other senses, it seems that the only realization she comes to about purgatory and hell is of the presence of the fiend she describes in the fifth revelation. She summarizes her understanding as seeing three things:

> I see sport, that the devil is overcome; and I see scorn, that God scorns him and he will be scorned; and I see seriousness, that he is overcome

[10] See Joan Nuth, *Wisdom's Daughter: The Theology of Julian of Norwich* (New York: Crossroad, 1991) 162–69; she emphasizes Julian's orthodoxy in this matter.

[11] The Fourth Lateran Council (1215) declared that at the resurrection of the dead those who have done evil will suffer eternal punishment along with the devil. The Second Council of Lyons (1274) asserted that immediately after death those who die in mortal sin or even original sin descend into hell, where they suffer different kinds of punishment. Nonetheless on the day of judgement all will appear in their bodies before God to give an account of their deeds. See Wolfgang Beinert and Francis Schüssler Fiorenza, eds., *Handbook of Catholic Theology* (New York: Crossroad, 1995) (= HCT) 327.

[12] The Second Council of Lyons taught that the souls of the dead who have not yet done appropriate penance for their sins are cleansed by purifying punishments *(poenae purgatoriae)*. These punishments can be mitigated by the intercessions of the living faithful. See HCT 562. This was repeated in the Council of Florence, 1439, possibly after Julian's death. It seems that this teaching was well known in Julian's day.

by the blessed Passion and death of our Lord Jesus Christ. . . . And
when I said that he is scorned, I meant that God scorns him, that is, because he sees him now as he will forever. For in this God revealed that
the devil is damned . . . for I saw that on Judgment Day he will be generally scorned by all who will be saved, of whose salvation he has had
great envy. For then he will see that all the woe and tribulation which
he has caused them will be changed into the increase of their eternal joy.
And all the pain and the sorrow that he wanted to bring them into will
go forever with him to hell (5:13.202).

Ultimately the devil, the personification of the non-being of sin, the
instigator of pain and suffering, is damned to an abyss of meaninglessness where pain and sorrow dwell eternally with their inflicter.[13] Paradoxically, the medley of well-being and woe becomes a game, play that
results in laughter ("of this sight I laughed greatly" 5:13.201), because
Christ in his Passion transfigures all the pain and suffering that the
devil inflicts. Because, thanks to that transfiguration, increasing suffering for love becomes joy, the cross increases our eternal joy and the
devil goes to hell. Significantly, it is not human beings damned to hell
but the devil who goes to hell with the sorrow and pain he inflicts on
us. All the pain that the devil inflicts leads to an increase in our joy.

In considering the possibility of eternal damnation Julian tenta-
tively questions a point of view assumed in her era: the collective
damnation of the Jews: "I saw nothing so exactly specified concerning
the Jews who put him to death; and nonetheless I knew in my faith that
they were eternally accursed and condemned, except those who were
converted by grace" (13:33.234). Through this unfortunate example she
suggests that even in confronting the worst sin the Church could imagine there is always a sin/grace dialectic that favors the grace of God.
She can never discount the presence of grace and suggest that anyone
is damned. Christ has the last word: "I shall make all things well."

Thus Julian can confidently speak of "all mankind that shall be
saved," or those "that will *[shall]* be saved *[safe]*" (13:27.225), or say that
"Jesus is in all who will *[shall]* be saved *[safe]*, and all who will be saved
[safe] are in Jesus" (14:51.276). She remarks: "I speak of those who will
be saved, for at this time God showed me no one else" (1:9.192). Julian
comes to the conclusion that all humankind "shall" be saved. The various derivations of this phrase have an important theological meaning
for her. "All," as we have noted earlier, conveys a universal sense of all
human beings having being in God. "Shall" designates the necessity of

[13] It is noteworthy that Julian does not use concrete imagery to describe hell.
Hell is where pain and suffering dwell. Cf. Marion Glasscoe, ed., *English Medieval
Mystics* (London: Longman, 1993) 232.

salvation occurring and implies that salvation will inevitably come to fruition. "Saved" or *safe* integrates two theological perspectives that inform Julian's soteriology. Salvation means that human beings, created with being in God in a relationship of *oneing* with the Trinity, will return to God, and salvation is about deliverance from the non-being of sin. "Saved" draws on the perception of being delivered, rescued, or protected from impending danger.[14] Thus the phrase "all that shall be saved" integrates the theological perspective that human beings are being rescued or saved, throughout life, from the non-being of sin. From another perspective, *safe* in Middle English can designate a receptacle for safe storage, a secure place for protecting things.[15] In this sense, theologically speaking, *safe* echoes Julian's images of being enclosed in the Trinity. The purpose of the journey of salvation is to find a secure dwelling place in God. *Safe* can also denote being uninjured, whole, healthy, or well.[16] In this context *safe* relates to Julian's idea of salvation as a condition in which all is well. The phrase "all that shall be *safe*" discloses that salvation is about being safe in God, well, and one in God. Thus the variations on the phrases "mankind that shall be saved" or those "that shall be *safe*" encapsulate Julian's idea of universal salvation. The human journey is from God to God. Our destiny is to be saved from the non-being of sin, to be one in God, to be well.

IV. THE LAST THINGS

Julian presents a depiction of the last judgement in which she gives a glimpse of what it will be like when "all is well." This vision reflects her understanding that what occurs in historical time is brought to completion in the eschaton:

> . . . when the judgment is given, and we are all brought up above, we shall then clearly see in God the mysteries which are now hidden from us. And then shall none of us be moved to say in any matter: Lord, if it had been so, it would have been well. But we shall all say with one voice: Lord, blessed may you be, because it is so, it is well, and now we see truly that everything is done as it was ordained by you before anything was made (16:85.341).

Julian is referring to the final communal judgment at the end of time.[17] The Fourth Lateran Council defined this as the time when all

[14] *NSOED* 2695. "Saved," however, is also related to "safe" through the Old French *sauf*.

[15] *NSOED* 2665.

[16] Ibid.

[17] The idea of the last judgment was based on Matt 24:1-51 and Rev 20:1–21:8.

souls resume their bodies and appear in person before Christ for the last or general judgment.[18] At the judgment their happiness or misery is experienced in bodily aspect. We can see Julian's inability to envisage the last judgment as a day of retribution when we compare her description to an illumination of the Last Judgment from *The St. Omer Psalter,* painted near Norwich in Julian's day.[19] Within the initial D, which begins Psalm 109, *Dixit Dominus,* Christ seated in judgment raises his hands and shows his wounds from the Passion, while graves lie in rows in the foreground and the dead are rising ready for judgment. Although the imagery that emphasizes Christ's Passion, even in his glory, is consistent with Julian's theology of the cross, her understanding of the last judgment is significantly different. In stark contrast to Julian's comment, "we shall then clearly see in God the mysteries which are now hidden from us," the characters rising from the graves have their faces turned away from Christ. They cannot see clearly. Their body language and facial expression communicate an ambience of fear. In a time when most art and literature conveyed this *parousia* of Christ as a terrible day at the end of the world when hidden sins would be revealed and punished with inescapable retribution, Julian does not mention either the pardoning or punishing of sin. Instead she describes the end-time as a time when "all is well" and all say with one voice, "all is well." The last judgment evokes a song of praise expressed with pleasure and *kindly courtesy:* "blessed may you be." "It is well" affirms undeniably that everything is as God intended it to be.

Heaven

Julian also describes heaven in a more concrete way as a wonderful banquet. This seems to be a transcendent intellectual vision:

> I saw our Lord God as a Lord in his own house, who has called all his friends to a splendid feast. Then I did not see him seated anywhere in his own house; but I saw him reign in his house as a king and fill it all full of joy and mirth, gladdening and consoling his dear friends with himself, very familiarly [*homely*] and courteously, with wonderful

[18] For a summary of the controversy over whether the last judgment transpired before or after the beatific vision see Paul Blinski, *Medieval Death: Ritual and Representation* (London: The British Museum Press, 1996) 212–14. By Julian's day Pope Benedict XII had issued a bull, *Benedictus Deus,* proclaiming that the beatific vision was given to the just before the last judgment.

[19] Psalm 109, The Last Judgment, from *The St. Omer Psalter.* Richard Marks and Nigel Morgan, *The Golden Age of English Manuscript Painting 1200–1500* (New York: George Braziller, 1981) 81.

melody in endless love in his own fair blissful countenance, which
glorious countenance *[cheer]* fills all heaven full of the joy and bliss of
the divinity (6:14.203).

Through the metaphor of a banquet Julian presents heaven as the fulfillment of the reign of God, the completion of this earthly life in eternity. Julian envisages heaven as a great feast like that in the parable of
the banquet (Luke 14:15-24) where God, who is head of the house, calls
all friends to solemn festivity to celebrate the fulfillment of the reign of
God. Unlike Luke's parable, however, Julian does not focus on those
invited who do not respond. At the banquet Julian envisages, each has
a *oneing* presence to the other.

The banquet gives a description of the fullness of joy, in which all at
the banquet are immersed. They share the blessings of creation, engage in
union and communion with each other, and ultimately experience the
fulfillment in God of who they really are. This eternal joy reflects the
joy Julian saw in the crucified Christ, which includes his union with all
humanity and the transformation of suffering. As the lord imparts eternal
joy, praise wells up. The communion of saints become one with the
"wonderful melody of endless love," which comes from the "glorious
cheer" of the lord. The scene discloses a vision of a future ruled by a loving
God, a future full of joy when we will live in peace with one another in
a wholeness that can come only when human beings are one with God.

Further contemplation of the joyous community at the banquet
reveals three degrees of bliss: "The first is the honor and thanks from
our Lord God which he will receive when he is delivered from pain"
(6:14.203). In concentrating on bliss, Julian stresses the continuity between what is built up in history and what constitutes the kingdom of
God at the end of time. She moves away from an image of a cataclysmic
end of the world when individuals will be judged for what they have
not done and toward the honor and thanks we will receive simply because of who we are. The second degree of bliss reveals how "all the
blessed in heaven will see the honor of the thanks" (6:14.203). There is a
communal dimension whereby individuals are bound to God and to
one another. The "dialectical tie between selfhood and otherness" that
the Holy Spirit activates in time comes to completion. The third degree
of bliss discloses how this glory "will last forevermore" (6:14.204). The
praise of the communion of saints in union with God lasts forever.

V. THE BEATIFIC VISION

A second analogy that Julian uses to describe eternal life is the depiction of heaven as a continuation of the prayer of *beholding*. This re-

flects Pauline eschatology, "for now we see in a mirror, dimly, but then we will see face to face" (1 Cor 13:12). She presents heaven not as something external to our present experience of God but as anticipated and known in time through our continual prayer:

> And so we shall by his sweet grace in our own meek continual prayer come into him now in this life by many secret touchings of sweet spiritual sights and feelings, measured out to us as our simplicity may bear it. And this is done and will be done by the grace of the Holy Spirit, until the day that we die, still longing for love. And then we shall all come into our Lord, knowing ourselves clearly and wholly possessing God, and we shall all be endlessly hidden in God, truly seeing and wholly feeling, and hearing him spiritually and delectably smelling him and sweetly tasting him. And there we shall see God face to face, familiarly *[homely]* and wholly. The creature which is made will see and endlessly contemplate God who is the maker; for so can no man see God and live afterwards, that is to say in this mortal life. But when he of his special grace wishes to show himself here, he gives the creature more than its own strength, and he measures the revelation according to his own will, and it is profitable for that time (14:43.255).

In this vision of heaven we see another description of eternal *oneing* whereby we come to know ourselves in union with the fullness of divine life. Julian uses all the senses, seeing, feeling, hearing, smelling and tasting, to describe the quality of *oneing* experienced in eternal life. The context suggests that she is elaborating on her personal experience of prayer. Through the use of vivid, sensual imagery Julian suggests that the incomprehensibility of eternity can only be illustrated as a vision of love. Her concentration of sensual imagery points to an integration between spiritual and bodily knowing and loving. It also implies that, paradoxically, in death we finally become fully human, attaining the completion of every part of our being in God.

Attention to each of the senses helps Julian convey the glorious, ineffable delight and enjoyment of God in eternal life. Each sense distinguishes the dynamism of the joy that ensues when love is central. "Knowing ourselves clearly" points to the merging of knowledge in the beatific vision as we see ourselves in God, and knower and the known become one. "Wholly possessing God" and "being endlessly hidden in God" describe the transformation we experience as God carries us into the embrace of divine love. This enables us to become one with the meaningful whole, to possess God, to be in God,[20] and to

[20] Wolfgang Riehle, *The Middle English Mystics*. Translated by Bernard Strandring (London: Routledge and Kegan Paul, 1981) 128.

know that God is all in all. Feeling is often used as a synonym for the perception of transcendental reality, for spiritual knowledge.[21] It conveys bodily-felt knowledge and also vision or insight. In this context "wholly feeling" is similar to "savoring," which Julian uses in her definition of prayer. It describes unrestrained freedom and love. "Hearing spiritually" is the internalizing of God's communication with us that occurs when we listen with the ear of the heart. "Delectably smelling" intimates the ultimate act of union with God. It alludes to Scripture passages such as the descriptions of the lovers in the Song of Songs who drip with the scent of choice ointments and herbs[22] or the woman who anoints Jesus' head with precious nard (Mark 14:3; Matt 26:7). "Sweetly tasting" implies mystical enjoyment of God. Although often linked with the blessed sacrament, in this context tasting denotes the eternal consuming of God.[23] Tasting, as in "taste and see the goodness of God" (Ps 34:8), also denotes internalizing spiritual knowledge, receiving wisdom, or savoring divine love. Julian's use of the spiritual senses points to eternal *oneing* as the complete fulfillment of the human being. Nevertheless, the possible metaphorical nature of the senses leaves us with an inconclusive answer as to whether she conceives of union with God in a purely spiritual dimension or as fulfillment in the physical dimension.

Reference to all these senses assists Julian in giving an interpretation of the teaching on the beatific vision that was promulgated by Pope Benedict XII in 1336 in the bull *Benedictus Deus*. The document describes the eternal beholding of God face-to-face after death, asserting that the souls of the elect "see the divine essence with an intuitive vision and even face to face without the mediation of any creature by way of object of vision; rather the divine essence immediately manifests itself to them plainly, clearly and openly, and in this vision *they enjoy the divine essence*."[24] Roger De Ganck highlights the essential meaning behind the notion of the beatific vision:

> . . . vision of God and union with him in the beyond are spoken of as being *multifariam multisque modis*, in multiple and various ways, as for instance the vision of God face to face (1 Cor 13:12), to see God as he is

---

[21] Ibid. 110.

[22] Ibid. 115.

[23] Ibid. 107–108. Riehle points to the translators' discomfort with this image and their choice to replace "swallowing" with the less vivid word "smelling" or even "following."

[24] Josef Neuner and Jacques Dupuis Collins, eds., *The Christian Faith in the Doctrinal Documents of the Catholic Church* (rev. ed. London: Collins, 1983) 685.

(1 John 3:2), to be with Christ (Phil 2:23), expressions often (though not always) emphasizing the individual's final beatitude. What all these expressions attempt to convey is oneness with a God who, paradoxically, remains incomprehensible.[25]

Although Julian never uses the words "beatific vision," her description of "coming in to our Lord" has a similar emphasis on the intuitive vision and immediate face-to-face experience of God. In this perfect contemplation of God, which God gratuitously imparts, the blessed experience a transparency to the absolute nature of divine love and become one with God, who paradoxically remains incomprehensible.

By describing the blessed nature of the face of God, Julian alludes to the enjoyment of seeing the divine essence, which becomes an experience of *oneing:* "The highest bliss there is, is to possess God in the clarity of endless light, truly seeing him, sweetly feeling him, peacefully possessing him in the fulness of joy; and a part of this blessed aspect of our Lord God was revealed" (16:72.320). *Beholding* the blessedness of God in the clarity of endless light is the highest beatitude we can experience. Through repeating the imagery used in her descriptions of *beholding,* Julian continues her description of the *oneing* experienced in the face-to-face vision:

> . . . the more clearly that the soul sees the blessed face by the grace of loving, the more it longs to see it in fullness, that is to say in God's own likeness. For even though our Lord God dwells now in us, and is here with us, and embraces us and encloses us for his tender love, so that he can never leave us, and is nearer to us than tongue can tell or heart can think . . . (16:72.320).

The image of the blessed face of God designates the sacredness and holiness of the face-to-face vision and the supreme delight of the experience of *oneing.* The glimpses we have in this life of this face, through grace, make us long all the more for the final face-to-face encounter. Meanwhile, "we can never cease from mourning and weeping, seeking and longing, until we see him clearly, face to his blessed face, for in that precious sight no woe can remain, no well-being can be lacking" (16:72.320). In this vision woe will no longer exist. The *exitus reditus* will be complete when we see the fullness of God's "blessed face" and know in the fullness of joy that "all shall be well."

---

[25] Roger De Ganck, *Beatrice of Nazareth: A Three Volume Study.* Part 3: *Towards Unification with God: Beatrice of Nazareth in Her Context* (Kalamazoo: Cistercian Publications, 1991) 535.

In the phrase "all shall be well" Julian encapsulates her eschatology, which takes from the phrase its distinctive spirit. All are included in the fulfillment of *oneing*. Julian can never imagine that the love of God is less mighty than sin and the power of evil. Though she never goes against Church teaching on the possibility of damnation, ultimately Julian laughs because the fiend is overcome for all time. Multiple images of heaven work together to create a dynamic sense of final *oneing* in the eschaton where we will finally see for ourselves, in the fullness of joy, that "all is well." Thus Julian's eschatology focuses on elements of continuity and transformation. On the one hand there is a line of continuity between the present and the future, a direct link between beginnings and endings. At the same time, however, there is an equally important dimension of discontinuity and transformation that emphasizes completion and fulfillment. There is an accent on consummation and the possibility of surpassing joy in the face-to-face vision in eternity. "In the third" we will finally have our fulfilling.

Part Six

What Was the Meaning?

. . . what was our Lord's meaning? (16:86.342).

10

Julian's Spiritual Understanding and Its Relevance for Today

I was answered in spiritual understanding (16:86.342).

At the end of the *Showings* Julian indicates her desire to know God's meaning: "And from the time that it was revealed, I desired many times to know in what was our Lord's meaning. And fifteen years after and more, I was answered in spiritual understanding" (16:86.342). This chapter draws together what Julian has come to understand about the nature of salvation, summarized in the word "love" and the celebrated song of hope: "I shall make all things well." As we have discovered, we can see this ourselves because all our life is "in three." "In the first" we have our being, "in the second" we have our increasing, and "in the third" we have our fulfilling. We can now collate the major aspects of Julian's soteriology. After pointing to the intrinsic relationship between theology and soteriology and drawing out the implications of Julian's hermeneutic of *beholding*, I will review the aspects of her soteriology of *oneing: oneing* in being, *oneing* through the crucifixion, *oneing* through the servant, *oneing* through Christ the deep wisdom of the Trinity our mother, *oneing* through the Holy Spirit, and *oneing* in the eschaton.

I. All Theology is Soteriological

Julian demonstrates how Christian theology is by its very nature soteriological. All reality is set in a soteriological context from God to God. It is an *exitus reditus*. All the theology expressed in the *Showings* relates to soteriology, from our *oneing* through the Trinity, our being in God, to our increasing in Christ and our fulfillment through the Holy Spirit. There is no separate theology of the Trinity, christology, theology of nature and grace, pneumatology, eschatology. Julian does not present doctrines that inform these theologies and then add insights revealed in the concrete events of salvation history. Theology and soteriology are intrinsically integrated. No theology of the Trinity or of creation, nature, or grace can ever be conducted in isolation. On the negative side this integrated approach makes it difficult to interpret specific aspects of the theology that informs Julian's soteriology without placing an artificial structure on the text. On the positive side, however, this integration keeps before us the interrelationship between all events in salvation history and the complexity involved in attempting to interpret the meaning of salvation.

A Hermeneutic of Beholding

Julian's soteriology begins and ends in *beholding,* a connecting thread that runs through the entire *Showings. Beholding* unites themes and integrates meaning. It draws the reader into the language of the text, inviting understanding. *Beholding* makes the movement in understanding circular: from *beholding* our being in God to *beholding* the Passion to *beholding* the motherhood in God to *beholding* in existential experience through prayer to the *beholding* experienced in the beatific vision. Yet this is not a tightly closed hermeneutical circle. The hermeneutic is dialectical. It embraces paradox and invites dialogue between theory and experience. Interpreting the text is sacramental: it encourages participation in the meaning that unfolds. The way of interpretation that mystical literature invites can make an important contribution to the interpretative process by giving another lens through which to understand the mystery of the divine. Julian's *Showings* engage the interpreter in contemplative knowing. They enable the expression of ideas not readily communicated in other ways of doing theology.

Julian's way of *beholding* corporeal sights, words forming in her understanding, and spiritual sights challenges those who think that theology cannot be expressed in metaphorical language that creates such ethereal categories. Because Julian's soteriology is not highly structured, themes and topics are not dealt with in logical order. Nevertheless, the language that emerges through Julian's rigorous reflection on this way of expressing mystery can inform other methods of theological reflection. Julian's method presents insights often lost in a more classically argued approach that prizes linear thinking as the only logical outcome of reflection on the meaning of existence. Julian's use of metaphor challenges the bias of the tradition toward predominantly left-brain thinking. She gives us a contemplative method of interpretation that balances knowing and loving.

The Revelations of Divine Love, I have argued, deserve to be classified as public (dependent) revelation. Julian's writings are an important source of reflection on how God reveals God's self in the lives of women. They are a source of theological reflection that the tradition must embrace if it is to express with authenticity the story of the whole people of God. However, Julian's writings should not be confined to the corpus of "women's literature." Julian has the depth of a great theologian. Her writing about salvation has an important contribution to make to men and women who want to understand more about soteriology.

A Trinitarian Soteriology of Love

In a time when Christian theology is rejuvenating the doctrine of the Trinity, Julian's trinitarian soteriology has a definite contribution to make. She creates a distinctive trinitarian soteriology that integrates God, Christ, Spirit, and world. Her doctrine of the Trinity affirms that the being of God is love. It belongs to God's nature to be in relationship with humanity and its history. Her theology of presence reveals that God's presence is reliable and constant. The sharing of divine love is irrevocable. The triune God's whole being and activity are involved in salvation. This deeply trinitarian soteriology provides a balance often lost in a soteriology that is confined to christology. Julian's soteriology is a reminder that Christians believe in a triune God.

Julian's soteriology is a theology of love. By identifying the essence of the Godhead as *charity unmade* Julian makes a significant theological point about the being of God as love, namely that God is active from all eternity as love. That love is always in relation to creation is essential to the very meaning of loving. It is impossible to conceive of God's inner life, *charity unmade*, without seeing how God relates as *charity made* and *charity given*. For Julian the doctrine of the Trinity is not simply a set of received formulations about the inner life of God that do not inform Christian life. Her doctrine of the Trinity intrinsically includes the relationship of the Trinity to creation. A soteriology that unites God's being and doing can give our contemporary world a way of developing a dynamic theology of divine presence.

Julian's presentation of the divine-human relationship as a *perichoresis* not only in the mutual giving and receiving of divine love within the Trinity but in the sharing of love with humanity implies that human beings exist within divine life. Human beings are an important, if not necessary, dimension of the loving of the Trinity. Thus there are not two sets of trinitarian relationships, one within the divine being and the

202 What Was the Meaning?

other in history. The one mystery of communion encompasses God and humanity reciprocally enclosed in each other. If Julian's stress on the dynamic relational indwelling of the Trinity in humanity is taken seriously it means that love is at the center of all reality. Shared divine love is the fundamental source from which we have being. This creates an ontology of being-in-relationship, which means that the Trinity is bound to humanity and its history in an unalterable covenant initiated in love and destined to be upheld despite sin in the world. Human beings can only be understood in relation to the love within the Trinity. An awareness of this life of communion in which we exist enables us to be more attentive to what this gift means and to respond to the gift. It creates a sense of wonder and awe. It humbles, frees, and empowers. It calls us to participate fully in divine life.

Julian creates a soteriology of *oneing*. There is an ontological *oneing* when humanity is created *one* with the Trinity and an existential *oneing* as humanity continues to be *oned* through the working of the Son and Holy Spirit. The movement of this *oneing* reflects the Plotinian notion of *exidus reditus*. A soteriology of *oneing* creates an evolutionary sense of a transforming union of ever-deepening love. Human beings, created with the potential to be one with God, are continually drawn into the mystery of God's unfolding plan of salvation, of further *oneing*. The idea of *oneing* leads to a soteriology that is not limited to salvation from sin or understood as a hierarchical ascent of steps to God. *Oneing* creates a soteriology of *koinonia*, total communion. This dynamic oneness between God and humanity undermines any inherent dualism that sets divine and human in opposition. *Oneing* describes the intrinsic participation of the life-giving love of God in human lives and designates the constancy of divine revelation.

The pattern of *exitus reditus* from being in God to fulfillment in God shifts emphasis away from a juridically fashioned soteriology to one that focuses on the presence of trinitarian love in human beings and the dynamic sharing of this love that continues through history. The implication is that salvation is not an afterthought to the divine plan initiated because human beings went astray, but rather is an essential part of divine providence from origin to fulfillment. A model of soteriology based on the cyclic flow of love from emanation to return creates a cosmic, universal, evolutionary, transformational soteriology that embraces historical time and eternity. This expands our understanding of God's salvific will by shifting emphasis away from one act that saved humanity toward expressing the whole of reality as salvific. This perspective, that the whole of reality is cast in a salvific context, responds better than some other perspectives to a modern concern to find salvific meaning in the totality of life's experiences.

II. A Soteriology of *Oneing* in Being

Because all things have being through the love of God there is a fundamental unity between God and all things in creation. Julian understands creating as an organic process in which God's work of creating is never isolated from keeping and loving. God is intimately present to all things. Julian's insistence on the immanence of God in creation affirms that there is an indestructible continuing relationship between God and creation. This undercuts the dualism between God and nature by stressing the innate affinity between God and creation, suggesting that creation is expressive of *who God is* as love. Creation is God's gift and promise. A soteriology that shows how creation has being in God can make an important contribution to contemporary creation theology. In a time when the future of creation is at risk, this perspective on the holiness of all things can teach reverence and care for creation, because creation is important in God's plan for salvation.

A true *oneing* between human beings and God demands some affinity with God in our nature or *kind*. Julian emphasizes that human beings are inherently oriented toward God because they are bound to God by nature. Our substance is kept whole and safe in God. Our soul is made in the image and likeness of the Trinity. We have a *godly will* and a *kindly will*. These loci of *oneing* show how there is something in us that is God-like, something that resembles God's nature, something that longs to return to its source. These *oneings* restlessly draw us to deeper union with the divine, or, as the psalmist says, deep calls to deep (Ps 42:7). The implications of the multiple *oneings* between human beings and God, established at creation for all time, affirm the inviolable value of human nature. Furthermore, because of ontological *oneing* in being, theology is anthropology and anthropology is theology: to say something about God is to say something about human beings. Negatively, Julian could be accused of being almost pantheistic, of placing too much stress on human likeness to God. Positively, her anthropology consistently reveals how it is possible that human beings will become divinized. In a world that often denies the inherent dignity of each person this perspective encourages belief in the innate goodness of human beings.

An anthropology based on substance and sensuality enables Julian to develop a unique anthropology that envisages salvation as the coming to wholeness of both the spiritual and bodily aspects of human nature in God. Though Julian's lack of clarity in defining exactly what she means by substance and sensuality is frustrating, there is enough evidence based on her use of the terminology to conclude that these words express her attempt to overcome the body/spirit split and spiritualization of the human person that was so prevalent in her day and that still scars theological anthropology. Reframing our understanding of human beings as substance (who we are in God) and sensuality (how we exist in the world) enables us to appreciate that our destiny is for divine life in God as spiritual/embodied beings. The journey to God is toward participation in divine life by our becoming fully Christ-like in the fullness of Christ's humanity. This does not mean an abandonment of the most human aspect of ourselves, our sensuality, but a full integration of it. Because we are sensual beings, enfleshed spirits, physical matter is our unique and special means of reaching spiritual perfection. Julian can inform contemporary society about the holiness of the body, sensual knowing and experiencing.

The multiple *oneings* between ourselves and Christ extend from the eternity of God and bridge the void between eternity and history to establish a union with Christ for all time. The *oneing* of human sensuality in Christ in the Incarnation reveals conclusively that God dwells in our humanity. Humanity is of value to God. Humanity is holy. This perspective encourages a respect and reverence for our deepest humanity by awakening us to the presence of Christ within each human being and the desire of God for each person to be whole. People sensitized to an awareness of their inherent goodness can be happy, peaceful people able to share that goodness with others. The implication of the *oneing* of Christ in sensuality is that we are not human people trying to be holy. We are holy people learning to be human. Salvation takes place within human nature, within the world; it is not escape from human nature and the world.

Julian makes love the motivating factor in the Incarnation by teaching that for love God creates and for love God becomes human. In this perspective God did not intend to create human beings and then, subsequently, decide to become human in order to "fix up" what went astray in creation. Human nature was always intended for the Son. This emphasis on Christ's humanity shifts the archetype for what it is to be human away from Adam. It replaces it with Christ, the actualized, fully human being who unites substance and sensuality. Nevertheless, human beings are not always Christ-like. There is something incomplete within human nature that prevents total *oneing* with the divine. An important consequence of the Incarnation is that Christ reveals how we can transcend this incompletion, because Christ takes our sensual soul and unites it to our substance. In Christ the work of creation continues. Julian can make a valuable contribution to the desire of contemporary theologians to relate christology to anthropology more completely. She demonstrates that if we want to know what authentic humanity is we can discover this in Christ.

Within Julian's vision of our gifted origins humanity is never envisaged as disconnected from the love of God. Negatively, though Julian has an image of the love of God grounding all things, present in all things, loving all things, we may wonder why God's love has not affected creation more completely. Though Julian never entertains the concept of what we would call process theology, her understanding of *charity unmade, charity made,* and *charity given* presents a God deeply involved in the process of *oneing* and affected by what happens in this *oneing*. A soteriology of *oneing* gives a more adequate answer to the modern protest against soteriologies that emphasize the impassibility and immutability of God or present a God who intervenes in history in a spasmodic and inconsistent manner. In Julian's soteriology God is constantly involved in the process of *oneing*.

III. A Soteriology of *Oneing* in the Crucifixion

Julian's theology of the cross is expressed as *oneing* in suffering, *oneing* in love, and *oneing* in joy. Her theology of the cross exposes suffering. It presents a stark reminder that the journey to God is cruciform. Suffering not only enters the body of God through Christ; suffering extends to the world. All creation is drawn into the meaning of Christ's suffering. Through her concentration on suffering Julian reminds us that there is no sense in which the pain reflected on the tortured body of Christ or the pain of creation can be denied. She challenges us to confront existential suffering. Julian shows us how to face darkness, to enter the darkness of Christ's suffering and to find divine light. Significantly, the suffering of the cross is never an end in itself or an excuse for glorifying and accepting suffering. Christ's Passion marks a creative moment in salvation history that draws us into its meaning and enables us to know love and joy.

Julian's depictions of the suffering of Christ powerfully convey that in a time of great existential suffering only an image of a suffering compassionate God will address the pain of the world. Julian suggests that the pain reflected on the dying body of Christ is divine love suffering with us. This theological perspective that accentuates Christ's sharing in human suffering makes explicit that human beings are in relationship with a God who suffers. Christ reveals that the very nature of God is to suffer for love, to take the suffering of humanity to God's own being, to be a saving God through *oneing* in suffering. Julian never conceives of a God unmoved by human suffering.

Julian's theology of the cross addresses the problem of sin in creation and the divine response to sin. Within the shadow of the cross she sees a creative tension. God is in all things and does all things, yet existential alienation, insecurity, and meaninglessness confront the truth of salvation seen in God's universal love. Faced with this dichotomy, Julian is in no doubt that the Passion exposes the effects of sin on the human condition. Significantly, however, in this model of redemption Christ is divine love, one with human suffering in a relationship of *oneing*. Julian resists interpreting the meaning of the cross as a propitiatory sacrifice by which Christ substitutes himself for sinners and becomes the passive victim who is sacrificed to God for the sins of the world in order that humanity will not be eternally damned. Christ's death on the cross is a continuation of the work of *oneing*. Suffering on the cross is an act of love.

Redemption takes on a cosmic dimension that includes the individual, the Church, creation, and all things. Sin is understood in a cosmic sense as the absence of good. This makes Julian's soteriology less privatized than some others. It shifts emphasis away from a model of redemption that accentuates the guilt and blame attributed to Adam and inherited by humanity. It is not what humanity is saved *from* that is central. Rather, Julian's soteriology centers on what humanity is created and saved *for*. We are made to be in a relationship of *oneing* with the divine. Julian does not concentrate on a personal mysticism that details the inner life of the individual alone; rather she presents a theology of divine presence in the midst of the sin and suffering of the community, transforming suffering to joy. Although Julian gives little attention to individual free choice and the ability to commit the most life-denying sin, she is unable to separate divine love from human freedom or sin. This stress on the absolute interrelationship between God and humanity gives a more adequate answer to a contemporary need to find communal meaning and hope in the midst of existential alienation and despair. It creates a paradigm shift away from attributing individual blame and punishment to sinners, toward hope. Thus she makes possible the integration of an image of a suffering God who ceaselessly works to draw all reality into the meaning of love.

Beholding love comes to a climax when Julian contemplates the wound in Christ's side. Through the cross Christ draws all into the heart of God, a place large enough for all peoples to rest within, in peace and love. These images reveal the present reality of divine love active in human lives. They become images of eternity. The images communicate that those who love know something of eternity. Those who love experience a call beyond and know that love is our beginning, love is our present, and love is our end. We may criticize Julian for her lack of reference to the life and ministry of Christ and her sentimental, romantic imagery. Nevertheless, the imagery she uses makes the cross central, powerfully conveying that the cross is a story of love. The inclusive nature of the invitation into the heart of God awakens universal hope.

It reveals that love calls all peoples forth beyond the temporal. Love cries out for fulfillment. Love gives a glimpse of human potential, a hint of who we are in Christ and the life of communion we are meant to live. Contemporary society can benefit from a poignant reminder of the unconditional love expressed by the crucified Christ.

Although profoundly christocentric, Julian's theology of the cross is ultimately a theology of the blessed Trinity, which is our salvation. The whole point of the Incarnation, Passion, death, and resurrection is to mediate the life of the Trinity to humanity. This is an occasion for trinitarian joy. The cross enables us to share in the fullness and communion of God's triune life incorporating past, present, and future. The connection between the cross and the Trinity is not always clearly drawn out in theology. Julian excels at making this bond explicit. She reminds us that the whole doctrine of the Trinity that includes God, Son, and Spirit is essential for salvation. It is the triune God who saves. A theology of the cross that is "the blessed Trinity of our salvation" helps correct soteriologies that neglect the trinitarian dimensions of christology.

Christ's *blessed cheer* reveals that we are completely drawn into the life of the Trinity. We have hope. In *beholding* Christ more glorified Julian shows how Christ is "I am he that is all." Christ communicates how trinitarian love permeates all things by compassionately sharing suffering and drawing all things into trinitarian joy. In our lives we already participate in Christ's joy and have a glimpse of the joy that is to come. This theology of joy, which reveals how struggling with the ambiguity of existence so powerfully reflected in the cross leads to an awareness of joy, is badly needed in a world that attempts to cover up and avoid facing the truth of the brokenness of human reality. Julian teaches us how to face our brokenness and to see the love of God in the midst of incompleteness. She instructs us how to find light in the midst of darkness, transformation and growth in chaos, and well-being in woe. She teaches us that the journey of the cross is the way of trinitarian joy.

A theology of *glorious asseth* signifies that the journey of Christ through the cross is a journey of transformation, exaltation, glorification, eschatological fullness, and completion. It is a journey of *oneing*. The *glorious asseth* reveals the unequivocal solidarity of God with the cause of humanity, especially at the point at which humanity is most vulnerable and most at risk, namely death itself. This expression of divine love at the moment of the death of Christ, symbolized by the resurrection, reveals that there is a gratuitous offer of a radically new life for all humanity. The purpose of Christ's redemptive work is to make us "heirs with him in bliss." When Julian recognizes Christ as "I am he that is all" she gains a glimpse of how "all shall be well." The glory of the cross gives a promise of human glory. In our world that cries out for hope, the *glorious asseth* keeps alive the hope that "all shall be well."

IV. A Soteriology of *Oneing* Through the Servant

Julian's parable of the lord and the servant is a distillation of her soteriology. The parable metaphorically presents the history of salvation from the experience of the Fall, to transformation, to glory. It gives a valuable vignette that can assist contemporary theologians in developing new models of redemption.

Julian examines the Fall from two perspectives: the good will of the servant who does not anticipate his fall and the pain the servant encounters after he endures loss of union with God after falling. The servant's consistent desire to do the will of the lord affirms the essential goodness of humankind. Although the Fall intrudes and causes disharmony in the union between God and creatures, God's perseverance in total commitment to creation ensures that human beings are not abandoned because of it. Julian's shift of emphasis from a willful act of disobedience by the servant to the good will of the servant who accidentally falls in the slade has significant implications for her soteriology. Rather than stress the one act that condemned all humankind, she accentuates the great pains the servant experiences after the fall. Her perspective has biblical precedent in Rom 7:15, "I do not understand my own actions. For I do not do what I want, but I do the very thing I hate." Disoriented by sin, we forget our natural love for God and become blind to the experience of divine love. Julian's concentration on the brokenness of humanity separated from God deflects attention from a historical fall caused by sin toward considering the physical and spiritual pain of sin that is a consequence of seclusion from God.

The blindness of the servant and his inability to know himself enables Julian to interweave the essential goodness of humankind and the shadow side of human nature. The metaphor of blindness synthesizes the view of sinners as blameworthy with God's perspective, which identifies the effects of sin with human incapacity to see the deepest truth: that humanity has a *godly will*, made in the image and likeness of the Trinity. Julian's concentration on the *godly will* of creatures rather than their perverse will contributes to an appreciation of the fact that the definition of what it means to be human includes the notion of human beings as graced creatures.

Julian's image of a feudal lord holds together a respect for God's mystery and transcendence and a responsive God's compassion for the pain of the human condition. Through her portrait of the lord she indirectly critiques classical theism's model of an impassible God by presenting a biblical view of God who has a rich emotional life, who feels love, compassion, pity, mercy, and concern for the suffering of the servant. This image of a compassionate God reveals how joy exists in the midst of suffering, offering hope in face of despair. The fidelity of a compassionate God gives confidence that "all shall be well." This enables human beings to withstand enormous hardship and to extend compassion to others.

Through the parable Julian shows how Christ, the servant, plays a central role in the work of human salvation. He endows creation with an abundance of grace through his work as gardener, his union of will with the Father, the double aspect of the servant as humanity and Christ, his fall into the maiden's womb, and his identification as the wisdom of the Father and the Head of the body. Julian emphasizes the creation-centered nature of Christ's work for redemption. As gardener Christ displays a vulnerability to human experience that reflects solidarity with human well-being. He labors with humanity to restore harmony to the garden. The focus on human nature as the treasure in the earth that is essential to God's happiness creates an anthropology that only comprehends human nature in relation to God. Conversely, we can only understand God in relation to humanity.

The fall that brings life and the fall that brings death reveal the great paradox that the fall of Christ ultimately reveals his glory. The servant shows that God constantly cares for humankind because the moment human beings fall, the Son falls, revealing that creation and Incarnation are intrinsically linked. In God's providential plan creation could never be left separated from Christ. Christ is in all who will be saved and all who will be saved are in Christ. Because humanity is in Christ the fall becomes a *felix culpa*. There is a new creation that re-creates humankind even more fully in union with God than we were before the fall. The servant experiences all the pain and degradation of the human condition on the cross, even to the extent of journeying to hell. In meeting humankind in suffering, the Son offers a share in transformation to resurrection life.

The identification of the servant with Christ, Adam, and all humankind points to an ontological union between Christ and humanity. When we relate this to Julian's understanding of Christ as the perfect human who models the complete *oneing* between substance and sensuality the implication is that human beings, in the truth of who they are, are the *imago Christi*. Human beings are one with Christ. We have the same identity as Christ. Therefore our destiny is to be fully Christ-like. We are called to be totally human as Christ is human, one in substance and sensuality. The blurring of the boundaries between Christ and humanity affirms that Christ's story is the human journey of salvation.

Some may say Julian has gone too far. We are not Christs. What Julian communicates, however, in this christology is a profoundly Pauline concept: all things come together in Christ. The Incarnation means that human nature will be made whole in Christ.

Julian recognizes hope for salvation that is partially realized in this life and fully realized in eternity. The parable shows how God's whole existence is tied up with the redemption and liberation of human beings. In Julian's vision of heaven the servant takes humanity with him when he sits at the right hand of the Father. What is unique about Julian's interpretation of heaven is the stress on the joy that God experiences in our salvation. Humanity becomes the glory of God, the crown of Christ and his reward. The parable facilitates a theology of hope. It affirms that human beings can be sure of the constancy of God's love.

V. A Soteriology of *Oneing* Through Christ, Deep Wisdom of the Trinity, Our Mother

The idea that the deep wisdom of the Trinity is our mother reveals to Julian how Christ continues the work of *oneing* from creation to fulfillment. The three interrelated *beholdings* of motherhood in God disclose ontological and existential *oneing*. They demonstrate how, in Christ, human beings come from God and return to God through the working of grace. As theologians search within the Christian tradition for ways to give equal status to a complete humanity, embodied and spiritual, male and female, Julian's christology has a significant contribution to make. Her christology of the deep wisdom of the Trinity our Mother can serve as a prototype for the way in which all human beings are one in Christ.

When Julian attributes motherhood to Christ's work in history she finds its source in the very nature of God, the deep wisdom of the Trinity. This christology provides an important interpretation of the way in which creatures may be said to be born of God. With the ground of humankind founded in mother wisdom we can only discover where we came from, who we are, our purpose and destiny in Christ, who gives birth to humanity from all eternity. This revolutionizes soteriology in that Christ images a twofold feminine manifestation of the divinity, wisdom and mother, in the male physical form of Jesus of Nazareth. Thereby all individuals, both male and female, can see themselves reflected in the image of Christ. In Julian's soteriology the mother/wisdom image works with the maleness of Christ to reveal that Christ gives birth to a complete humanity, male and female. Therefore all humankind, regardless of gender, has the potential for participating in the divine nature by being *oned* to Christ.

Because mother wisdom is the paradigm of all wisdom and knowledge, yet also nurtures us as a mother would physically attend to a child, the value of being wise in mind and responsive to human needs also extends to both women and men. Because Christ is the divine exemplar the image enables Julian to dissolve classic gender distinctions that equate the masculine principle with the intellect and the feminine principle with affectivity. Through Christ the possibility of reflecting the wisdom of God and of caring as Christ cares is available to all who are born in Christ.

The three *beholdings* of the motherhood of God demonstrate how human beings are bound to God by nature and by grace. This relationship between nature and grace is important for developing a soteriology that goes beyond the dualism of classical theology expressed in authors such as Thomas Aquinas who view nature and grace separately or even in opposition to each other. Julian creates a unity within the distinction between nature and grace. She maintains a balance between the significance of nature created in Christ the mother of *kind* and the presence and working of grace through Christ the mother of grace. For Julian every human being comes into the world graced by God. Every human being is called by God into a relationship of *oneing*. This divine call has a real effect on the very being of humankind; the implication is that the human person is intrinsically turned toward God. Grace is not an extrinsic supernatural reality bestowed on humanity as a consequence of sin, but rather is the indwelling of Christ, the mother of grace, within human nature as a free, unmerited presence. Julian creates a harmony between nature and grace.

A theology of grace needs to be reclaimed and given new vigor and energy in our contemporary theology. Julian's way of describing grace as grounded in our sensuality, in the working of Christ the mother of grace, and in the presence of the Holy Spirit in us gives us fresh images and new ways of understanding grace that can make us more attentive to this divine reality in human lives. Too often in Christian theology grace has been intellectualized, systematized, and categorized. Julian's way of describing grace draws attention to the intimacy of the presence and working of grace. Furthermore, in Julian's theology of grace human beings are not undeserving of grace nor do they need to earn grace. Julian's nuanced view of the nature/grace relationship retrieves an often neglected aspect of theology: that grace is an intrinsic aspect of human nature.

Like grace, mercy contributes to the healing of humanity. In response to sin, the mother of mercy and grace meets us as children who need motherly care and love. Through this image of the mother responding to the needs of a child Julian becomes confident that "all shall be well." Salvation is grounded in the faithfulness of God actualized through Christ's work of mercy. The world needs mercy. The Church needs mercy. Julian's depiction of divine mercy can assist in reforming a Church too ready to condemn people who are different. Julian teaches that the only way God ever treats human beings is with mercy.

Although Julian does not develop an extensive sacramental theology she relates the Eucharist to her soteriology. The gift of Christ's self as food is not viewed as a sacrifice, however, but as parental nourishment that brings life to humanity. Her image of Eucharist reinforces her theology of presence and the faithfulness of God in the ongoing care of humanity. This linking of the Eucharist to Christ's care for humanity as a mother gives it a vital christological character.

Julian's ecclesiology creates a model of the Church imbued with the presence of Christ. Christ is the Church. She envisages Church not as an institution but as a graced people, "all the blessed common," indwelt by Christ. This ecclesiology points to the Church as a salvific reality where divine love dwells and is expressed personally and communally. The implication of Julian's view of the Church as "all the blessed common," bound to God by nature and by grace, gives value to the whole people of God. It is a pertinent reminder that it is a model of communion that marks the Church as blessed.

VI. A Soteriology of *Oneing* Through the Holy Spirit

Julian brings her theology of love to completion by associating *charity given* with the Holy Spirit, who is the divine gift, the active power of love and divine grace present in history. Through this relationship of love Julian completes her trinitarian view of God's presence and action for the sake of human beings. The significant role she gives to the Spirit in the sharing of grace lends her soteriology a vital, existential character. In our climate, where theology is reclaiming the significance of the Holy Spirit in salvation history, Julian's theology of the Holy Spirit provides a significant missing link in reflection on soteriology by creating an important bond between theology and spirituality. This responds to our contemporary consciousness, which demands that theology be intrinsically connected to praxis.

Julian's theology of the Holy Spirit lays a foundation for an eschatology that embraces both this world and eternity. The role she gives the Holy Spirit in the present experience of fulfillment and the hope for its future realization in the eschaton provides a valuable example of the ways in which this unresolved tension between present and future may harmonize. It is not salvation in this world *or* salvation in eternity: the already and the not yet are in dialectical tension. Julian's pneumatology, which extends her theology of grace, has an important contribution to make to soteriology today. It awakens us to the presence of *charity given* (or grace) in our humanness. It reminds us that we stand now in the face of and experience something of the eternal in the presence of the Holy Spirit in human lives. In other words, the presence of the Holy Spirit gives proleptic access to the eternal in the present. Julian's pneumatology leads the way to a radical unity between the mystical and the practical, contemplation and action, salvation now and salvation in the eschaton.

The Holy Spirit communicates the content of God's saving revelation by teaching us how to know. Julian's stress on knowledge of God, knowledge of self in nature and grace, and knowledge of self as against sin and weakness affirms the intrinsic connection between God and human nature. Access to God occurs through human beings, not outside human nature and experience. We have a basis for believing that human nature will be divinized. Although we may criticize Julian for an unbalanced interiority, the point to her idea of self-knowledge is that it makes us conscious of who we essentially are in God in nature and grace. Knowing enables us to come to an awareness that the God we meet after death is not a stranger to us but a God we know in this life. The God we hope to be one with is, in a sense, already one with us. The work of the Holy Spirit is to help us truly know this *oneing*. Our world can only benefit from people who are attentive to the work of the Holy Spirit in encouraging self-reflection. Ultimately the presence of the Spirit, teaching us to know ourselves, does not lead to introspection. Rather, the Spirit teaches us to be true to our God-like nature while at the same time teaching us about love and loving.

Julian's theology of prayer extends the link between theology and spirituality by giving primacy to human experience. It reinforces the interconnection between experience now and hope for eternal life. In her view prayer gives an experience of *oneing*, a foretaste of the joy to come. Julian falls short, however, in not presenting a spirituality that focuses on political dynamism within all aspects of life. Positively she excels at presenting how all humanity is in total relationship with God and can respond to God's presence in prayer. She develops a convincing theology that all our living is prayer. This appreciation of all of life as prayer assists our awareness of the potential holiness of all life-experience.

VII. A Soteriology of *Oneing* in the Eschaton

Julian's eschatology, which arises from her awareness of the action of the gracious Spirit of God in the creation, in the Church, and in individuals, gives images of hope for final *oneing* in the eschaton. Significantly, the idea that "all shall be well" is not limited to life after death. "All shall be well" is something that begins in this life. Julian's eschatology can contribute to our contemporary understanding of eschatology, which seeks to move away from the monism of salvation limited to this world and the dualism of salvation that will only occur in the next world. Her sense of the immanence of God in creation and in human nature, balanced with her understanding of the transcendence of God expressed in her images of the beatific vision, helps us create a delicately nuanced eschatology that embraces past, present, and future.

All aspects of Julian's theology are eschatological. Her trinitarian theology, christology, pneumatology, anthropology, and ecclesiology all express hope in final fulfillment. Through integrating the *reditus* or fulfillment with all aspects of her theology Julian helps us move beyond the two extremes in which salvation is viewed only from the perspective of present reality or only from the perspective of life after death. While the *reditus* includes *oneing* in the eschaton, *oneing* is not conceived of as a mystical union that bypasses life-experience or material creation. The hope for the face-to-face vision of God flows out of our living. Julian always presents a theology of hope. Although she expresses hope for the individual in the context of a community of hope, she stresses the communal dimension of hope. Still, there is a certain unresolved paradox. On the one hand there is the interdependence of human beings and communal redemption, and on the other the individual care of God for each person and individual salvation. This tension between individual and community keeps before us the importance of not allowing the individual to be absorbed into some impersonal collective. It also monitors too great a stress on personal relationships with God, as if all people and the wider created order are not intrinsically in relationship. Julian provides a model of spirituality that balances the personal and the communal.

Within the tradition there are two polarized positions on the nature of salvation. One is expressed in the optimistic doctrine of *apokatastasis,* which considers all creatures to be saved. The other, more pessimistic view inherited through Augustine is that large numbers of people are predestined to be damned. Neither of these extreme positions seems appropriate today. Julian presents a moderate doctrine of universal salvation. She creates a bridge between a simplistic view that denies the power of evil and a cynical view that stresses the perverse, sinful nature of humankind. In keeping with orthodox Church teaching, the overwhelming weight of Julian's soteriology affirms the universal salvific will of God as the context in which all questions about salvation must be examined. Though she deals with judgment, heaven, and hell, her focus is always on the promise that "all shall be well," which embraces all things and all human experience in all creation. Julian finds every reason to conclude that God wishes well-being for all. She interprets the events of Christ's Passion, death, and resurrection as having universal significance. She draws this out powerfully in her interpretation of the parable, in the identity she perceives between Christ, Adam, and the servant, and brings it to completion through her dynamic theology of grace. Julian helps us express a modified doctrine of universal salvation based on hope grounded in "the blessed Trinity of our salvation," where all of history moves toward a definite goal of *oneing* in God. This ability to envisage universal salvation opens the way for Christians to develop an inclusive soteriology that embraces all peoples, religions, cultures, and classes.

Relationality is central in Julian's soteriology. She always views salvation in terms of humanity's relationship of *oneing* with the Trinity. Salvation is a journey from God to God. Salvation is maturation, increasing, fulfilling. Julian's eschatology, like all eschatology, presents a special problem because we are not dealing with interpretation of past events or present experience. Negatively, Julian shares the limitations and possible futility of such an endeavor. Her analogies are culturally conditioned; they require additional interpretation for a contemporary world. Her depiction of heaven and the beatific vision leaves some ambiguity. She does not confront the tension between the immortality of the soul and the expectation of bodily resurrection. Nevertheless, rather than speculate about details in the unknown experience of the eschaton Julian emphasizes hope for divine intimacy with individuals in such a way that the promise and fulfillment transcend all threats from the non-being of evil. Her analogies point to promise. They speak of final transformation, fulfillment, and well-being. Julian's eschatology informs the meaning of human existence, the goals of human life. In short, as Julian understands salvation, when we die and face God it is not the brokenness of the human condition or our feeble attempts to respond to divine love that will form our destiny. It is our gifted origin, our being in God, increased through Christ and brought to graced fulfillment through the Holy Spirit that ultimately saves.

A number of future directions for a study of Julian's soteriology suggest themselves. Her thought deserves to play a significant role in the articulation of a contemporary soteriology because it presents an approach often disregarded in a tradition biased against mystical literature and the expression of women. Julian integrates a wide range of important aspects of soteriology often overlooked in a tradition that has focused on the sinfulness of the human race. Her stress on a theology of love and her christology of Christ the deep wisdom of the Trinity our mother can help reform our images of God and prevent problems with gender distinctions before theologizing begins. Julian's soteriology deserves a significant place in theological education for both its method and its theology.

In a world that is in danger of losing sight of the fact that "all shall be well," Julian's soteriology has something to contribute to hope. Her reflections reveal the fundamental unity between all things: God, creation, and humanity. They illumine an integral unity between past, present, and future. Her essentially trinitarian theology celebrates the presence of God in history. At the same time it generates hope that our present experience of divine love will come to eschatological fruition for all creation, all things, in the fullness of God's time. Her *Showings* reveal how we can see that *all manner of things shall be well.*

Bibliography

MANUSCRIPTS OF THE *SHOWINGS*

London. MS British Museum. Additional 37790 fols. 97-113 (Amherst).

Paris. MS Bibliothèque Nationale. Fonds anglais 40 (Paris).

London. MS British Museum. Sloane 2499 (Sloane 1).

London. MS British Museum. Sloane 3705 (Sloane 2).

London. Westminster Archdiocesan Archives MS (Westminster).

Upholland. MS St. Joseph's College (Upholland).

EDITIONS OF THE *SHOWINGS*

Long and Short Text

Reynolds, Frances (Sister Anna Maria). *A Critical Edition of the Revelations of Julian of Norwich (1342–c.1416) Prepared From All Known Manuscripts*. Ph.D. dissertation, University of Leeds, 1956.

A Book of Showings to the Anchoress Julian of Norwich. 2 vols. Edited by Edmund Colledge and James Walsh. Toronto: Pontifical Institute of Mediaeval Studies, 1978.

Long Text

Julian of Norwich. A Revelation of Love. Edited by Marion Glasscoe. Exeter: University of Exeter Press, 1976 (rev. editions 1986, 1993).

The Shewings of Julian of Norwich. Edited by Georgia Ronan Crampton. Teams Middle English Texts Series. Kalamazoo: Medieval Institute Publications, 1994.

Short Text

Julian of Norwich's Revelations of Love: The Shorter Version. Edited by Frances Beer. Middle English Texts 8. Heidelberg: Carl Winter, 1978.

MODERNIZATIONS AND TRANSLATIONS

Long and Short Text

The Revelations of Divine Love of Julian of Norwich. Translated by James Walsh. London: Burns and Oates, 1961.

Julian of Norwich Showings. Translated by Edmund Colledge and James Walsh. Classics of Western Spirituality. New York: Paulist, 1978.

Long Text

Comfortable Words for Christ's Lovers: Being the Visions and Voices Vouchsafed to Lady Julian, Recluse at Norwich in 1373. Edited and translated by Dundas Harford. London: R.A. Allenson, 1911.

Julian of Norwich: A Revelation of Love. A New Translation by John Skinner. Evesham: Arthur James, 1996.

Julianna of Norwich: Revelations of Divine Love. Translated by M.L. Del Mastro. New York: Doubleday Image, 1977.

A Lesson of Love: The Revelations of Julian of Norwich. Edited and translated by John-Julian, O.J.N. New York: Walker and Company, 1988.

Revelations of Divine Love. Edited and translated by Clifton Wolters. Harmondsworth: Penguin, 1966.

Revelations of Divine Love Recorded by Julian Anchoress at Norwich Anno Domini, 1373. Edited by Grace Warrack. London: Methuen, 1901 (2nd ed. 1907)

Revelations of Divine Love Shewed to a Devout Anchoress, by Name Mother Julian of Norwich. Edited and translated by Henry Collins. London: Thomas Richardson and Sons, 1877.

Revelations of Divine Love Shewed to a Devout Ankress by Name Julian of Norwich. Edited by Dom Roger Hudleston, O.S.B. London: Orchard Books, 1927.

XVI Revelations of Divine Love, Shewed to a Devout Servant of our Lord, Called Mother Juliana, an Anchorete of Norwich: Who Lived in the Days of King Edward the Third. Edited by Serenus Cressy. London: R.F.S. Cressy, 1670.

XVI Revelations of Divine Love, Shewed to a Devout Servant of our Lord, Called Mother Juliana, an Anchorete of Norwich: Who Lived in the Days of King Edward the Third. Edited by Serenus Cressy with a forward by George Hargrave Parker. London, 1843.

XVI Revelations of Divine Love, Shewed to a Devout Servant of our Lord, Called Mother Juliana, an Anchorete of Norwich: Who Lived in the Days of King Edward the Third. Edited by Serenus Cressy with a forward by I. T. Hecker. London, 1864.

XVI Revelations of Divine Love Shewed to Mother Juliana of Norwich. Edited by Hugh Serenus Cressy with a preface by George Tyrell. London: Kegan Paul, Trench, Trübner, 1902.

Short Text

Comfortable Words for Christ's Lovers, Being the Visions and Voices Vouch-safed to Lady Julian, Recluse at Norwich in 1373. Edited and translated by Dundas Harford. London: R. A. Allenson, 1911.

A Shewing of God's Love: The Shorter Version of Sixteen Revelations of Divine Love by Julian of Norwich. Edited and translated by Anna Maria Reynolds. London: Longmans, Green, 1958.

The Shewings of Lady Julian Recluse at Norwich, 1373. Edited and translated by Dundas Harford. London: R. A. Allenson, 1912.

Selections

"Julian of Norwich: The Westminster Text of a Revelation of Love," edited by Hugh Kempster. *Mystics Quarterly* 23 (1997) 177–245.

"The Upholland Anthology: An Augustinian Baker Manuscript," edited by Hywel Wyn Owen and Luke Bell. *Downside Review* 107 (1989) 274–92.

SECONDARY LITERATURE

Abbott, Christopher. "Piety and Egoism in Julian of Norwich: A Reading of Long Text Chapters 2 and 3," *Downside Review* 114 (1996) 267–82.

_____. "His Body, The Church: Julian of Norwich's Vision of Christ Crucified," *Downside Review* 115 (1997) 1–22.

_____. *Julian of Norwich: Autobiography and Theology.* Cambridge: D. S. Brewer, 1999.

Aers, David, and Lynn Staley. *The Powers of the Holy: Religion, Politics and Gender in Late Medieval English Culture.* University Park, Pa.: Pennsylvania State University Press, 1996.

Allchin, Ann. "Julian of Norwich Today," *Fourteenth-Century English Mystics Newsletter* 6 (1989) 11–26.

Allen, Christine. "Christ Our Mother in Julian of Norwich," *Studies in Religion* 10 (1981) 421–28.

Allen, Hope Emily. "Some Fourteenth Century Borrowings from Ancrene Riwle," *Modern Languages Review* 18 (1922) 1–8.

_____. "Further Borrowings From Ancrene Riwle," *Modern Languages Review* 24 (1929) 1–15.

_____. *English Writings of Richard Rolle: Hermit of Hampole.* Oxford: Clarendon Press, 1963.

Baker, Denise Nowakowski. "Julian of Norwich and Anchoritic Literature," *Mystics Quarterly* 19 (1993) 148–60.

_____. *Julian of Norwich's Showings: From Vision to Book.* Princeton, N.J.: Princeton University Press, 1994.

Baldwin, Anna. *The Triumph of Patience in Julian of Norwich and Langland.* Rochester, England: D. S. Brewer, 1991.

Barker, Paula S. Datsko. "The Motherhood of God in Julian of Norwich's Theology," *Downside Review* 100 (1982) 290–304.

Bartlett, Anne Clark, ed., with Thomas Bestul, Janet Goebel, and William F. Pollard. *Vox Mystica: Essays on Medieval Mysticism in Honour of Professor Valery M. Lagorio.* Cambridge: D. S. Brewer, 1995.

Bauerschmidt, Frederick Christian. *Julian of Norwich and the Mystical Body Politic of Christ.* Notre Dame, Ind.: University of Notre Dame Press, 1999.

Bhattacharji, Santha. "Independence of Thought in Julian of Norwich," *Word and Spirit* 11 (1989) 79–82.

Bozak-DeLeo, Lillian. "The Soteriology of Julian of Norwich," in John Apczynski, ed., *Theology and the University.* Annual Publication of the College Theology Society 33 (1987). Lanham, Md.: University Press of America, 1990, 37–46.

Bradley, Ritamary. "The Motherhood Theme in Julian of Norwich," *Fourteenth Century English Mystics Newsletter* 2 (1976) 25–38.

_____. "English Mystics: a Progress Report on Scholarship and Teaching," *Religious Education* 73 (1978) 335–45.

_____. "Patristic Background of the Motherhood Similitude in Julian of Norwich," *Christian Scholar's Review* 8 (1978) 101–113.

_____. "Julian's Doubtfulle Drede," *The Month* 242 (1981) 53–57.

_____. "Julian of Norwich on Prayer," *Analecta Cartusiana* 106 (1983) 136–54.

_____. "Mysticism in the Motherhood Similitude of Julian of Norwich," *Studia Mystica* 8 (1985) 4–14.

_____. "Perception of Self in Julian of Norwich's Showings," *Downside Review* 104 (1986) 227–39.

_____. "Metaphors of Cloth and Clothing in the Showings of Julian of Norwich," *Mediaevalia* 9 (1986 for 1983) 269–82.

_____. "Julian on Mary," *Anima: an Experimental Journal of Celebration* 15 (1989) 108–112.

_____. *Julian's Way: A Practical Commentary on Julian of Norwich*. London: Harper Collins, 1992.

_____. *Not For the Wise: Prayer Texts from Julian of Norwich*. London: Darton, Longman and Todd, 1994.

Busshart, Helen. M. *Christ as Feminine in Julian of Norwich in Light of the Psychology of C. G. Jung*. Ph.D. dissertation, Fordham University, 1985.

_____. "Christ as Feminine in Julian of Norwich in the Light of the Psychology of C. G. Jung," *Mystics Quarterly* 11 (1985) 83–84.

_____. "Julian of Norwich: God's Love and the Experience of Dying," *Contemplative Review* 12 (1979) 6–13.

_____. "Julian of Norwich: God's Love and the Experience of Dying," *Contemplative Review* 13 (1980) 24–28.

Caspar, Ruth. "'All Shall Be Well': Proto-typical Symbols of Hope," *Journal of the History of Ideas* 42 (1981) 139–50.

Clark, John P.H. "'Fiducia' in Julian of Norwich," *Downside Review* 99 (1981) 97–108, 214–29.

_____. "Predestination in Christ According to Julian of Norwich," *Downside Review* 100 (1982) 79–91.

_____. "Nature, Grace and the Trinity in Julian of Norwich," *Downside Review* 100 (1982) 203–20.

_____. "Time and Eternity in Julian of Norwich," *Downside Review* 109 (1991) 259–76.

Colledge, Edmund, and James Walsh. "Editing Julian of Norwich's Revelations: A Progress Report," *Medieval Studies* 38 (1976) 404–27.

Colledge, Eric, ed. *The Medieval Mystics of England*. London: John Murray, 1961.

Cooper, Austin. *Julian of Norwich: Reflections on Selected Texts*. Homebush: St. Paul Publications, 1986.

Corless, Roger. "The Dramas of Spiritual Progress: the Lord and the Servant in Julian's Showings 51 and the Lost Heir in Lotus Sutra 4," *Mystics Quarterly* 11 (1985) 65–75.

_____. "Comparing Cataphatic Mystics: Julian of Norwich and T'an-luan," *Mystics Quarterly* 21 (1995) 18–27.

Dreyer, Elizabeth. "Julian of Norwich: Her Merry Counsel," *America* 139 (1978) 55–57.

Durka, Gloria. *Praying With Julian of Norwich*. Winona, Minn.: St. Mary's Press, 1989.

Durley, Maureen Slattery. "Guilt and Innocence: The Coincidence of Opposites in Julian of Norwich's Parable of the Lord and the Servant," *Revue de l' Université d' Ottawa* 50 (1980) 202–208.

Flinders, Carol Lee. *A Comparison of the Short and Long Text of the Sixteen Revelations of Divine Love by Julian of Norwich*. Ph.D. dissertation, University of California, 1972.

_____. *Enduring Grace: Living Portraits of Seven Women Mystics*. San Francisco: HarperSan Francisco, 1993.

Flood, H. R. *St. Julian's Church, Norwich and Dame Julian*. Norwich: Wherry Press, 1936.

Foss, David B. "From God as Mother to Priest as Mother: Julian of Norwich and the Movement for the Ordination of Women," *Downside Review* 104 (1986) 214–26.

Furlong, Monica. *The Wisdom of Julian of Norwich*. Oxford: Lion Publishing, 1996.

Furness, Jean. "Teilhard de Chardin and Julian of Norwich: a Rapprochement," *Mystics Quarterly* 12 (1982) 67–70.

Gatta, Julia. *A Pastoral Art. Spiritual Guidance in the English Mystics*. London: Darton, Longman and Todd, 1986.

_____. "Julian of Norwich: Theodicy as Pastoral Art," *Anglican Theological Review* 63 (1981) 173–81.

Gilchrist, Jay. "Unfolding Enfolding Love in Julian of Norwich's Revelations," *Fourteenth-Century English Mystics News Letter* 9 (1983) 67–88.

Glasscoe, Marion, ed. *The Medieval Mystical Tradition in England*. Exeter: Exeter University Press, 1980.

_____. "Means of Showing: An Approach to Reading Julian of Norwich," in James Hogg, ed., *Spätmittelalterliche Geistliche Literatur in der Nationalsprache.* Analecta Cartusiana 106. Salzburg: Institüt für Anglistik und Amerikanistik, 1983, 155–77.

____. *The Medieval Mystical Tradition in England.* Cambridge: D. S. Brewer, 1984.

____, ed. *The Medieval Mystical Tradition in England: 1V.* Cambridge: D. S. Brewer, 1987.

____. "Visions and Revisions: A Further Look at the Manuscripts of Julian of Norwich," *Studies in Bibliography* 42 (1989) 103–120.

____. *The Medieval Mystical Tradition in England: V.* Cambridge: D. S. Brewer, 1992.

____. *English Medieval Mystics.* London: Longman, 1993.

____. *The Medieval Mystical Tradition in England, Ireland and Wales: VI.* Woodbridge: Boydell and Brewer, 1999.

Hanshell, Deryck. "A Crux in the Interpretation of Dame Julian," *Downside Review* 92 (1974) 77–91.

Heimmel, Jennifer P. *God is Our Mother: Julian of Norwich and the Medieval Image of Christian Feminine Divinity.* Salzburg: Institüt für Anglistik und Amerikanistik, 1982.

Hide, Kerrie. "The Influence of Late Medieval Crucifixion Images in the Showings of Julian of Norwich," *Religion, Literature and the Arts Project: 1996 Conference Proceedings.* [Sydney]: The Conference, 1996, 265–71.

____. "The Showings of Julian of Norwich as a Lectio Divina," *Tjurunga* 49 (1996) 39–50.

____. "The Parable of the Lord and the Servant: A Soteriology for Our Times," *Pacifica* 10 (1997) 53–69.

____. "Sweet Touchings of Grace: Reflections on the Theology of Grace from Julian of Norwich," *Presence: The Journal of Spiritual Directors International* 3 (1997) 6–12.

____. "The Deep Wisdom of the Trinity Our Mother—Echoes in Augustine and Julian of Norwich," *The Australasian Catholic Record* 4 (1997) 432–44.

Janda, James. *Julian: A Play Based on the Life of Julian of Norwich.* Minneapolis: Winston, 1984.

Jantzen, Grace M. *Julian of Norwich: Mystic and Theologian.* Great Britian: S.P.C.K., 1987.

____. *Power, Gender and Christian Mysticism.* Cambridge: Cambridge University Press, 1995.

_____. *Julian of Norwich*. New ed. New York: Paulist, 2000.

John-Julian, Father. "Thankyng in Julian," *Mystics Quarterly* 15 (1989) 70–74.

Knowles, David. *The English Mysical Tradition*. New York: Harper, 1961.

Knowlton, Mary Arthur. *The Influence of Richard Rolle and Julian of Norwich on the Middle English Lyrics*. Mouton: The Hague, 1973.

Krantz, M. Diane F. *The Life and Text of Julian of Norwich: The Poetics of Enclosure*. Studies in the Humanities. Literature—Politics—Society 32. New York: Peter Lang, 1997.

Lagorio, Valery M., and Ritamary Bradley. *The 14th-Century English Mystics. A Comprehensive Annotated Bibliography*. New York: Garland, 1981.

Lagorio, Valery M. "Variations on the Theme of God's Motherhood in Medieval Mystical and Devotional Writings," *Studia Mystica* 8 (1985) 15–37.

Lang, Judith. "'The Godly Wylle' in Julian of Norwich," *Downside Review* 102 (1984) 163–73.

Lawler, John. "Notes and Observations: A Note on the Revelations of Julian of Norwich," *Review of English Studies* n.s. 11 (1951) 255–58.

Leech, Kenneth, and Benedicta Ward. *Julian Reconsidered*. Oxford: S.L.G., 1988.

Lewis, Muriel. "After Reflecting on Julian's Revelations of Behovabil Synne," *Studia Mystica* 6 (1983) 41–57.

Llewelyn, Robert. *Love Bade Me Welcome*. London: Darton, Longman and Todd, 1984.

_____. *Julian: Woman of Our Day*. London: Darton, Longman and Todd, 1985.

_____. *With Pity Not Blame. The Spirituality of Julian of Norwich and the Cloud of Unknowing For Today*. 3d. ed. London: Darton, Longman and Todd, 1994. Published in U.S.A. as *All Shall be Well: The Spirituality of Julian of Norwich for Today*. New York: Paulist, 1985.

Lichtmann, Maria R. "I Desyrede a Bodylye Syght: Julian of Norwich and the Body," *Mystics Quarterly* 17 (1991) 12–19.

_____. "Julian of Norwich and the Ontology of the Feminine," *Studia Mystica: Women and Mysticism* 13 (1990) 53–64.

Logarbo, Mona. "Salvation Theology in Julian of Norwich: Sin, Forgiveness, and Redemption in the Revelations," *Thought* 61 (1986) 370–80.

Louth, Andrew. "The Influence of Denys the Areopagite on Eastern and Western Spirituality in the Fourteenth Century," *Sobornost* n.s. 4 (1982) 185–200.

Lucas, Elona K. "Psychological and Spiritual Growth in Hadewijch and Julian of Norwich," *Studia Mystica* 9 (1986) 3–20.

Mastro, M. L. del. *The Stairway of Perfection.* New York: Doubleday Image, 1979.

_____. "Juliana of Norwich: Parable of the Lord and Servant—Radical Orthodoxy," *Mystics Quarterly* 14 (1988) 84–93.

McEntire, Sandra J. *Julian of Norwich. A Book of Essays.* New York: Garland, 1998.

Mahan, Susan. *The Christian Anthropology of Julian of Norwich.* Ph.D. dissertation, Marquette University. Ann Arbor: UMI Dissertation Services, 1988.

Maisonneuve, Roland. *L'Univers Visionnaire de Julian of Norwich.* Ph.D. dissertation, Sorbonne University, 1978.

_____. "Julian of Norwich and the Prison of Existence," *Studia Mystica* 3 (1980) 26–32.

Marshall, D. E. "St. Thomas Aquinas and Mother Julian on Charity," *Life of the Spirit* 7 (1953) 335–41.

Maud'huit, R. "The Three Wounds of Julian the Recluse," translated by D. Sloate and H. Terris. *Studia Mystica* 3 (1980) 24–25.

McCaslin, Susan. "Vision and Revision in *Four Quartets:* T. S. Eliot and Julian of Norwich," *Mystics Quarterly* 12 (1986) 171–78.

McConnell, Helen H. "From Shame to Joy: Julian of Norwich, Companion on the Journey to Spiritual Wellness," *Studies in Formative Spirituality* 14 (1993) 395–405.

McLaughlin, Eleanor. "'Christ My Mother': Feminine Naming and Metaphor in Medieval Spirituality," *Saint Luke's Journal of Theology* 18 (1975) 228–48.

_____. "Julian's Death Into Life," *Living Light* 20 (1987) 28–35.

McLean, Michael. *Guide Book to St. Julian's Church and Lady Julian's Cell.* Norwich, 1979, revised 1981.

McNamer, Sarah. "The Exploratory Image: God as Mother in Julian of Norwich's Revelations of Divine Love," *Mystics Quarterly* 15 (1989) 21–28.

Meany, Mary Frances Walsh. "The Image of Christ in the Revelations of Divine Love of Julian of Norwich." Ph.D. dissertation, Fordham University, 1975.

Members of Julian's Shrine. *Enfolded in Love: Daily Readings with Julian of Norwich.* London: Darton, Longman and Todd, 1980.

Miller, Gayle Houston. *Imagery and Design in Julian of Norwich's Revelations of Divine Love.* Ph.D. dissertation, University of Georgia. Ann Arbor: UMI Dissertation Services, 1988.

Moffett, John. "God as Mother in Hinduism and Christianity," *Cross Currents* 28 (1978) 129–33.

Molinari, Paul. *Julian of Norwich: The Teaching of a Fourteenth Century Mystic.* London: Longmans, Green, 1958.

_____. "Love Was His Meaning: Julian of Norwich, Six Centuries Later," *Fourteenth-Century English Mystics News Letter* 5 (1979) 12–33.

Nuth, Joan. *Love's Meaning: The Theology of Julian of Norwich.* Ph.D. dissertation, Boston College and Andover Newton Theological School, 1988.

_____. *Wisdom's Daughter: The Theology of Julian of Norwich.* New York: Crossroad, 1991.

_____. "Two Medieval Soteriologies: Anselm of Canterbury and Julian of Norwich," *Theological Studies* 53 (1992) 611–45.

Okulam, Frodo. *The Julian Mystique: Her Life and Teachings.* Mystic, Conn.: Twenty-third Publications, 1998.

Oldfield, Alan. *Revelations of Divine Love of Julian of Norwich: Paintings by Alan Oldfield.* Sydney: Macquarie Galleries, 1988.

Olson, Mary. "God's Inappropriate Grace: Images of Courtesy in Julian of Norwich's Showings," *Mystics Quarterly* 20 (1994) 47–59.

Palliser, Margaret Ann, O.P. *Christ Our Mother of Mercy: Divine Mercy and Compassion in the Theology of the Shewings of Julian of Norwich.* Berlin and New York: Walter de Gruyter, 1992.

Pamchelli, Debra Scott. "Finding God in the Memory: Julian and the Loss of the Visions," *Downside Review* 104 (1986) 299–317.

Parsons, John Carmie, and Bonnie Wheeler, eds. *Medieval Mothering.* New York: Garland, 1996.

Paul, Sr. Mary. *All Shall Be Well.* Oxford: S.L.G., 1976.

Peloquin, Carol Marie. "All Will Be Well: A Look at Sin in Juliana's Revelations," *Contemplative Review* 13 (1980) 9–16.

Pelphrey, Brant Charles. *Julian of Norwich: A Theological Reappraisal.* Ph.D. dissertation, University of Edinburgh, 1978.

_____. "Uncreated Charity: The Trinity in Julian of Norwich," *Sobornost* 7 (1978) 527–35.

_____. *Love Was His Meaning: The Theology and Mysticism of Julian of Norwich.* Salzburg: Institüt für Anglistik und Amerikanistik, 1982.

_____. "Spirituality in Mission: Lessons from Julian of Norwich," *Cross Currents* 34 (1984) 171–90.

_____. *Julian of Norwich: Christ our Mother,* edited by Noel Dermont O'Donoghue. The Way of the Christian Mystics 7. Wilmington, Del.: Michael Glazier, 1989.

Peters, Bradley. "The Reality of Evil Within the Mystic Vision of Julian of Norwich," *Mystics Quarterly* 13 (1987) 195–202.

_____. "Julian of Norwich and Her Conceptual Development of Evil," *Mystics Quarterly* 17 (1991) 181–88.

_____. *Julian of Norwich and the Composition of Mystical Experience.* Ph.D. dissertation, University of Iowa. Ann Arbor: UMI Dissertation Services, 1992.

_____. "Julian of Norwich and the Internalized Dialogue of Prayer," *Mystics Quarterly* 20 (1994) 122–30.

Phillips, Helen, ed. *Langland, the Mystics, and the Medieval English Religious Tradition: Essays in Honour of S. S. Hussey.* Cambridge: Boydell and Brewer, 1990.

Pollard, William, and Robert Boenig, eds. *Mysticism and Spirituality in Medieval England.* Cambridge: D. S. Brewer, 1997.

Reynolds, Frances (Sister Anna Maria). "Some Literary Influences in the Revelations of Julian of Norwich," *Leeds Studies in English and Kindred Languages* 7 (1952) 18–28.

_____. "Julian of Norwich," *Month* 24 (1960) 133–44.

_____. "Love is His Meaning," *Clergy Review* 58 (1973) 363–69.

_____. "Courtesy and Homleness in the Revelations of Julian of Norwich," *Mystics Quarterly* 5 (1979) 12–20.

_____. "Julian of Norwich: Woman of Hope," *Mystics Quarterly* 10 (1984) 118–25.

Riehle, Wolfgang. *The Middle English Mystics.* Translated by Bernard Strandring. London: Routledge and Kegan Paul, 1981.

Rudd, Jay. "Nature and Grace in Julian of Norwich," *Mystics Quarterly* 19 (1993) 71–81.

Ryder, Andrew. "A Note on Julian's Visions," *Downside Review* 96 (1978) 299–304.

Sayer, Frank Dale, ed. *Julian and her Norwich: Commemorative Essays and Handbook to the Exhibition "Revelations of Divine Love."* Norwich: Julian of Norwich 1973 Celebration Committee, 1973.

Sprung, Andrew. "We Nevyr Shall Come Out of Hym," *Mystics Quarterly* 19 (1993) 47–62.

Stone, Robert Karl. *Middle English Prose Style: Margery Kempe and Julian of Norwich.* Mouton: The Hague, 1970.

Tamburr, Karl. "Mystic Transformation: Julian's Version of the Harrowing of Hell," *Mystics Quarterly* 20 (1994) 60–67.

Thouless, Robert H. *The Lady Julian: A Psychological Study.* London: S.P.C.K., 1924.

Tugwell, Simon. "Julian of Norwich as a Speculative Theologian," *Fourteenth-Century English Mystics News Letter* 9 (1983) 199–209.

Upjohn, Sheila. *In Search of Julian of Norwich.* London: Darton, Longman and Todd, 1989.

_____. *Why Julian Now? A Voyage of Discovery.* London: Darton, Longman and Todd, 1997.

Vinge, Patricia Mary. *An Understanding of Love According to the Anchoress Julian of Norwich.* Elizabethan and Renaissance Studies. Salzburg: Institüt für Anglistik und Amerikanistik, 1983.

Walsh, James. "A New Thérèse," *Month* 206 (1958) 150–59.

_____. "God's Homely Loving: St. John and Julian of Norwich on the Divine Indwelling," *Month* 19 (1958) 164–72.

_____. "A Note on Sexuality and Sensuality," *The Way.* Supplement 15 (1972) 86–92.

_____. *The Blissful Passion of our Lord Jesus Christ: Mother Julian of Norwich.* Worchester: Stanbrook Abbey Press, 1973.

Warrack, Grace. *All Shall Be Well: Selections from the Writings of the Lady Julian of Norwich* A.D. *1373.* London: A.R. Mowbray, 1925.

Watkins, Renée Neu. "Two Women Visionaries and Death: Catherine of Sienna and Julian of Norwich," *Numen: International Review for the History of Religions* 30 (1983) 174–98.

Watson, Nicholas. "Classics of Western Spirituality II: Three Medieval Women Theologians and their Background," *King's Theological Review* 12 (1989) 56–63.

_____. "The Composition of Julian of Norwich's Revelation of Love," *Speculum* 68 (1993) 637–83.

Webb, Geoffrey. *Julian of Norwich: A Light in the Darkness*. London: Rivington, 1980.

_____. *Suffering: The Jews of Norwich and Julian of Norwich*. London: Diocesan Council of Christian-Jewish Understanding, 1981.

Webster, Alan. "Julian of Norwich," *Expository Times* 84 (1973) 228–30.

Windeatt, Barry A. "Julian of Norwich and Her Audience," *Review of English Studies* n.s. 28 (1977) 1–17.

_____, ed. *English Mystics of the Middle Ages*. Cambridge: Cambridge University Press, 1994.

Wolters, Clifton. "Julian of Norwich Commemorative Celebration, 1373–1973," *Ampleforth Journal* 78 (1973) 57–67.

_____. "Two Spiritualities: A Superficial Survey," *Fourteenth-Century English Mystics Newsletter* 5 (1979) 16–27.

Wright, Robert E. "The 'Boke Performyd': Affective Technique and Reader Response in the Showings of Julian of Norwich," *Christianity and Literature* 36 (1987) 13–32.

Index